ECONOMIC PERSUASIONS

Studies in Rhetoric and Culture

Edited by **Ivo Strecker**, Johannes Gutenberg University Mainz and Addis Ababa University, **Stephen Tyler**, Rice University, and **Robert Hariman**, Northwestern University

Our minds are filled with images and ideas, but these remain unstable and incomplete as long as we do not manage to persuade both ourselves and others of their meanings. It is this inward and outward rhetoric which allows us to give some kind of shape and structure to our understanding of the world and which becomes central to the formation of individual and collective consciousness. This series is dedicated to the study of the interaction of rhetoric and culture and focuses on the concrete practices of discourse in which and through which the diverse and often also fantastic patterns of culture—including our own—are created, maintained, and contested.

Volume 1
Culture & Rhetoric
Edited by Ivo Strecker and Stephen Tyler

Volume 2
Culture, Rhetoric, and the Vicissitudes of Life
Edited by Michael Carrithers

Volume 3
Economic Persuasions
Edited by Stephen Gudeman

Economic Persuasions

∎ ∎ ∎

Edited by
Stephen Gudeman

Berghahn Books
New York • Oxford

First published in 2009 by

Berghahn Books

www.berghahnbooks.com

©2009, 2012 Stephen Gudeman
First paperback edition published in 2012

All rights reserved. Except for the quotation of short passages for the purposes of criticism and review, no part of this book may be reproduced in any form or by any means, electronic or mechanical, including photocopying, recording, or any information storage and retrieval system now known or to be invented, without written permission of the publisher.

Library of Congress Cataloging-in-Publication Data

Economic persuasions / edited by Stephen Gudeman.
   p. cm. — (Studies in rhetoric and culture ; v. 3)
Includes bibliographical references and index.
ISBN 978-1-84545-436-4 (hbk.) -- ISBN 978-0-85745-663-2 (pbk.)
   1. Economic anthropology. 2. Rhetoric—Social aspects. 3. Persuasion (Rhetoric)
 I. Gudeman, Stephen.
GN448.2.E36 2009
306.3—dc22

2009012947

British Library Cataloguing in Publication Data

A catalogue record for this book is available from the British Library

Printed in the United States on acid-free paper.

ISBN: 978-0-85745-663-2 (paperback) ISBN: 978-0-85745-664-9 (ebook)

Contents

List of Figures	vii
Preface	ix
1. Introduction Stephen Gudeman	1
2. Simplicity in Economic Anthropology: Persuasion, Form, and Substance James G. Carrier	15
3. When Rhetoric Becomes Mass Persuasion: The Case of the Concept of Interest Richard Swedberg	31
4. The New Social Science Imperialism and the Problem of Knowledge in Contemporary Economics William Milberg	43
5. The Persuasions of Economics Stephen Gudeman	62
6. Conversations Between Anthropologists and Economists Metin M. Cosgel	81
7. "The Craving for Intelligibility:" Speech and Silence on the Economy under Structural Adjustment and Military Rule in Nigeria Jane I. Guyer with LaRay Denzer	97

8. Mass-gifts: On Market Giving in Advanced Capitalist Societies 118
   Nurit Bird-David and Asaf Darr

9. The Persuasive Power of Money 136
   Keith Hart

10. The Money Rhetoric in the United States 159
    Ruben George Oliven

11. The Third Way: A Cultural Economic Perspective 176
    Arjo Klamer

Contributors 201

References 204

Index 224

Figures

■ ■ ■ ■ ■ ■

Figure 4.1. Three Modes of Economic Persuasion — 54

Figure 11.1. The Spheres that Dominate the Political and Economic Discussions — 191

Figure 11.2. Four Spheres Make a Complete Picture — 196

Preface

∎ ∎ ∎ ∎ ∎ ∎

The contributions to *Economic Persuasions,* which is the third volume in the *Studies in Rhetoric and Culture* series, were originally presented in July 2005 at the University of Mainz as part of the Rhetoric Culture Project. An initial conference on rhetoric culture theory, inspired and led by Ivo Strecker, was convened during 2002 at Mainz. Attended by anthropologists and scholars from related disciplines, it became the springboard for a subsequent series of conferences on topics such as religion, social relations, politics, and economics. This volume's editor was a participant in the initial conference, but he harbored reservations about assembling a group of scholars interested in addressing the intersection of rhetoric, anthropology, and economics. The home of rhetoric seemed to be in politics, language, semiotics, and expressive culture, and not in anthropology or in its overlaps with economics. These doubts were unfounded, because it proved very easy to convene a group of scholars around the idea of persuasion and economy. Our diverse group included anthropologists, economists, and a sociologist; their topics ranged from ethnography to theory, and from history, to texts, to art. The many postings, discussions, and dialogues on rhetoric culture that emerged after the initial planning conference inspired our contributors along with the opportunity of trying to develop, with like-minded scholars, a different way of thinking about economy.

A large, intellectual venture, such as the rhetoric culture series, comes to fruition through the commitment, encouragement, and hard work of a group of individuals. Ivo Strecker, influenced by the work of Stephen Tyler, developed the idea of an encompassing rhetoric culture project, and our contribution would not have emerged without his unflagging support and encouragement. We also owe special thanks to Felix Girke, who co-organized the economics conference with this editor, and who plans to edit a second volume on economics and rhetoric. Christian Meyer, Jean Lydall, and Anna-Maria Brandstetter contributed in many ways to the success of our meetings in Mainz. The Volkswagen Foundation generously funded our conference with the others, and we were especially pleased that the publisher, Marion Berghahn, was able to attend our conference sessions.

I close with thanks to our contributors, who were faced with a new challenge in thinking about economy in terms of rhetoric and culture. The study of market economies traditionally has been the province of economists just as everyday small-scale economies have provided the grounds for anthropological research: a breach separated the two fields so that a convincing comparative economics never developed. The essays that follow help to bridge this gap and offer an exciting way of comparing economies.

CHAPTER 1

Introduction

Stephen Gudeman

■ ■ ■ ■ ■ ■

As the transition from socialism to market economy gathered speed in the early 1990s, many people proclaimed the final success of capitalism as a practice and neoliberal economics as a science. But with the uneven achievements of the "transition," the deepening problems of "development," the continuation of boom and bust cycles in market societies, persistent unemployment, widening of the wealth gap, and expressions of resistance, the discipline of economics is no longer seen as a mirror of reality or as a unified science. How should we understand economics and, more broadly, the organization and disorganization of material life?

In the meanwhile, economists are crossing disciplinary boundaries in impressive numbers and attempting to apply their models to an ever-increasing range of social phenomena. Some economists also have discovered anthropological notions such as culture and figurative speech. Today, economists speak about social and cultural capital, as well as signals and information. Even the hallowed and notoriously ambiguous anthropological term, "gift," (as well as "reciprocity") has been encompassed within the rationalistic rhetoric of economics; however, anthropologists and economists use the terms very differently. For their part, anthropologists have not reached into this cross-disciplinary space nor fully used their ethnographic and analytical tools to offer alternative interpretations. Given its notion of culture, what does anthropology contribute to our understanding, explanation, and "predictions" about economies and economics?

In this book, we have approached these issues by asking a new question. Why is economics persuasive? How does it convince us? Or, what persuades us to participate in everyday economic life? We are not asking about the persuasions given by market incentives or about individuals balancing rewards and costs in their decisions, as in the language of economists, but about the persuasions of economy that stimulate, focus, cajole, and invite us to act in certain ways. This rhetoric is public and private, as well as spoken, written, and acted. Such persuasions often lie hidden in the gap between economics and anthropology.

Our essays were first presented within a set of conferences on "rhetoric culture," the meaning of which was discussed through all of the prior sessions. The preceding volumes in this publication series explore the idea in depth. A central thread in all of these conversations to which we responded is that language and actions are performances that we deploy to move others and ourselves in action and conceptually. Rhetoric, as in political speech, can be used to lead, align, beckon, and bring people to a particular perspective. These performances are rooted in culture, context, memory, and shared (and not so shared) understandings. But the task of addressing economy in terms of rhetoric posed a special challenge. Other sessions in the conference series addressed everyday poetics, politics, religion, and kinship. Most of us can envision a link between these parts of life and rhetoric. Addressing the connection between rhetoric and economy, however, created a challenge for both the anthropologists and the economists who contribute to this book. If anthropologists had always been aware of the rhetorical aspects of social life, where had they written about economy? And if economists had always been talking about and writing down graphs, curves, and equations, where was the rhetoric? As if to underline the challenge, our conference on economy was the ultimate session in the larger conference series. Could anything fruitful emerge?

We used the occasion to bring together anthropologists and economists (as well as a sociologist) to speak to the puzzle and to engage in a conversation across the disciplines. Because we were in a dialogue, we were trying to persuade each other, both our fellow disciplinarians and our counterparts, of the power of our views. On the idea of persuasion as the theme, we agreed at the outset. But as the work proceeded, it proved to be increasingly profitable, because—as the essays demonstrate—the toolkit of rhetoric smartly aligns with much of economic theory and practices, and with economic anthropology as well (although that may be because we are all voices within a long "Western" conversation). The reader will find that by "thinking rhetorically," the contributors to this volume find shared ground and open exciting spaces for exploration as they show how their different approaches have more in common than is usually supposed.

We use the word, "rhetoric," in the original (Platonic and Aristotlean) sense of persuasion. But what makes an analysis of material life in economics or in anthropology persuasive? And what makes a form of material life persuasive to its practitioners and to others? In economics, the Chicago-trained Deidre McCloskey (1985, 1994) was the pioneer in the study of economic rhetoric, and her writings have been influential outside of the field.[1] Others have pursued a broadly rhetorical line, such as Arjo Klamer (1983), who has written on conversations, and Philip Mirowski (1989), who has explored the metaphors of general equilibrium theory that were drawn from physics. Related as well are writings in feminist economics, postmodern economics, and a variety of heterodox approaches in economics. Anthropology, with its emphasis on culture, semiotics, pragmatics, language, myth, ritual, and everyday life, has long displayed an interest in rhetoric, as the other volumes in this series attest. In the past decades, some anthropologists (Bird-David 1992; Gudeman 1986; Sahlins 1976) have tried to bring the culture concept to ways of thinking about economics, but the idea of developing a rhetorical approach has been slower to develop.

But what does the word, rhetoric, really mean? Some people associate rhetoric with the use of tropes, such as metaphor or metonymy; on this view, it may be opposed to deduction or logic. Some use rhetoric to refer to modes of presentation in speech and gesture; others link rhetoric to dialogue, interaction, and communication. More broadly, rhetoric can be seen as a way of bringing about a feeling or emotion in others. Of course, rhetoric sometimes means just the opposite: it is hot air, sophistry, and just talk, if not misdirection. The philosophically inclined might claim that through rhetoric the "real" is constructed, while others offer the perspective that rhetoric has to do with multiple and unstable meanings that require interpretation by both speaker and listener. Still others may prize a rhetorical perspective because it leads to the analysis of a speaker and listener's positions.

We draw on some of the traditional divisions that the concept of rhetoric evokes. For example, in rhetorical studies, the form of an expression may be separated from its content, or how something is said may be separated from what is said. Some of the classical terms used to capture this division are *res* or substance, and *verba* or expression, as well as *logos* (content) and *lexis* (style). Today, we might talk about figures of speech and the subject being conveyed. In Marshall McLuhan's words, we could also speak about medium and message. But the divisions are arbitrary, because the two aspects overlap and interact, and they are emphasized differently by disciplines and cultures. In the West, we often prize the substance or meaning of discourse over its form, but it is the interaction or dialectics of the two that provides an important thread in this volume. In economics, as the reader will find, the form of a presentation conveys a good part of its meaning and persuasive power; in a word, form becomes content. For example, when metaphoric associations tell us about the local meaning of money, are we not looking at the impact of how something is said on its content? And when supply and demand curves specify price, are we not defining price through a mode of expression? It works in reverse as well, because we could see graphs and metaphors as outcomes of struggles to express something we experience or think we know. These struggles to express and to use expressions to formulate knowledge are common to both anthropology and economics. And they lead us into perplexing issues about epistemology, methodology, history, and ethnography. The reader thus will find that we weave reflections about these issues into our consideration of economic persuasions. We want to persuade the reader that "thinking rhetorically" is a profitable way to think about economy.

The Cast of Essays

If the study of rhetoric begins with Aristotle's discussion of political persuasion, James Carrier's essay ends with the way political power and control are achieved through rhetoric. Rhetoric, says Carrier, is about the devices we use to persuade others and concerns the form as opposed to the substance of a communication. To invoke Marshall McLuhan again, it is the medium and not the message. Carrier admits that this division is "formal," but it is persuasive. We rely on the form of a communication, suggests Carrier, for its simplicity, which makes for good aphorisms and understandable public policy, as in the neoliberal wave that has swept Britain and the United States. Simplicity lends itself to prescribing and controlling world events, just as it offers clarity and consistency.

With this view of rhetoric, Carrier turns to the most well known dispute within economic anthropology, which is that between the "formalists" and the "substantivists." The terms repeat the crucial division in rhetorical studies and suggest why the formalists claimed "victory" in the debate, because by focusing on the "medium," they were more persuasive. But it was never this simple. For one part, the debate replicated a long-standing division between anthropology and economics as disciplines. For another, as William Milberg discusses in this volume, economics may be undergoing a change that brings it closer to the concerns of anthropology. I might add that several generations of students have found the formalist/substantivist debate to be "rhetorical" as well, although in the pejorative sense of the term.

Carrier leads us through the main points of the debate. Is economy the product of individuals choosing through the exercise of calculative reason, or is it a set of social relationships and institutions? Are economic processes forged in local and historical contexts or are they transcendent forms? The formalist approach is persuasive for its universalism, because it presumes that humans across cultures are alike in their mental predisposition. The substantivists are more particularistic with their insistence on the importance of variation and context. This difference in methodologies and epistemologies reflects broader debates infecting many disciplines, such as that between lumpers and splitters, or between anti-relativists and relativists.

The formalist/substantivist debate is dialectical because each side actually employs both faces of rhetoric, although with different emphases. Substantivists start with the substances of economy, which are land and labor. The two make up the content and the context of their discourse. But these substances assume different forms in different societies, according to the transaction type (or form) in which they are exchanged, which include reciprocity, redistribution, and markets, and the transaction forms are institutionally framed. For substantivists, it might be said, every economy is typologically or "formologically" different. In contrast, formalists are looking at the invariant form of the individual who is a purposeful actor, or *homo economicus*. So far, so good, but this rational actor operates by drawing on the subjective content of preferences, which are distinct to him. For formalists, the form may be comparable across all human beings, which is the claim of many economists, but the substance of that action, which is made up of preferences, is not, otherwise why would rational calculators exchange? Thus, the dialectical terms of rhetoric are echoed in the debate between formalists and substantivists. One finds form in transactions that are institutionally framed; the other finds form in the acts of individuals. Formalists must presume substances just as the substantivists presume form, even if their contents and forms are differentially emphasized.

Carrier offers us a punch line to this debate: the idea of simplicity. Not all forms, he suggests, are alike; some are more persuasive than others. The formalists' "form," he suggests, is simple and abstract. The substantivists' form, which is transaction types, is threefold and linked to institutions. On the ground, these transactions also are mixed and not always clearly discernible. The substantivist approach does draw on the device of simplicity, at the social if not the psychological level, but it is a more complex simplicity. Thus, are we left with an ambiguity? Was the great debate between formalists and substantivists in economic anthropology about content or form? We have always considered it to be a controversy concerning the content of economy, but perhaps it was truly rhetorical. At the least, a rhetorical approach that looks at how we persuade helps us understand the issues at stake.

Richard Swedberg's account of our shifting uses of the word, interest, reprises many of our themes, but in a different language and with a more philosophical and sociological turn. Swedberg argues that disciplines appropriate words for their own purposes, and these meanings dominate other possible uses, especially as they spread across several disciplines. Why do some uses become more persuasive than others? For many of us, the word "interest" means the return we pay for the use of someone else's money, however, Swedberg uncovers other uses of the word in economics and sociology, which reveal some of the rhetorical differences between the disciplines. Tracing the history of these uses, he suggests that their reconsideration may offer fresh ways of thinking about economy.

Swedberg first recounts the stillborn use of the concept of interest in sociology. Paying special attention to Simmel's work, he suggests that Simmel drew on the Kantian distinction between form and content in which interest, referring to content, provided the driving force or motive for interactions that took different forms. According to Simmel, sociology was to leave the exploration of the content of interest to other disciplines. Although his notion of content was broader than economists entertained, Simmel subordinated it to the relationships or form in which it was expressed; and he thought that the same interest might have a different form in different associations (which is not unlike exercises in rhetoric that call for variations in style while preserving meaning). Conversely, the same social form might rest on different interests. In contrast to Simmel, Weber argued that interests lend stability to actions and that interest-driven behavior pervades all domains of life and is vital to the form of social action and organization. For Weber, interests covered almost the entire range of human experience and were seemingly more stable than the obligations and expectations of formal groups in which they were expressed.

Swedberg contrasts these multifaceted notions of interest in earlier sociology to the narrow use of the word "interest" in economics. After Adam Smith, the term was cleansed of explorations into the subjective states of actors and replaced by the concepts of *homo economicus* and preferences. But preferences or interests could be known only when revealed in choices, so even socially shaped actors dropped out in the abstract theory. With this development, the difference between sociology and economics sharpened. For Simmel, interest was motive or content, while form was the shape of the interactions in which it appeared; for Weber, interests were sturdy, but varied by context. In economics, however, interest became a form, whereas the contexts within which it was realized were elided. Swedberg's analysis points us to the interesting dialectical transformation that what began as shifting content or substance in early sociology became the invariant form in economics. His analysis of the word, interest, also suggests why the formalist/substantivist debate in economic anthropology became so heated, because it had much to do with how we conceive humans in society. The formalists in anthropology took the position of economists; the substantivists were like sociologists. They splintered the dialectics of rhetoric.

But nothing stands still, and the form versus content debate may be long in the tooth given changes in economics and anthropology. William Milberg returns us to the general topic of persuasion in his survey of changes in the methodologies and theories in economics. He asks how and why economics has become so persuasive, despite its sometimes-indirect relevance to what actually happens. His argument crosscuts, if not confounds, some of the traditional classifications in rhetoric. Milberg shows how economics has moved from a view of economy as an ordered and complete system (or form), which was an assurance against uncertainty, to a more pragmatic sense of incompletion, although the yearning for simplicity persists.

Focusing on his discipline's shifting questions, Milberg shows how the criteria of persuasion and "progress" in economics have changed and moved slightly closer to some of anthropology's traditional ones. Milberg identifies three phases or paradigms in economics during the past century. First, practitioners relied on a hypothetico-deductive method that involved the notions of partial equilibrium (Marshall), general equilibrium (Arrow and Debreu), optimization, the first welfare theorem, and scarcity. In this paradigm, progress was judged by the elegance of the formulation and its robustness in the sense that if the same results could be achieved by using less restrictive assumptions than before, the new model was considered to be more persuasive. The deductive rigor of this rhetoric brought it closer to physics (and persuaded us to support capitalism).

A transition—often contested within the discipline—occurred with the rise of the "New Economics" in which the possibility of achieving general equilibrium was abandoned, although the anchor of rational choice was retained. As the search for overall systematicity and completeness was forsaken, new subfields in economics arose. In this period, the discipline shifted toward a more inductive approach, and with it, results contrary to the earlier deductions were found in the analysis of international trade, monopolistic competition, increasing returns to scale, and growth. Rational choice played a role in explaining these findings, but the vision of consistency shifted from the overall economy to the subfields. Robustness was no longer so prized, although the problem of allowing for contingency, given the ad hoc hypotheses, was avoided by assuming rational choice. Assessing progress in the discipline became more difficult. For anthropologists, the shift from deduction to induction as a mode of persuasion in economics is ironic, because this distinction was the central theme in the 1941 Frank Knight–Melville Herskovits debate.[2] Knight, the well known economist, accused Herskovits, and other anthropologists, of practicing induction as opposed to the rigorous deductive methods employed in economics.[3] Fifty years later, the tables have turned, except that most anthropologists have abandoned induction (which is the other side of the coin to deduction) in favor of constructivism, narratives, and other means of persuasion!

Finally, according to Milberg, in the 1990s, economics began to evince another shift, this time toward empiricism and more reliance on the use of statistics—terms like "significance" are used now with their statistical meaning. The disadvantage is that statistics draws on probabilities but not certainty, so that the achievement of definite knowledge is no longer possible, and as economics becomes more pragmatic it becomes difficult to judge what constitutes progress. With this turning, the image and anchor of *homo economicus* is almost booted out the door. There is a fascinating consequence of this change that Milberg terms, "The Kletzer Effect." As Milberg suggests, statistical results can be interpreted, attributed with diverse meanings, and put to different uses. If he is correct, the difference between anthropology and economics narrows even further, because interpretation is a central method and persuasive device in anthropology.

By his analysis, then, the rhetoric of economics has shifted considerably from the logos or reasoning of deduction to induction and then to pragmatics and statistics. According to some of the cynics that he cites, it has even become chicanery with its emphasis on the stylistic (or lexis) device of statistics, especially when the statistical notion of significance takes on a broader meaning than is supported by probability theory.

Milberg has one more lightening bolt in his locker. In light of these changes, he sees an increasing move in economics toward the study of institutions (the New Institutionalism), especially institutions that have to do with property rights. By drawing on this approach, he suggests, economics will carry out a new imperialism of the other social sciences and may resurrect the image of *homo economicus*. In the next chapter, however, I offer a contrary story. Harold Demsetz presented one of the original and most cited articles that began the shift toward the New Institutionalism; my contribution attacks this essay by deconstructing its circular rhetoric. The conversational merry-go-round of economics and anthropology continues!

I interweave themes we have encountered in the essays by Carrier, Milberg, and Swedberg, such as different modes of knowing and forms of persuasion. Focusing on the concept of property, I highlight the different ways that economists and folk justify and explain their holdings. Both have narratives of legitimation, but the stories are worlds apart. Folk understandings, as made evident in tales, myths, and other verbal performances, are varied and have no predictable form. People often rely on rhetorical devices, such as metaphor and part-for-whole relations in their justifying narratives. Locally contested and discussed, these stories legitimate the shared holdings that I call a base. Standard economics employs a different rhetoric and displays a breach or tension in its stories. Often contemporary economics begins with Locke's story of possessive individualism and the extension of personal labor to objects that creates possession of them. This narrative uses rhetorical devices, such as metaphor and metonym. But the neoclassical narrative, as exemplified by the work of Harold Demsetz, silences these content-filled stories to employ a different mode of reason. His story persuades by use of calculative reason, deduction, and the expectation of achieving efficiency in competitive trade, which are hallmarks of formal economics. Examining the way that Demsetz applies this deductive mode to an ethnographic case (which Demsetz does in order to provide an aura of realism and beginnings), I find that Demsetz's narrative misconstrues the ethnographic content and turns solipsistic. His rhetorical form has no touchstone outside of itself. But the Demsetz story, which has been absorbed within the New Institutional Economics, has become persuasive in and outside of economics. Just as this case illustrates the tension between communicating by medium (derivational form) and by message (ethnographic content), it also suggests how the former often colonizes the latter in mentality and on the ground. The contrasting narratives employed by an economist and by a people, with their different rhetorical emphases, reflect the epistemological difference between economics and anthropology, even if in practice the two are often mixed together.

Metin Cosgel is interested in the differences between economics and anthropology as well, but he draws on the trope of conversations to explore the contrast. Cosgel finds that in the social sciences, anthropologists and economists talk to each other less than each does with other disciplines. They do not draw on one another's works as made evident in citation patterns, nor do they attend the same professional conferences. What is the difference between the two? Is it a divergence in assumptions, in the use of mathematics, in subject matter, in methodologies, or in models? These explanations, says Cosgel, are not persuasive, because such differences do not stop economists from conversing with scholars from other disciplines. Cosgel then explores two models of specialization (Adam Smith and Charles Babbage), which have aided economists, and applies these to conversation types. With this move, Cosgel shifts our focus from the different subject matter of the two fields to their conversational forms. Adopting a rather pragmatic perspective, he asks whether there is a difference in the problem each discipline attempts to solve. Economists try to discover how to align incentives or bring different interests together (as Swedberg observes); anthropologists try to make sense of dispersed interests. If one discipline asks how unlike interests can be joined, the other asks what people share. Anthropologists thus face the problem of finding out what they do not know (or even know how to find) in ill-defined contexts; economists encounter the problem that people may keep information about their interests secret. Each discipline socializes or disciplines its practitioners to converse and persuade in a particular way, which explains our lack of dialogue and sometimes-mutual antagonism. Cosgel concludes that by exploring our rhetorical differences, and drawing on our respective comparative advantages (as in classic trade theory), we may each benefit from cross-fertilization. In the language of economists, we can both benefit from "spillovers"; in the language of anthropologists, we can benefit from culture contact and "diffusion."

Jane Guyer finds that even when conversations take place among people who share interests, wish to reach agreement, and seemingly understand one another, "economics talk" may swirl out of control. She traces through a public debate in Nigeria during the 1983 to 1999 period of military rule and structural adjustment. Her central theme, which she takes from Hayek, concerns our everyday "craving for intelligibility" (rather like Cosgel's description of anthropologists) and Hayek's admonition that we should all "submit" to the unpredictable outcomes of markets rather than the predictable outcomes of central planning and authoritarian regimes. Hayek's view is linked to the Austrian distinction between market uncertainty, for which outcomes cannot be probabilistically calculated, and risky results to which probabilities can be attached. We should trust, he argues, that spontaneous order emerges through the invisible hand process, and we should accept our ignorance about the future. As Guyer shows, the rhetoric used in the Nigerian economic debates drew on the neoclassical perspective in which markets reach or are supposed to reach equilibrium or stasis and in which the concept and experience of uncertainty has no place. The neoliberal promise of certainty, however, was never fulfilled, even as the Nigerian people and media kept calling for a degree of certainty and closure.[4]

Guyer shows that Nigerians did not agree about what was happening in "the economy" or even whether there was "an economy." Government voices suggested there was an economy, which they knew how to manage; however, most people's experience of wildly fluctuating prices, unpredictable supplies, and worsening material conditions denied this political talk. People searched for and disagreed about "basic" concepts, such as "the deficit," "the surplus," "a subsidy," "price stability," and "benchmarking." Most Nigerians wanted to have a sense of certainty about the economy, but market results were uncertain and the meanings by which the market was understood were disparately defined and were contested. This confusion fed into the difference that was drawn between the near term and the future, especially by the International Monetary Fund. According to the structural adjustment rhetoric, one had to accept short-term difficulties and perplexities in the service of reaching long-term economic growth and stability through the market process. The steps between these stages, however, were never made clear or "simple," to invoke Carrier's distinction, and a gap opened up between the long-run promise and everyday hardship. A contested rhetoric emerged to fill this seemingly chaotic space. People wanted a feeling of certainty or intelligibility in everyday life, but abstract, simplistic terms such as freedom, democracy, the nation, and sacrifice were not satisfying. Guyer's rhetorical analysis shows how the debate swung back and forth between substance and expression, or between what was communicated and how it was conveyed. This shifting rhetoric may leave us with the sense that an economy can become so inscrutable that we can only search for terms to tame it or accept the limits of our knowledge, which was Hayek's argument.

Nurit Bird-David and Asaf Darr turn our attention to rhetoric in practices and to a topic that has occupied anthropology since Malinowski and Mauss. What is a "gift" and how is it different from a commodity? Are market exchanges of goods for money different from reciprocity or delayed gifting between acquaintances, friends, and strangers? Did anthropologists invent the category, "gift," in opposition to market trade, or does it have an ethnographic application? If, as many anthropologists claim, reciprocity is a distinct mode of exchange, what is the relation between their distinction and actors' practices? Drawing on ethnography from market contexts, Bird-David and Darr offer a new perspective on this puzzle by employing a pragmatic and rhetorical approach. They look at "mass-gifts" that are offered by retailers in Israel and at "samples" that are provided by wholesalers in the United States. In both cases, these gifts are offered as persuasions to purchase. Do these prestations create mutuality and a commitment to purchase the object? Alternatively, are they a price reduction that invokes a sense of thrift or a product sample that provides needed information before purchasing? If the gift accompanies the commodity that is sold, does it imply that the seller is reciprocating the payment with a "free" gift or is the seller simply providing full value? This market practice confounds our traditional separation between gifts and commodities, which sometimes exemplifies the opposition between anthropology and economics. How should we interpret these practices?

According to Bird-David and Darr, mass-gifts and samples help convince people in markets to transact. But there are local limits on their meaning. In some contexts, gifts cannot be offered because they would be seen as bribes. For example, purchasing agents in electronic companies can accept product samples but not lunches, although once a market trade is established a lunch may be accepted. Bird-David and Darr reveal how the rhetoric of the gift and of mutuality is appropriated to enhance market sales, suggesting that market transactions are being mystified or veiled as if they were mutuality in order to create a long-term relationship. In these rhetorical practices, substance and expression, or content and form, are contradictory. Such actions, filled with conflicting meanings, require contributions from both anthropology and economics not as alternatives or complements, but as dialectical voices that are joined in practices. Bird-David and Darr show how anthropology and economics as conversations about sharing knowledge and about aligning interests (to follow Cosgel) are both a part of economy.

Keith Hart and Ruben Oliven attend to that central tool in market economies: money. Traditionally, the analysis of "modern" money has been the province of economists who address interest rates, currency exchange, inflation, and a host of issues. Anthropologists used to talk about "primitive" currency and ask whether or not it shares features with market money. Both Hart and Oliven bring a more rhetorical approach to money if in different ways.

Hart has already provided a number of studies of money, but here he adds a fresh perspective by asking a central question: how does money persuade? How do we communicate through money, and what are we saying when using currency? We use money, of course, to persuade others to give up what they possess. Hart asks a deeper question: how have we endowed money with the capacity to convey both local and personal meanings, and joint and cross-cultural meanings? Perhaps, he suggests, its persuasive power lies in its capacity to mediate between the abstract and the singular.

Drawing on a range of writers to explicate money's power, Hart first invokes Spengler, in whom he finds a dialectical perspective that brings together and opposes number as magnitude and as function (relationships). Each signals constancy in variability; but, if one directs us to the concretely sensual, the other leads us toward infinite potential. According to Spengler, there is an historical transition from money as magnitude to money as abstraction, but Hart sees the dialectic as a universal property of money, which is the source of its persuasive power. We have faith in money, yet we are aware that this commitment must be collectively shared. Money is a tool for realizing one's wants; however, these can be fulfilled only through the shared medium that enables others to do the same; money binds us together even as we compete for it in a community. Money's rhetorical force is based on this dialectic that invokes content and form, message and medium, substance and expression. Without the capacity to convey personal meanings, money as an abstraction would lose its power. In this age of global capitalism, we increasingly use money in its abstract sense, which may be why local or community currencies also have been flourishing.

Ruben Oliven's essay fills the ethnographic space that Hart outlines. A Brazilian anthropologist, Oliven offers a set of ethnographic observations about everyday money practices in the United States. Money, he shows, is both meaningful and an empty medium. It is a measuring rod, a means of exchange and a store of value; but what is this "value" in local terms? Oliven recounts the

US everyday figures of speech about money. If I look at the hegemonic power of market rhetoric and the way it cascades into economic theories and into economic practices, Oliven considers how monetary associations cascade in daily life. Rhetoric here refers to how money is discussed and communicated, or its contents versus its form. Part of money's "value" lies in its pervasive and persuasive power to express US history, the life cycle, food, cleanliness, pathologies, religious differences, and even values insured by the Constitution. Money in the US is animate, and when it talks, it conveys a "universal" language that "all" of us understand as it soaks up many meanings that appeal. These US persuasions differ markedly from those in Brazil. If people thought they were not being rhetorical with money, they would be wise to read Oliven, for it is through such quotidian sayings and practices, as Hart argues, that money achieves its persuasive power.

Arjo Klamer draws the essays to a close with a model of economy that brings together perspectives from both economics and anthropology. Like other scholars, he is concerned about the rhetorical emphasis on form in economics. In its place, he offers a four-part, overlapping model of economy that consists of the oikos (the house), the social, the market, and the state. His model centers on incommensurate values and institutions, but their overlaps and the separate constituents are continually open to conversation and negotiation. Klamer thus addresses the content of values as well as their creation and modification in dialogue; in fact, the idea of economy as a conversation has long been a motif for him (1983) as it has been for myself (Gudeman and Rivera 1990), as Cosgel observes. Because values are a part of culture, Klamer observes, economy is never an independent domain. We converse about economy within the context of cultural values and "doing good." Going beyond the traditional idea that economics is a prescriptive discipline, Klamer revives the idea of economics as a moral science, which strikes a welcome chord with many anthropologists who—following Durkheim—see their field as a moral science. Klamer refers as well to the market as a conversation and even suggests that a significant part of the Gross Domestic Product is made up of conversations! Here, he is attacking the idea that individual preferences, which make up demand, are independently given. They are socially influenced and negotiated through conversations. Klamer even envisions the entrepreneur in terms of his persuasive powers and the conversations in which he engages. Ultimately, for Klamer, economic values and transactions are only a way or means to generate support for other value domains, such as art, rituals, and a heritage, which are its contents. With this perspective, he joins Aristotle in seeing material action as something done "for the sake of" something else rather than something done "for its own sake."

The Outcome

Economic Persuasions focuses in two directions: toward the similarities and differences in the rhetoric of anthropology and economics, and toward the rhetoric of people as they experience material life. One set of issues revolves around the different disciplinary rhetorics: are there epistemological differences between anthropologists and economists? Do they employ contradictory methodologies? Or, have their traditional fields of study been so different—small ethnographic societies and large industrial ones—that they have little in common? Why are the two disciplines unable to persuade one another of their own positions? From the second perspective, we have asked what illumination anthropologists can offer by exploring the language of everyday material life in both market societies and elsewhere. What persuades people in the realm of consumption or in economic policy making? And why has the rhetoric of economics so often become the legitimating force for taking action in everyday life?

We have approached these and similar questions in view of the fact that rhetoric in relation to material life can be understood in several ways: it is a method of analysis; it is constitutive of the world; and it is part of our analytical discourses. We can analyze the utterances of the Chair of the US Federal Reserve as a way of persuading people to believe in the economy, and as a way of constituting a world for us—a world of "objects," such as "the economy," "inflation," and "productivity." We can also look at our disciplinary discourses as constitutive techniques for seeing, being, and talking in the world, and as different styles. Whatever the mode, the exertion of influence and power over others and ourselves is woven into these ways of approaching economy. We make a world for ourselves through rhetoric. We invite the reader into this world and to join the conversation about this unexplored side of economic life.

Notes

1. Keynes, of course, long ago published his *Essays in Persuasion* in hopes of directing us to "our real problems—the problem of life and of human relations, of creation and behaviour and religion" (1932: vii).
2. The essays are reprinted in Hersokovits (1965).
3. As we observed, this same difference partly divided the formalists from the substantivist, as discussed by Carrier.
4. Hayek's themes suggest a pragmatic approach, which might connect him to John Dewey who, in 1929, published *The Quest for Certainty*, in which he saw culture as providing the certainty that humans seek. It was an anti-essentialist or anti-foundationalist position, just as Dewey was a defender of open, free speech as in the Nigerian debate.

CHAPTER 2

Simplicity in Economic Anthropology
Persuasion, Form, and Substance

James G. Carrier

■ ■ ■ ■ ■ ■

One, among the many, ways of defining rhetoric is that it is devices that are intended to persuade. Viewed thus, one could decide that all human communication, verbal or otherwise, is rhetorical. Were our task simply to chart the bounds of the use of rhetoric, there would be little left to say. But this view has an important corollary. That is, to see rhetoric as persuasive devices is to imply that it is independent of the content being communicated: the devices that do the urging are independent of the end toward which the audience is being urged.

Taking such a view separates rhetorical form from communicative substance. This separation of form and substance is familiar in Western academic thought, but, on closer inspection, it is not always so clear. This chapter presents a case where that separation dissolves. It does so by considering simplicity in intellectual debate. On its face, simplicity is a matter of form rather than substance, and it is potent rhetoric: simple arguments and pithy aphorisms appeal, it seems, in and of themselves. However, simplicity is not only formal, for it is associated with some substantive positions.

A point of entry into the relationship of simplicity, form, and substance—the concern of this chapter—is a dispute between two groups of anthropologists interested in economy. Appropriately, this dispute is called the formalist–substantivist debate. It played itself out in the 1960s and was not so much resolved as abandoned; commonly, it is assigned to the dustbin of disciplinary history. This debate is interesting in itself, but it is also part of a debate that has existed, does exist, and will continue to exist in the social sciences more generally. That debate is, ultimately, about how we should understand humans and their actions. The substance of the arguments made and the positions taken at various stages in that debate differ, but their forms remain recognizable over the last hundred years and more. These forms are rhetorical, for they are devices that persuade. However, and in testimony to the fragility of the boundary between form and substance, these forms appear to be linked to analytical content, and that content has consequences.

In presenting the formalist–substantivist debate as the most visible instance of a longer running intellectual debate, I am of course invoking my own simplifying and formal rhetoric. The works of various writers over more than a century get collapsed into a neat and relatively timeless binary opposition between essentialized positions. To say this, however, is only to observe that I am a creature of a cultural tradition, one that I have in common with the bulk of my likely readers and that offers a set of intellectual tools and contains a set of intellectual values. To bemoan this cultural position seems pointless; however, to ignore it is dangerous. This chapter deals with one aspect of that danger: the potentially unfortunate consequences of separating rhetorical form and communicative substance in an unreflective way.

The Formalist–Substantivist Debate

The 1960s debate was the first, and perhaps only, time that there was a sustained public discussion about the nature of economy among anthropologists and between anthropologists and at least some economists.[1] A pivotal figure in the debate was an economist and historian, Karl Polanyi, and the name for the debate came from a distinction he drew between two meanings of "economic" (Polanyi 1957: 243). One meaning is "formal," concerned with "the logical character of the means–ends relationship," and hence with the choice of alternative ends in a situation of scarcity of means. The other meaning is "substantive," concerned with the way we supply ourselves with "the means of material want satisfaction," and hence with the activities and institutions through which people secure their livelihoods. Following this distinction, the groups engaged in the debate were called "formalists," those who tended to see economy as a form of decision making, and "substantivists," those who tended to see economy as activities and as social relationships and institutions.

The debate was sparked by the appearance of *Trade and Markets in the Early Empires* (Polanyi, Arensberg, and Pearson 1957). In this collection, Polanyi extended some of the arguments laid out in his earlier *The Great Transformation* (Polanyi [1944] 1957), which analyzed the emergence of market economy in England and Western Europe, primarily in the nineteenth century. Polanyi argued that the English market economy was in no sense a natural development, as some earlier thinkers would have it. Rather, it was the hard-won accomplishment of political-economic interests, which were able to generate a string of legislation that would bring that economy about in the face of popular resistance. In other words, the development of the English market economy was a process that was historically contingent and hence needed to be explained by contextual factors.

This line of argument was pursued in different ways by the contributors to the later *Trade and Markets in the Early Empires,* who laid out analytical positions or described economic systems in ways that treated economic practices and values as contingent on the larger context in which they occurred. They also pointed to the ways that economic systems were institutionalized and even were a function of their institutionalization. That is, the institutions in which economic activities occurred were not approached as the consequence of the decisions and actions of individual economic transactors. Rather, those institutions had an existence and force of their own, typically resting on areas of social life that are not economic in any self-evident way, such as the political system or the kinship system.[2]

More narrowly, Polanyi (1957) argued that there are three broad types of economic transaction: reciprocity, redistribution, and exchange. Each of these types entails different institutions and practices, and all three are likely to exist to some degree in every society. While they may coexist, societies can be characterized in terms of the predominance of one or another of them. Of the three, the exchange form (effectively, market transactions between autonomous individuals) predominates in Western capitalist societies, and in these societies the economy comes closest to being a distinct realm, disembedded from other important social institutions. Also, in such societies, the concept of the rational, calculating individual not only predominates as a cultural image, but also reflects the orientation common among people exchanging with each other. This is the sort of orientation Adam Smith ([1776] 1976: 18) pointed to when he wrote: "It is not from the benevolence of the butcher, the brewer, or the baker, that we expect our dinner, but from their regard to their own interest."

Polanyi's argument was attractive to anthropologists working in non-Western, noncapitalist societies, who were, reasonably enough, looking for ways to help them make sense of the self-evident differences between what they observed in the field and the capitalist market economies that dominated the West (a classic example is Sahlins 1963). Not surprisingly, *Trade and Markets in the Early Empires* generated substantial interest. As well, it generated an articulated opposition, the writers of which who came to be identified as formalists. The formalist criticism had three noteworthy aspects. The first was that the substantivists had their facts wrong. Formalist critics argued that throughout the world, people make economic decisions on the basis of the sort of rational calculation that, they said, Polanyi's model treated as predominant only in exchange systems such as the capitalist West.

The second, and related, aspect of this criticism was that the substantivists were romantics who were disenchanted with the modern world.[3] This disenchantment, critics argued, led them to create an imagined alternative, a Golden Age in which societies were full of harmonious souls who were interested in collective well being rather than maximizing their gain. According to one pair of influential formalists (LeClair and Schneider 1968: 11), the substantivist desire to construct such a Golden Age meant that, "it is necessary to define markets out of existence in earlier societies in order to preserve the perception of earlier societies as in some sense ideal."

The third common criticism was that substantivists got their theory wrong. Formalists argued that substantivists, with few exceptions, did not understand the economic theory that they were attacking, which was effectively neoclassical economics. Rather, according to critics, the substantivists attacked "an already outmoded concept of an 'economic man'" (LeClair and Schneider 1968: 4) that no self-respecting economist would espouse. While the concept may have seemed outmoded to LeClair and Schneider, it has proven remarkably durable (see, in their different ways, Ferber and Nelson 1993; Sahlins 1996). Indeed, it is a central figure in the issues addressed here, and I will return to it from time to time.

I have sketched the debate between the formalists and the substantivists, a debate that, as I said at the outset, generally is consigned to the dustbin of history. Though it may be a creature of the 1960s, it deserves our attention in view of the issues that were at stake.

The debate was about the most rewarding way to understand important aspects of people's collective lives. The formalists urged an approach based on what they took to be a human universal, the calculation of costs and benefits with the goal of achieving the greatest possible benefit for the least possible cost. Because this is a common attribute, the way that people make decisions can properly be abstracted from the social contexts in which those decisions occur, and analyzed in its own right (this abstraction from context is valued strongly in the modern West: see Carrier 2001). The substantivists argued that this is by no means a common human attribute, but is apparent only in certain times and places. Because they are not a common attribute, decisions can only be approached in terms of the social contexts in which they occur; and because these contexts are analytically prior to people's decisions, contexts are the proper object of study.

I said earlier that my argument contains its own simplifying rhetoric. That simplification appears in what I have said about the formalists and substantivists, though it reflects the tone of the debate between them, if not the considered positions of the different participants. Those on one side of the debate were concerned with the form of economic decision making. However, that form has a substantial element: the individual preferences by which people assign different values to the alternatives that they confront. Equally, those on the other side of the debate were concerned with the substance of the means and institutions by which people satisfy their material wants. However, that substance has a formal element as well, which was important for Polanyi and his fellows—the types of transactions, social relations, and institutions that the substantivists identified. Thus, it is that, in their understanding of economy, both sides of the formalist–substantivist debate attended to both form and substance. For the formalists, the pertinent form and substance were located in the mentality of the economic actor; for the substantivists, they were located in the social transactions and relations in which that actor was involved.

However, the complex nature of the intellectual position of each side in the debate was simplified, and its relevance reduced, by the form of the debate itself. Not surprisingly, those on each side of the debate tended to define themselves by their difference from those on the other. Formalists emphasized rational calculation of means in relations to ends as a human constant; substantivists emphasized the social contexts and institutional patterns of economic activity.

Put differently, in this debate, the formalists put forward positions that were methodological-individualist and that were universalist in that they saw all humans as having the same mental predisposition, which was to maximize their return in transactions. At a fundamental level, their world is uniform; what differences do appear are relatively insignificant epiphenomena of a prior uniformity. Conversely, the substantivists put forward a methodology that was sociological, which was seeing people in terms of their social context. In being sociological, their methodology implies a particularist approach: the formalist universal human tendencies are replaced by attention to context, difference, and division. At a fundamental level, their world was diverse.

Given these issues, we should not wonder that the debate was abandoned rather than resolved. After all, how can we resolve the difference between universalism and particularism, the difference between a focus on individuals and a focus on the relations in which they exist, the difference between neutral rationality and contextual social value? The only things that should cause us to wonder are that anyone would think the debate is over, and that any group could declare that its side won.

The Debate Perennial

In being about such fundamental issues, the formalist–substantivist debate was but one manifestation of a perennial debate in anthropology, and in the social sciences more generally. I want to trawl the history of the discipline now to show some of the ways that that debate has appeared. Arguably, both sociology and social anthropology began in the last quarter of the nineteenth century with the work of Emile Durkheim, and I will begin there.

A central work of Durkheim's is *The Division of Labour in Society* ([1893] 1984). In it, he did battle with an English social-evolutionist, Herbert Spencer. As Durkheim presented it, Spencer's claim was that the basis of society was individuals' transactions with each other, as exemplified by contract. Moreover, social evolution was the gradual elimination of the collective restrictions on these transactions; the transactions were gradually abstracted as their social contexts lost constraining power. Those restrictions had been a feature of militarism, an evolutionary stage in which internal diversity was subordinated to the uniformity that would provide the society's strength in a dangerous world. As Durkheim ([1893] 1984: 150) phrased it, Spencer was arguing that "with the decline of militarism and the ascendancy of industrialism, the power as well as the extent of [collective, social] authority diminishes, and as freedom of action increases, so does the relationship of contract become more general."

Spencer's model was not just descriptive, but was evaluative as well, social evolution being both natural and good. Not only were individuals increasingly being liberated from social constraint, but it was good that this was happening. People were best left alone, free to be autonomous individuals. Spencer, then, wanted us to strip away the hindrances to what Adam Smith ([1776] 1976: 17) called people's inherent "propensity to truck, barter, and exchange one thing for another." As Durkheim ([1893] 1984: 152) phrased it, for Spencer, "society would be no more than the establishment of relationships between individuals exchanging the products of their labour"; or, in Margaret Thatcher's words of a century later, there is no such thing as society.

Spencer's model presupposed, of course, that individuals, their desires, and propensities existed well before the rise of the stage of industrialism. Were this not the case, it would make no sense for him to argue that they were suppressed in the earlier stage of militarism. Durkheim said that Spencer was incorrect. Individuals and their desires are not prior to society; they did not exist independent of their context, becoming increasingly visible as social constraints upon individuals were reduced with the rise of industrialism. "In fact, if in lower societies so little place is allowed for the individual personality, it is not that it has been constricted or suppressed artificially, it is quite simply because at that moment in history it did not exist" (Durkheim [1893] 1984: 142). The individuals and the transactions that Spencer described are, then, functions of their social contexts.

The disagreement between Durkheim and Spencer does not match perfectly with the disagreement between the substantivists and formalists. However, there is a family resemblance. Spencer, at least as Durkheim rendered him, saw a world of uniformly motivated individuals who differed primarily in the constraint they faced. In contrast, Durkheim saw a world of qualitative difference between societies, the attributes of which were crucial for shaping what it was that their members were and what they wanted to or could do.

If Durkheim is arguably the founder of social anthropology, Bronislaw Malinowski is arguably the founder of the discipline in its modern form. And in his work, we see similar concerns, though more ambiguously than is the case with Durkheim. The first and most famous of his volumes of Trobriand Island ethnography is *Argonauts of the Western Pacific* (1922), a work that many take as the foundation of economic anthropology. Malinowski wrote that work in part against what he presented as an important element of the economic thought of his day. That was the idea of "the Primitive Economic Man … an imaginary, primitive man, or savage, prompted in all his actions by a rationalistic conception of self-interest, and achieving his aim directly and with the minimum of effort" (Malinowski 1922: 60).

Such a figure has two features. The first is that this Man is Economic, and hence has the eye for self-interest that Adam Smith ascribed to the butcher, brewer, and baker. The second feature is that this Economic Man is Primitive, in the sense of being primal. Because the Trobriands were a Primitive society, its inhabitants provided instances of humanity in the raw, free of the sort of social and cultural overlay that would obscure the basic human tendencies. Because, one imagines the argument to go, these are people who exist "untrammelled by convention and social regulations" (1922: 92), we should see human economizing in its pure form.

Malinowski strongly rejected this "preposterous" (1922: 60) notion, and argued: "Quite the reverse is the case" (1922: 96), though on grounds very different from Durkheim's. Whatever the status of Economic Man, the people that Malinowski observed in the Trobriands were not primitive. They may have lacked the trappings of Western civilization, but that did not mean that they were asocial, with neither custom nor culture to restrain them. They did not, in fact, behave in the way that Economic Man in primitive society should. For example, "work is not carried out on the principle of least effort. On the contrary, much time and energy is spent on wholly unnecessary effort, that is, from a utilitarian point of view" (Malinowski 1922: 60). Similarly, while Trobriand Islanders may like to acquire things, "the social code of rules, with regard to give and take by far overrides his natural acquisitive tendency" (Malinowski 1922: 96).

In asserting that Trobriand Islanders did not accord with the construct of a Primitive Economic Man, Malinowski was challenging the construct's assumption that real, existing societies identified as primitive lack the moderating constraints of the civilized world. His complaint, then, was with the assumption that people like those in the Trobriands were effectively asocial. In his criticism, however, Malinowski was arguing in favor of a uniform world, accessible more or less directly to us all. The social conventions may vary from place to place. However, the underlying human psyche, such as the Trobrianders' "natural acquisitive tendency," is the same.

Trobrianders are not, it seems, so very different from ourselves. And Malinowski's assertion of this lack of difference was driven home in his disagreement with another of the founders of economic anthropology, Marcel Mauss. In *The Gift* ([1925] 1990), Mauss had used Malinowski's Argonauts to illustrate the ideas of the gift and of societies of the gift, and one should recall that Mauss famously rooted the institutions and practices of the gift in the distinctly nonmodern sort of thought exemplified in the Maori concept of the hau, the spirit of the gift. Malinowski would have none of it. "The honourable citizen," he said in rebuttal, "is bound to carry out his duties, though his submission is not due to any … mysterious 'group sentiment,' but to the detailed and elaborate working of a system … [in which there] comes sooner or later an equivalent repayment or counter-service" (Malinowski 1926: 42).

In contrast to Mauss, then, Malinowski was similar to Spencer and the formalists in that he saw the world as populated by individuals who were more or less alike. A Trobriander may do things differently from a Londoner or a Parisian, but the differences were insubstantial, for those people's underlying rationality and propensities were the same, a sameness apparent when these people's judgments and decisions are abstracted from their contexts and viewed in formal terms. On the other hand, Mauss, like Durkheim and the substantivists, located people in their social settings, which definitely were not more or less alike. For Mauss, to abstract the person and the decision from the context is nonsensical, for these exist only in terms of their context. Indeed, Mauss ([1938] 1985) echoed Durkheim in arguing that that the very notion of the individual, self-interested or otherwise, is a creature of socio-historical context.

Just as these issues were salient in the discipline before the debate between the formalists and the substantivists, so they remained salient afterwards. However, because subsequent work is more recent, I can attend to it more briefly.

An obvious place where these issues were addressed is the distinction between gift and commodity, articulated most famously in the work of C.A. Gregory (esp. 1980; 1982). He describes two forms of economic life, one dominated by the gift and the other by the commodity, two forms that differ in systematic ways. Most broadly, Gregory (1980: 640) says that the circulation of commodities revolves around "the social conditions of the reproduction of things," while the circulation of gifts revolves around "the social conditions of the reproduction of people." More narrowly, he argues that in commodity relations, transactions are voluntary (at least formally), objects are alienated from the transactors, and the transactors themselves are neither linked with nor obligated to each other. In gift relations, on the other hand, transactions are mandatory, objects are inalienably linked to the transactors, and the transactors themselves are mutually obligated and related (see Carrier 1995a: chap. 1).

This sort of bifurcation, which echoes Polanyi's distinction between types of transaction systems, is not, of course, unique to Gregory. For example, Louis Dumont contrasted an integrated and hierarchical India with an individualist and economistic West in a pair of magisterial books, *Homo Hierarchicus* (1970) and *From Mandeville to Marx* (1977). Similarly, in *The Gender of the Gift*, Marilyn Strathern (1988) contrasted Melanesia with the modern West in terms that echo both Gregory's and Dumont's arguments. For Strathern, the West is the land of possessive individuals transacting impersonal things, while her Melanesians are dividuals, partible persons inevitably linked to each other and to the things that they produce and consume, give and take. And as with Dumont and Polanyi, she simplifies the complex social systems that she invokes (Carrier 1992).

For these writers, the world is by no means populated by people who are fundamentally alike and using the same mental calculus, in the way that the world is for the formalists, Spencer, and Malinowski. Rather, forms of thought and action, and the associated social institutions, vary from region to region, if not from society to society.

Echoes of the formalist side of the debate reverberate as well. One instance of this is optimal foraging theory, which became important in the discipline at about the same time that Gregory and Dumont were writing (see Foley 1985). Optimal foraging theory rests not on the assumption that humans share common attributes, but on the assumption that all animals, and indeed all living things, share common attributes. These are the attributes of evolutionary fitness and comparative reproductive advantage. In its basic form, optimal foraging theory is a way of assessing and explaining the ways that living beings search for, secure, and use resources, most notably food. In this, birds (e.g., Richardson and Verbeek 1986) and hunter–gatherers (e.g., Hill et al. 1984) are creatures having the same imperatives, just as these hunter–gatherers traveling their territory looking for food are the same as people browsing the web searching for information (Pirolli and Card 1998).

Optimal foraging theory is based on the assumptions of Darwinian evolution, in which motivations and reward are, at least in principle, clear and uncontestable. Physical survival and reproductive advantage spring from forces we take as being beyond the social realm. However, its expansion to areas of life other than getting food and to results other than biological reproduction drives home the point that optimal foraging theory is a frankly economistic model. Accordingly, decisions and actions are viewed formally, as being shaped by marginal utility: hunting in groups rather than as individuals, like continuing to search a particular territory or web site rather than moving on to a different one, occurs because the net return from one course of action rather than another is greater. However, as was the case with the formalists, the substantial preferences that define utility for an individual are taken for granted rather than investigated. In this, the theory blends fairly seamlessly into the approach of Gary Becker. He represents perhaps the classic Chicago theoretical economist, and was awarded a Nobel Prize in 1992. Although he is not an anthropologist, Becker is worth mentioning here because he symbolizes the growing general influence of economistic models throughout the social sciences in the 1980s.

His intellectual project is the relentless expansion of the ambit of formal economic modeling beyond the realm of the market transactions that were its original focus, to all areas of living, including decisions about family life and relations (e.g., Becker 1991), religious belief (e.g., Becker 1996), and crime (e.g., Becker 1968). In all of these realms of social life, Becker seeks to explain what people do in terms of the marginal utility of alternative courses of action that are rationally evaluated. The scope of this vision was described by Assar Lindbeck (1992), in the speech he gave when presenting Becker with the Nobel prize: Becker was being recognized for producing "a theory of rational choice, i.e. of purposeful behavior." For Becker, then, it is not only that people are fundamentally all the same, operating with the same mental calculus regardless of their individual utility functions, but it is as well that all areas of life are the same, as those people apply the same calculus to everything they do (see Fine 1998).

Simplification and Abstraction

I have reviewed some of the debates and orientations that existed or were reflected in anthropology since the founding of the discipline, which point to a recurring tension between two approaches. One construes the world as made of individuals who are fundamentally alike, with the corollary that people's actions should be investigated and explained in terms of their basic alikeness, and with the further corollary that the context of people's actions is relatively insignificant. The second approach construes the world as made of types of societies that are fundamentally different, with the corollary that people's actions should be investigated and explained in terms of their context. I will refer to these as the individualist and sociologist orientations in the balance of this chapter.[4]

In pointing to the individualist and sociologist aspects of these different positions, I do not mean that individualists ignore the social, or that the sociologists ignore the individual. For instance, some individualists argue that individual people's dealings have social consequences, producing complex structures that themselves have consequences, a position illustrated by the new institutional economics (promulgated in Williamson 1975). Equally, as I have noted in passing already, some sociologists argue that the ordering of social life affects the orientation of individuals (e.g., Bernstein 1971; Durkheim [1897] 1951; Mauss [1938] 1985). These efforts by some in each camp to account for, or colonize, the phenomena of concern to the other are significant, not least because they show that elaborated positions on each side of these debates can come to resemble positions on the other side. However, these colonizations are derivative of their respective orientations, in the sense that what they account for is treated as epiphenomenal, generated by the processes or operations that are viewed as basic. In Williamson's new institutional economics, for instance, economic patterns and institutions are the result of ontically prior individuals and their calculations and transactions, while in Durkheim's view of suicide, that most private of acts varies with changes in the ontically prior social order.

Of these two positions, the one that seems to have dominated in the past few decades is the individualist one, most visibly in the discipline of economics. It is, after all, Becker who was awarded the Nobel prize, not Gregory. This is true even in anthropology, in spite of its generally sociological orientation. Since the 1970s, there has been a move away from a concern with structure, constraint, and regularity, and toward a concern with process and individual agency. This move reached its peak in fin de siecle postmodernism and may be receding now, just as the popularity of a Becker-esque concern with rational choice shows signs of receding. There are many factors that can help account for the predominance of the individualist approach. Here, I want to point to one of them: the rhetorical appeal of simplicity.

At its most basic, the individualist argument is simpler than the sociological one. Spencer's market-going individuals are easy to understand, just like Malinowski's Trobriand Islander expecting a return. We can empathize with these individuals and the simple calculus that guides them, without the sort of effort that, for instance, Weber devoted to construing a Puritan's mental world. Life on the other side of these debates is more complex and resistant to easy comprehension. Opposed to Spencer's simple vision, in *The Division of Labour*, Durkheim had to develop and invoke a range of concepts and variables: organic and mechanical solidarity, conscience collective, retributive and restitutive legal systems, and the like. Similarly, Mauss struggled with the hau, the spirit of the gift, a notion sufficiently complex that it generated a minor industry of commentary and criticism (e.g., Parry 1986: 462–66; Sahlins 1972: chap. 4).

Simplicity's rhetorical attraction is significant, and this is certainly true for public debate. There, a clear and straightforward vision that cuts through a complex problem can have a powerful and comprehensive appeal. We are all somewhat seduced by the lure of cutting the Gordian knot, rather than untangling it. We can all, that is, sympathize with the thoughts of a British advocate of that public, late-twentieth-century form of individualism, neoliberalism. This man said that he was drawn to it by the way it "provides clear, consistent and above all, simple solutions to the problems thrown up by society and the economy" (Cockett 1994: 194). Simplicity helps drive the slogans that resonate over time: de Mandeville's aphorism that private vice leads to public virtue; Smith's assertion of the human propensity to truck, barter, and exchange. Their opponents rarely have so compelling a vision: their concern with context and difference puts them at a rhetorical disadvantage. The big battalions do not march under the banner of "It all depends!"

We can see this simplicity elsewhere in the public realm as well. For instance, a wave of reform that spread through the government in the United States in the 1970s and 1980s, and finding echoes in Britain, sought to make government more "business-like." This revolved around variants of cost–benefit analysis (MacLennan 1997). This technique required firstly that all projected costs and benefits of a proposed government policy be simplified, by being reduced to a single unit of measurement, money. The technique then simplified the decision making process into seeing whether the proposed policy had more cost or more benefit. The same recurs in policies intended to protect the environment. There, programs to impose individual transferable quotas on resource extractors, typically in fisheries, replace complex notions of skill, experience, and leadership, complex concepts of nationality, group membership, and entitlement in a common resource, with the capitalist logic of a market in licenses to exploit (e.g., Helgason and Palsson 1997). In such cases, there is the imposition of a single, uniform measure, money, which on its face eliminates divergence in opinion, value, or way of seeing the world.[5] There is also the imposition of a mechanical means for deciding, which is comparing monetized cost and monetized benefit. These impositions operate whether one is deciding who should catch cod, or deciding whether to build a bridge, or to support research on malaria, or to clear asbestos from a plot of land.

Simplicity, though, is not the property solely of the individualist approach, for it is found on the other side of the fence as well. However, as I noted above, it is of a different sort. It is not the supposition of a set of common human propensities, but the analytical supposition of uniformity among societies of different kinds, kinds often defined by the form of their social relations. Just as Polanyi laid out three forms of economic organization, so in *The Division of Labour* Durkheim distils a mass of evidence about different societies into two, seemingly homogeneous types. Likewise, Mauss reduced the world that he described to societies of the gift, archaic societies, and modern societies. While these models allow for differences among types of society, each of them elides differences among societies within each type, as each elides differences among the different people and realms of life found within societies of whatever type. As these examples show, however, the sociological side of the debate is less thorough-going in its simplification than the individualist side: Polanyi's three forms of economic organization, each with its own complex of properties, is a long way from the simplicity of the universal maximizing individual. This is not least because it allows the possibility of other types, while universalist approaches do not.

I do not present my point about simplification because I think it is novel. We have all been told about anthropological (and other) simplification and about some of its more baleful intellectual and social consequences (see, e.g., Carrier 1995b; Carrier and Miller 1998; Said 1978; not to mention much of the anthropology published since the 1980s). Even though the point is not novel, it is worth repeating. Simplicity, which in the analysis of social life typically means abstraction from context, is something that helps persuade us all. Perhaps for this reason, it is important that we remind ourselves of both its existence and its force. Doing so helps make it more visible and less taken for granted, which in turn helps make us more aware of its corollaries and consequences.

Simplicity's Rhetoric

As I have suggested, this simplification is not just one of those devices that persuade. Rather, it appears to have substantial consequences for how we approach the question of understanding people, their lives, and relationships. Rhetorical form and communicative substance are not, then, as distinct as we might suppose.

As the examples I described in this chapter indicate, simplicity tends to be accompanied by two things. The first is a tendency to construe social life in terms of rational actors and their mental calculus, a pass of Occam's Razor eliminating the entire social level that concerned the substantivists. The second is a tendency to seek causal models that account for social life and, in principle, allow one to predict and plan it, another pass that eliminates the significance of all that exists at the level of mere surface appearance. Becker, after all, did not get his Nobel Prize for his fine-grained description of people's criminality, religious beliefs and practices, or domestic relations, but for a theory of purposeful behavior. Applying that theory abstracts the principles taken to account for such behavior from the particular cases where Becker sees them manifest and presents them on their own in a concise form that comes close to that of logical propositions.

Among some academics, this sort of simplicity has corollaries that, once more, echo Becker's work. These revolve around ideas of rationality and efficiency, as in the rational and efficient use of natural resources (see Johnson 2004). This conjunction of simplicity, rationality, and efficiency echoes what some have identified as the Modernist project (e.g., Scott 1998). That conjunction has two aspects that are pertinent here. One is the desire to understand the world in a distinctive way (as in, e.g., Pryor 2005). The other, to use that understanding to predict and control the world, is more problematic.

This control of the world takes two forms. One is the desire to produce programs for action in the world that are portable, ranging from programs to restructure civil service organizations to programs to preserve commercial fishing stocks. Because people are fundamentally alike and guided by the same simple motives, the argument goes, these programs can be applied just about anywhere without substantial modification. The second form that this control takes is somewhat more complex, which is what is called virtualism (Carrier and Miller 1998). Here, the goal is not to assure that the abstract models adequately reflect the world that they seek to describe, but to assure that the world conforms to the models. In other words, those models cease to be just descriptive, but become prescriptive. So, for societies where economic organization and practice do not conform to abstract economic models, efforts are made not to bring the models into line with the organization and practice, but to bring the organization and practice into line with the models (as in, e.g., structural adjustment programs, see McMichael 1998; see also Miller 1998).

Because the models underlying these projects to control ignore context, they help make the projects themselves appear to be decontextualized, in the sense of being free of the debates and disputes about what ought to be done that are the realm of politics, which is to say the realm of the social and of divergent preferences. In this, such projects are almost inevitably anti-politics machines (see Ferguson 1990; see also Mosse 2005). This is not to say that these models are free of debate and dispute; certainly, they are not. However, those debates and disputes are hidden, embedded in transmuted form in the content of these models and the institutions that promulgate them, rather than being apparent in their application (see, famously, Kuhn 1970). The politics is there, then, but in the traces that it leaves; as well, of course, as in the greater authority possessed by those who proclaim and apply such models, compared to those who are the objects of the models and of the projects based on them.

Conclusion

I have sketched a set of debates in economic anthropology, and in the social sciences more generally, with two ends in view. One is to show how these debates circle around a basic opposition that is never resolved, but return to it repeatedly in somewhat different form. The second is more tentative, to argue that while simplicity is a device that persuades, it is more than just a formal rhetorical figure. Rather, it appears to have substantial aspects, illustrated both by the sort of worldview and by the activist and interventionist approach to social life with which is it associated. I do not claim that this worldview and this approach to social life are necessary corollaries of the sort of abstract simplicity I have described, but their association is real.

This abstract simplicity and the Modernist project with which it is associated have been criticized for their costs and failures (especially Scott 1998). However, it is important to recognize their successes (e.g., the eradication of smallpox), just as it is important to recognize the weaknesses of the apparent alternatives. The prime alternative in anthropology seems to be to search for agency, celebrate diversity, and cherish the heterodox. Too often, however, this seems to be reduced to a kind of *chacun à son goût* and the rhetoric of lifestyles freely chosen in something like a cultural supermarket. This brings us perilously close to the formalists' individualist view. As well, it is important to recognize that some degree of abstraction and attendant simplicity may well be necessary. After all, in the debates described here, the side that I have called sociologist invoked its own abstractions and simplifications.

It is not clear, then, that the basic debate I have described can be resolved. Rather, it seems likely that the two positions will continue to exist in some sort of tension. This is consonant with the way that Radcliffe-Brown (1952: 1–2) described the distinction between ethnography and comparative sociology. However, where he saw this distinction largely as one between gathering information (ethnography) and generalizing from it (comparative sociology), the half-century since Radcliffe-Brown described this distinction has made it clear that there is much more separating the two than just their function in the anthropological enterprise.

Equally, it is not clear that the distinction between rhetorical form and conceptual substance can be maintained in any rigorous way. Form and substance may be distinct logically, which is to say, formally. However, it appears that in the empirical, which is to say, substantive, case of the important and long running debate described in this chapter, this distinction dissolves. The reasons for the association of formal simplicity with certain substantive positions, and for the association of formal complexity with different positions, are beyond my competence, much less the scope of this chapter. However, until these reasons are discerned, the realm of rhetoric looks to be perilously close to the realm of culture and political debate; so close, indeed, that its independent existence appears problematic.

Notes

1. The core substantivist position is Polanyi, Arensberg, and Pearson (1957), followed by Bohannan and Dalton (1965). A treatment of that position is in Isaac (2005), describing the work of its prime thinker, Karl Polanyi. The most extensive formalist statement is the collection edited by LeClair and Schneider (1968), with briefer statements in Cook (1966b) and the resultant comment by Cancian (1966) and rejoinder by Cook (1966a). A sound summary of the debate is in Wilk (1996: 3–13), which foreshadows some of what I say here.
2. Polanyi was not, of course, the first to make these sorts of points, which are found in much of the work of the mature Marx, and in Weber's (1958) *Protestant Ethic.*
3. Two meanings of "romantic" apply here, though formalist critics referred only to one. The first was the tendency to see alien societies in isolation, untouched by Western civilization, a tendency described by Eric Wolf (1964: 11–12; invoked in Cook 1966b: 327). The second is the long-standing German Romantic criticism of the instrumentalism of capitalism (described in Kahn 1990; 1997).
4. These appear to have been the two main positions on offer, though others are possible. For instance, we could construe the world as made of societies that are fundamentally alike, or as made up of individuals who are fundamentally different. The former position seems never to have attracted much support in the social sciences. The latter position was apparent in Levy-Bruhl's (1923) idea of primitive mentality.
5. "On its face," because these divergences exist, but only in terms of assigning a monetary value to different benefits and costs (see, e.g., MacLennan 1997). Once a value is assigned, that divergence is made invisible. I pursue this point in the next section.

CHAPTER 3

WHEN RHETORIC BECOMES MASS PERSUASION
THE CASE OF THE CONCEPT OF INTEREST

Richard Swedberg

■ ■ ■ ■ ■ ■

THROUGH THE RISE OF NEOLIBERALISM from 1980 and onward, many ideas and concepts in mainstream economics have spilled into the realm of social science and have become a part of political ideology. This migration of ideas has placed pressure on the noneconomic social sciences to adopt economic concepts; and this pressure is ideological rather than scientific in nature. The attempt to persuade someone else—in this case the noneconomic social scientists—through reason and logic has been replaced by something much broader, what we may call *mass persuasion,* to speak like Robert Merton (1946).

This story has a macro dimension as well as a micro dimension; and in this article, I will focus on the latter. I am more concerned with the confusion caused by ideology intruding on other disciplines than with the evolution of neoliberalism and why there exists a certain affinity between its ideas and those in the economics profession. By taking a close look at one key concept in economics, *interest,* I propose to work out my argument about the spillover of economic ideas into political ideology.[1] I proceed historically, because I believe that without understanding the history of concepts, we cannot understand their meaning and how meaning may change over time. I will first show how economists appropriated and transformed the concept of interest for their own use, which they did very successfully; however, the product of their efforts was a singularly nonsocial concept of interest, which is not suitable for use in the other social sciences—even if the rhetoric has been persuasive.

The Economists' Concept of Interest

One of the great success stories of early social theory concerns the way that economists seized on the concept of interest, transformed it, and used it to lay the foundation for what was to become modern economic analysis. The first step in the process of turning the so-called analysis of wealth into modern economics was taken by Adam Smith in the late 1700s (e.g., Kirzner 1976). He famously used the concept of interest to connect economic activities at the micro level ("self-love," "interest") to what happened at the macro level ("the wealth of nations"). Using the famous image of the "invisible hand," he linked the two and created the idea of economy as an autonomous area of society with its own laws and principles. By proceeding in this manner, Adam Smith transformed into social science what Mandeville had earlier held up as a moral and scandalous paradox (*Private Vices, Public Benefits*; Mandeville [1714] 1981). The well known figures of the baker, the brewer, and the butcher are from Adam Smith's perspective self-interested or self-loving individuals—but they must also produce good merchandise to attract customers, and in so doing, they serve the interest of the general public. From Smith's viewpoint, all of this was part of a larger attempt to reconcile the existence of virtue with the existence of a commercial society, but posterity soon transformed Smith's ideas in a different direction (see for example, Tribe 1999).

The second and crucial step in the appropriation by the economists of the concept of interest came in the early nineteenthnineteenth century with the invention of the idea of *homo economicus,* a development that is usually associated with the work of John Stuart Mill (Persky 1995). In his attempt to define political economy in the 1830s, Mill proposed that economics should disregard everything except the economic interest or motive for "the desire of wealth" (Mill [1836] 1992: 137–39). By proceeding in this manner, the economist could bypass everything in economic actions but an idealized version of economic interest (as the profit-motive).

Mill's move yielded results, and by the end of the nineteenth century, most of modern price theory had come into being and was gradually extended from one area to another in economics. At the heart of this theory were the insights of marginal utility theory, which yielded the famous "Marshallian cross" of demand and supply (Marshall 1890). Exact (but formal) prices could now be analytically predicted as well as manipulated.

One negative aspect of this development in the use of interest was that economic theory became one-dimensional and profoundly nonsocial in nature, as it was based on the idea of *homo economicus.* Frank Knight's often cited list of what characterizes *homo economicus* includes items such as "complete rationality" and that "every member of society is to act ... in entire independence of all other persons" (Knight [1921] 1971: 76–81).

Modern economic theory had come off to a very successful academic start through its appropriation of the concept of interest, but it had also turned the idea into a single dimensional and nonsocial concept. In the 1930s, whatever was left of a subjective dimension of the economists' concept of interest was eliminated through the theory of revealed preferences, as extrapolated through his or her observed behavior (Samuelson 1938). This helped to eliminate whatever was left of the concrete actor's perception of the situation.

The Sociological Approach to the Concept of Interest, Part I (Georg Simmel et. al)

It becomes important precisely at this point to look at the way another group of social scientists—the sociologists—tried to appropriate and use the concept of interest in the nineteenth century for their purposes, because they followed a very different route from that of the economists and reached a different destination. They developed a concept of interest that was multi-dimensional as well as social in nature—a concept that fits today's noneconomic social scientists much better than the economic concept.

The story of this alternative concept of interest has long been forgotten and therefore deserves to be told in some detail. Key people in this effort include: Gustav Ratzenhofer (1842–1904), Georg Simmel (1858–1918), Max Weber (1864–1920), and Albion Small (1854–1926). Their ideas on interest, as we soon shall see, are situated at the center of their view of sociology, which makes it suitable for use by noneconomic social scientists.

In German-speaking academia, much attention was paid during the 1890–1920 period to Gustav Ratzenhofer's ideas that interest represents the driving force (*Urkraft*) of all social behavior and that it should therefore constitute the foundation of sociology (e.g., Ratzenhofer 1907; cf. e.g., Martindale 1960: 184–87, Timasheff 1967: 65–66). Ratzenhofer's ideas were effectively spread in the United States by Albion Small, who presented them in a very favorable light in *The American Journal of Sociology* as well as in *General Sociology* (Small 1900; 1905; cf. e.g., Kocourek 1917). Mention should also be made of Arthur Bentley, who studied under Small at the University of Chicago and is considered the father of the theory of interest groups (Bentley [1908] 1967).

Gustav Ratzenhofer was a well-known sociologist in his day, however, his work has not survived in contrast to that of Georg Simmel, especially Simmel's writings on sociology. As is well known, the key theoretical chapter in Simmel's *Soziologie* (1908) centers around the Kantian distinction between content and form. This famous chapter ("How Is Society Possible?") also contains a forceful argument about the need to take interests into account in sociological analysis. Simmel's most important ideas in this context are: (1) that it is precisely interests and similar forces that make people come together and form various social configurations; and, (2) that interests, on the one hand, and social configurations, on the other, are inseparably united in concrete reality (as opposed to in analytical thought). Simmel's key formulations in "How is Society Possible?" read as follows:

> Sociation is the form (realized in innumerable different ways) in which individuals grow together into a unity and within which their interests are realized. And it is on the basis of their interests (*Interessen*)—sensuous or ideal, momentary or lasting, conscious or unconscious, causal or teleological—that individuals form such units ... Any social phenomenon or process is composed of two elements: on the one hand an interest, a purpose, or a motive; on the other, a form or mode of interaction among individuals through which, or in the shape of which, that content attains social reality. (Simmel 1971: 24)

A common interpretation of Simmel's sociology is that sociology should only deal with the forms and should leave the content to the other social sciences. This, however, represents an oversimplified view of Simmel's position, which is considerably more difficult to nail down; and it also obscures his attempt to introduce interests into sociology. In reality, Simmel's approach on this issue is quite complex and he was well aware that forms without content cannot exist. Attention should also be drawn to Simmel's related argument that one and the same interest can be expressed in many different social forms, and that the same social form can give expression to many different interests:

> However diverse the interests [are] that give rise to ... sociations, the forms in which the interests are realized are identical. On the other hand, the identical interest may take on form in very different associations. (Simmel 1971: 26)

To illustrate his ideas, Simmel notes that an economic interest may take the form of, say, competition, but also whatever form it takes to realize an economic interest in a planned economy. And the social form of competition can be inspired by different interests—a political interest as well as, for example, a religious or a sexual interest.

THE SOCIOLOGICAL APPROACH TO THE CONCEPT OF INTEREST, PART II (MAX WEBER)

Simmel may have provided a general outline for a sociological concept of interest, but he did not elaborate his basic idea that interests constitute the main motives for people to associate with one another and for forming groups, organizations, and societies.

Instead, his friend and colleague Max Weber elaborated on the idea. While Weber's work on the special relationship (or "elective affinity") between ideas and interests is well known, little attention has been paid to the fact that he assigned a much more general role to the concept of interest in his sociology. Interests, he argued, are central to the formation of many types of social action and to the formation of many groups and organizations.

In the following pages, I first will present some facts about how often Weber used the concept of interest and where it can be found in his writings. Then I address the following question: what role did Weber assign to the concept of interest in his sections on social action and social groups in his general sociology in Chapter 1 in *Economy and Society*? I finally discuss the relationship between ideas and interests, taking as my departure Weber's famous statement that certain ideas operate like switchmen, steering interests in different directions (Weber 1946: 280).

The *term* interest (*Interesse*) is frequently used by Weber as is the *idea* of interest. To know exactly how often the word *Interesse* can be found in Weber's work necessitates the use of a kind of database that is currently not available, but which will presumably be available once the publication of Weber's *Collected Works* is complete. In the meantime, however, a rough estimate of the frequency of different terms in Weber's work can be established using a recent CD-ROM version of Weber's major texts (Weber 1999).

This source tells us that one can find the term *Interesse* throughout Weber's work, and that Weber uses it in many different ways (and not only in the sense of economic interest, as is typically the case among economists from the late nineteenth century and onward). According to Michel Peillon, who has himself tried to establish the frequency with which the term "interest" appears in *Economy and Society,* it can be found on every third page (Peillon 1990: 55, 61).

Weber speaks of many different types of interests, which is something that deserves a comment. We find, for example, references to "economic interests," "emotional and affective interests," "bodily interests," "market interests," and many other types of interests. Weber appears to have seen interests as spanning the whole human experience. He also felt that they could conveniently be grouped into two major categories: those that are related to the body ("material interests"), and those that are related to the noncorporal dimension of the human experience, such as values and ideas ("ideal interests").

Weber on Interests # 1: Regular Behavior that is Interest-driven

The term *Interesse* does not appear in the crucial first paragraph in Chapter 1 of *Economy and Society,* in which sociology and its tasks are presented, nor in the twenty pages explication that Weber appended to it. The term *Interesse* does play a prominent role in one of the first paragraphs in Weber's general sociology in Chapter 1, namely the important Paragraph 4, "Types of Action Orientation: Usage, Custom, Self-Interest."

According to this paragraph, certain empirical uniformities or regularities exist in social life and are of much relevance to the sociologist because they involve *types of behavior*. Three types are *usage* (or regular social action), *custom* (or social action that is of long standing), and social action "*determined by self-interest.*" The latter regularity is described as "a uniformity of orientations ... if and insofar as the actors' conduct is instrumentally oriented toward identical expectations" (Weber [1921–22] 1978: 29).

In his explication of the paragraph about regular social action, Weber uses the market to illustrate regular behavior that is interest-driven. If a market actor is (instrumentally) rational, he or she will orient his or her behavior in an impersonal way to other market actors, in order to realize his or her economic interest. The more this is done—that is, the more the behavior is oriented to what Weber in Paragraph 4 calls "identical expectations"—the more that market behavior will be rational and interest-driven. Weber also points out that actors who deviate from this behavior will harm themselves and cause difficulties for other actors and evoke their anger.

There is little that is particularly new or thought provoking in Weber's description of this type of behavior; however, he also points to some interesting qualities of interest-driven behavior. This type of behavior is often more sturdy than behavior that is oriented to norms: uniformities of this type "are far more stable than they would be if actions were oriented to a system of norms and duties which were considered binding on the members of the group" (Weber [1921–22] 1978: 30).

Second, Weber notes that economists have been fascinated by the fact that there exist interest-driven regularities of great stability. Indeed, this has been one of the circumstances that has made "economics [possible] as a science" (Weber [1921–22] 1978: 30). Marginal utility economics from the early twentieth century, of course, was based on the notion of interest-driven behavior—and had nothing to say about norm-driven or customary behavior.

Weber adds that interest-driven regular behavior, which figures so prominently in the economic sphere, can also be found "in all other spheres of action as well" (Weber [1921–22] 1978: 30). This means that it can be found, e.g., in politics, religion, intellectual life, and perhaps also in erotic life. Weber writes:

> This type, with its clarity of self-consciousness and freedom from subjective scruples, is the polar antithesis of every sort of unthinking acquiescence in customary ways as well as of devotion to norms consciously accepted as absolute values. (Weber [1921–22] 1978: 30)

Fourthly, Weber suggests that interest-driven behavior of the regular kind becomes more common as the world becomes more rational. This point, it can be added, is reminiscent of what may be referred to as the reflexive dimension of the concept of interest. Customs recede, Weber says, and are replaced by market oriented and similar types of behavior.

Lastly, immediately following paragraph 4, Weber makes the point that for an order to be stable, it cannot exclusively rest on interest (or violence); it also has to be seen as valid or binding (Weber [1921–22] 1978: 31–38). This legitimacy, as Weber terms it, comes about through norms ("conventions") and is sometimes enforced through law. Given the prevalence of legitimate orders in most societies, it seems clear that for Weber, interests are typically closely associated with norms.

Weber on Interests # 2: The Role of Interests in Associative Relationships or Associations

As Chapter 1 in *Economy and Society* progresses, the social phenomena that are discussed become increasingly complex, and Weber advances from social action, to social relationship, to organizations, and so on. This is also true for social phenomena that have something to do with interests, as exemplified by the advance from Paragraph 4 on "Types of Action Orientation" to Paragraph 9 on "Communal and Associative Relationships" (Weber [1921–22] 1978: 40–43). Although a communal relationship, according to *Economy and Society*, is characterized by a sense among the actors of belonging together, an associative relationship is characterized by the fact that it rests on interests that are rationally adjusted to each other or balanced against each other.

Associative relationships or associations, Weber states, can be found in their most pure version in three forms: (1) market exchange (where compromises between opposed interests are common); (2) instrumental associations based on the material interests of the members; and (3) associations devoted to a cause and of a value-rational nature. A modern corporation would be an example of an instrumental and interest-based association, and so would what Weber in *Economy and Society* terms interest groups (Weber [1921–22] 1978: 297–99). A sect, on the other hand, would be an example of a value-rational association.

Weber emphasizes that associative relationships or associations are conflictual in nature, in that they are based on interests that oppose each other. This means that there will either be compromises (as in the market) or a continuous opposition of interests (as in an instrumental association or *Zweckverein*).

Weber mentions rational market transactions as an example of associative relationships or associations, and this reminds us of his earlier discussion in

Paragraph 4 of interest-driven regularities. Little new is added to this type of phenomenon in Paragraph 9, except that Weber here focuses on the *interaction* between two market actors, which is typically brief.

But Weber also expands his use of the concept of interest in Paragraph 9 in an important way. Rational and interest-driven actions can be turned into something of a permanent nature, namely what Weber terms a *Verein,* and which may simply be translated as an organization. These organizations can be value-rational, as sects tend to be, or instrumentally rational, as firms tend to be; and it seems clear that the latter are common as well as important in contemporary society.

Weber on Interests # 3: The Concept of Class

Another social category in which the concept of interest plays a crucial role for Weber is *class*. According to Weber, the modern concept of class rests exclusively on economic interest. "The factor that creates 'class,'" we read in *Economy and Society,* "is unambiguously economic interest, and indeed, only interests involved in the existence of the market" (Weber [1921–22] 1978: 928). As opposed to Marx, however, Weber sees class more as a factor that decides the socio-economic fate of the individual than as a collective actor in its own right. To cite a concept that has become part of the language of modern sociology: which class an individual belongs to in a market economy will decide his or her "life chances."

In his discussion of class, Weber sometimes formulates himself in such a way that one gets the impression that he works with a quasi-biological or naturalistic concept of interest. Interests push and drive the actor to do something that is clearly social (say, to interact with other actors or to orient his/her action to others)—but these interests do not seem to be particularly social themselves. According to a formulation in *Economy and Society,* for example, "economic interest … is among the most fundamental and universal components of the actual course of interpersonal behavior" (Weber [1921–22] 1978: 601).

But this problem may be more apparent than real, and Weber sometimes reiterates the thesis on which all of his sociology rests, when he is talking about interests, namely, that the actor's subjective perception of his or her motive is essential for there to be an "action" in the first place. For example, Weber qualifies a statement about "the normal interests of the actor" with the words "as they themselves are aware of them" (Weber [1921–22] 1978: 3).

Weber's view of the actor's subjective perception of his or her interests is also touched on in his discussion of the notion of "class interest" (Weber [1921–22] 1978: 928–29). Weber notes that the concept of class interest immediately becomes "ambiguous" when one goes beyond the general statement that a huge number of people sharing the same economic interests are likely to behave in a similar way. Several factors, according to Weber, channel interest-driven behavior in different "directions" (Weber [1921–22] 1978: 929). One is the skill of the individual worker: whether he or she has a lot of talent for the task in question, just average talent, or no talent at all (Weber [1921–22] 1978: 929). Another factor that determines the "direction" of the interest-driven action in this case has to do with the extent to which collective social action is available to the actor—whether it is available to some extent, to a large extent, and also if organizations such as trade unions are present.

Before leaving the discussion of interest and Weber's concept of class, it should be noted that Weber famously contrasts the concept of class to that of status in *Economy and Society*. While the former is decided by economic interest and production, the latter has to do with honor, lifestyle, and consumption. Just as there is a "class society," there is a "status society" (Weber [1921–22] 1978: 306). If we look at the important chapter 4, entitled "Status Groups and Classes," we also note that Weber only uses the concept of interest in his discussion of class, not in his discussion of status. This, however, should not be seen as a sign that interests are somehow less important in a status society than they are in a class society. It is perfectly clear from Weber's analysis elsewhere in *Economy and Society* that people will fight just as hard for their interests in a status society as in a class society. Weber also uses the expression "status interests" at least at one point in his work (Weber 1991: 16). We are again encountering a case where Weber uses other words for interest, and where the absence of the term "interest" should not be equated with an absence of the idea of interest.

In the next section, we shall turn to Weber's famous discussion of "material and ideal interests," and a status society, which can perhaps be described as a type of society that rests on a different combination of interests than a class society. As opposed to a class society, the economic interests in a status society are not centered around the market, but around the processes of redistribution and reciprocity, to speak like Polanyi. Ideal interests also play more of a role in a status society, since honor and lifestyle are central.

Weber on Interests # 4: Interests and Ideas as Switchmen

When Weber in 1919–20 revised the text that was to serve as the introduction to *The Economic Ethics of the World Religions*, he added a classic passage:

> Not ideas, but material and ideal interests, directly govern men's conduct. Yet very frequently the 'world images' that have been created by 'ideas' have, like switchmen, determined the tracks along which action has been pushed by the dynamic of interest. (Weber [1920] 1946: 280; [1920] 1988: 252)

This passage, among the most cited and discussed in the secondary literature on Weber, is at the center of the few discussions that exist of the concept of interest in Weber's work. These discussions typically focus on the relationship between interests and ideas in Weber's work (Weber 1946: 63–64, Lepsius 1986).

A few exceptions to this trend deserve mention. One is Michel Peillon, who devotes a chapter to Max Weber in *The Concept of Interest in Social Theory*. Peillon carefully shows how Weber uses the concept of interest in his analyses of religion, law, the formation of groups, and a few other topics (Peillon 1990: 55–77). Walter Sprondel, another exception to the tendency to ignore the ubiquitous nature of the concept of interest in Weber's work, says, "Weber's concept of interest is situated on several levels; it is not analyzed and it lacks clarity in his work" (Sprondel 1973: 221).

Weber's phrase "material and ideal" demands comment. First, it should be noted that this expression (or expressions similar to it) appears in other places in Weber's work than in the quote with the switchmen (for the exact expression, see e.g., Weber [1921–22] 1978: 246 [twice], 315, 287, 1129; for similar expressions, see e.g., Weber [1921–22] 1978: 202, 224, 264). Talcott Parsons argues that with the term "ideal interests," Weber means such things as "interests in religious salvation, the interest in the growth of knowledge through scientific research and many others" (Parsons 1975: 668). Stephen Kalberg, who has devoted an article to Weber's concept of ideal interests, argues that this type of interest is situated at a different level than material interests, and also is primarily related to values (Kalberg 1985).

In contrast to Kalberg, another commentator notes that it is easy to misunderstand Weber's use of the term "ideal interests" in the passage about the switchmen, and not realize that "the emphasis has to be placed on 'interests' not 'ideal'" (Whimster 2002: 97). Weber, in brief, equates material and ideal interests, and what makes them similar is precisely that both are interests. To this statement it may be added that Weber does not only relate values to ideal interests. One of his points about early religion, for example, is that many of its "benefits" were material and not spiritual—such as long life, health, and wealth (e.g., Weber [1921–22] 1978: 399–400, 527).

It is clear that the quote about the switchmen is primarily about the relation of interests and ideas; and by ideas in this context Weber means different religious worldviews, such as Buddhism, Hinduism, and so on. The following comment by Stephen Kalberg is relevant on this point: "Weber generally uses the term 'ideas' (*Ideen*) in the nineteenth-century usage to refer to coherent views of the cosmos and man's place within it" (Kalberg 1979: 137n6).

The main emphasis, however, in Weber's famous quote is on what we may call the double relationship of ideas to interests. Ideas are, first of all, *not* what primarily drives or motivates human beings—interests are. Secondly, *some* ideas may orient people's actions in different directions. Weber's metaphor can be rewritten as follows: human actions are propelled forward, like a train at full speed—but only in the direction that the switchmen decide.

Concluding Remarks

After this long discussion of Weber's concept of interest, it is time to return to the concern expressed at the outset of this article, namely, the need for social scientists to resist the economists' rhetorical use of the concept of interest. This attempt at mass persuasion is unsuitable because the economists' concept of interest is one-dimensional and profoundly nonsocial in nature. Adding political weight to this concept, with the help of ideology, only increases the problem.

Much more suitable for adoption by the noneconomic social sciences is a different concept of interest, namely, the one that was developed by some sociologists during 1890–1920 and which today is largely forgotten. There are four key points on which this use of the concept of interest differs from its rhetorical use; and by way of concluding, I shall briefly state these points and comment on them:

Point # 1: The sociological concept allows for different types of interest.

Economists, ever since the invention of *homo economicus* in the mid nineteenth century, focus exclusively on one type of interest, namely, material interest. In reality, however, people assign fundamental values to a number of different activities in their lives and, respectively, are driven by a number of different forces. Just as people are driven by their economic interests, they can be driven by political interests, emotional interests, sexual interests, and so on. Max Weber reminds us of this through his famous phrase "material and ideal interests."

Point # 2: According to the sociological view, interests are to be understood as socially defined or constructed, not simply as given.

Economists make the assumption that people have economic interests, and then proceed to the analysis. Sociologists, in contrast, start from the assumption that interests always have to be socially constructed or defined. Legitimate sexual interests are, for example, typically defined in the law or in the mores. Different ruling groups may have different interests, with, for example, the

European aristocracy defining itself in terms of honor (an ideal interest), while the European bourgeoisie defines itself in terms of material wealth (economic interests).

Point # 3: *In sociological analysis, the actors' own view of their interests must be included in the analysis.*

In mainstream economic analysis, the actor is assigned an (economic) interest, which he or she then proceeds to realize, given restrictions in terms of resources, and so on. In sociological analysis, on the other hand, the actor's own perception of what his or her interests are must be taken into account. The actor may, for example, have difficulty in singling out some interest as central, in settling on one strategy rather than on another—and, for the analyst to get access to this crucial type of information, he or she has to take the actor's view into account.

Point # 4: *Sociologists argue that interests can only be realized via social relations or by taking other actors into account.*

In standard economic analysis, the element of social relations is ignored; this is not the case in sociology. The sociologist argues that in order to realize an interest, the actor will typically have to take other actors into account—say, by avoiding them, using them, questioning them or the like. Again, we come back to the main point of this article, namely, that in order for us to go beyond the economic concept of interest, backed up as it is today by neoliberal ideology, we need a type of analysis that allows us to take the social element fully into account.

Note

1. See also Milberg below on the ideological power of the fundamental theorem in economics.

CHAPTER 4

THE NEW SOCIAL SCIENCE IMPERIALISM AND THE PROBLEM OF KNOWLEDGE IN CONTEMPORARY ECONOMICS

William Milberg

■ ■ ■ ■ ■ ■

INTRODUCTION

What is it about economic argument that has made it traditionally so persuasive as to be widely viewed as the king of the social sciences? Many have accepted the dominant role of economics in the social sciences because of the perceived power of its first fundamental welfare theorem: the social optimality of a fully decentralized (privately owned) and competitive economy rooted in rational individual choice. In this chapter, I argue that mainstream economics largely abandoned this theorem almost twenty years ago and has subsequently moved through two new methodological phases. The first phase was a "New Economics" that emerged in the late 1970s, in which somewhat *ad hoc* models of rational choice generated unorthodox, indeterminate, and nonrobust conclusions about a variety of economic questions related to international trade, technological change, unemployment, economic growth, and development. The *ad hoc* and nonoperational nature of the models' conclusions subsequently pushed economists into a new, empirical mode, in which rational choice and microeconomic foundations were no longer the basis for assessing new knowledge or even for generating new hypotheses. In this latest methodological phase, the questions economists pose for purposes of research start from a variety of sources, and what distinguishes the research is its careful statistical analysis.

While the recent empiricist phase has left open the possibility of new, and even pragmatist, approaches to the pursuit of knowledge of the economy, more than anything it has led to a new source of imperialism of economics among the social sciences. In the earlier methodological phases, the economics profession's tentacles reached across the social sciences due to the power of its notion of agency, which is rooted in the form of "rational economic man," as discussed in earlier chapters of this volume. Today, economic research ventures onto the traditional terrain of the other social sciences with a different mode of persuasion: statistics applied to extensive sets of quantitative data. This new imperialism of economics in the social sciences leaves an explanatory void and an openness to competing interpretations of empirical evidence, the result of both old and new problems with empirically based knowledge. The theoretical void also is rapidly being filled with a narrow, rational choice-based, conception of institutions, which may be the most contentious aspect of the new approach, as Gudeman argues in this volume.

After describing these recent developments in economics, I will focus on some of the problems with the new empiricism as it has unfolded in contemporary research. I conclude with a discussion of the nature of the new intellectual imperialism of economics and of the particular conception of institutions that is emerging as central to the future of social inquiry.

Imagined Economies

The notion that a fully decentralized and competitive private ownership system with self-interested and rational actors leads to a socially optimal economic outcome is disarmingly simple (as Carrier suggests in this volume) and has been articulated with great mathematical eloquence, in particular in the works of Arrow and Debreu (1954) and Arrow and Hahn (1971), who use standard techniques of calculus, and by Debreu (1959), using concepts from topology. The idea is typically dated to Adam Smith's metaphor of the invisible hand, but it was not until the late nineteenth century, with the marriage of utilitarianism and differential calculus in economics, that rational individual choice provided the foundations for the principle.[1] When mathematical economics took hold in the United States after World War II, the pursuit of new economic knowledge was driven by notions of marginalism and the implications of general equilibrium. Alfred Marshall's utilitarianism, which dominated economic thought and teaching between the 1890s and the 1930s, focused on partial equilibrium and was presented in the social and historical context of Victorian

England. In his 890-page tome, *The Principles of Economics,* Marshall mentions general equilibrium and the work of the 1870 group only twice.

The shift that occurred in the US around the time of World War II was not about methodological individualism *per se,* although this was certainly an important feature of the American models. In the 1840s, John Stuart Mill had already made the case for methodological individualism in economic inquiry. The shift in the twentieth century was more about optimization. The key was the prominent role of scarcity. For Mill, economics was about the individual "desire for wealth" (Mill 1874: 138) and for Marshall, it was "the science of material welfare" (Hands 2001: 35). Not until Lionel Robbins' 1932 piece, "An Essay on the Nature and Significance of Economic Science," did choice under conditions of scarcity become the defining condition of the economic. "Economics," he wrote, "is the science which studies human behaviour as a relationship between ends and scarce means which have alternative uses" (Robbins 1932: 16).

The scientific goal of the marginalist project was the *generalization* of the logic of the beneficence of a purely competitive private enterprise system. Generalization was defined in the mathematical sense: if the same result could be generated with "weaker," that is, mathematically less restrictive, assumptions, then the model was termed more robust than the earlier model and constituted an advance in economic knowledge.[2] For example, if the current proof of the existence of general equilibrium relied on concave utility functions, then a proof that assumed preferences to be quasi-concave constituted progress in knowledge because it held under more general (less restrictive) conditions. The reliance on mathematics was seen by some as a weakness of economics—an effort to veil an ethical bias beneath scientific metaphor.[3] However, the clarity of its criterion for the progress of knowledge was viewed as a great scientific strength.

The influence of the first fundamental theorem of welfare economics on the imagination of social scientists is evident in the vitriolic discussions between those who embraced it and those who rejected it. Mirowski (2002) gives a detailed history of how computer technology fed economists' sense of the importance and modeling possibilities of rational individual choice in the outcome of markets and a variety of strategic games—principles promoted by financial support from the US government during the Cold War. But many social sciences other than economics (political scientists most notably) have embraced the rational choice approach.

Resistance to the model comes from resentment of its imperialism in social thought (the wrath against Gary Becker's theory of marriage and the division of labor is the most evident example), but also from those who prefer explanation over prediction, and rich social and cultural description of production and consumption rather than parsimonious mathematical formulas. The price of strict hypothetico-deductivism—narrow, unrealistic assumptions about agency and social interaction and mathematically tractable assumptions on consumer preferences, technology, and economic growth—is viewed by many social scientists as too high a price to pay for its benefits.

From where does the persuasive power of the economics metaphor and its first fundamental theorem come? Briefly, there are three sources: methodological, ideological, and sociological. The methodological strength is economics' individualism, axiomatic precision, deductive rigor, and tightly construed hypothetico-deductive approach that approximates, as many have noted, the methods and metaphors from physics, which is so often viewed as the ultimate hard science.

The second source of power is ideological, in that the fundamental theorem gives scientific support for free market capitalism in its purest form, that is, as a system of private property with no role for government.

The sociological explanation is that economists are in positions of power, with an advisory role in the executive office of most countries (or, as in several Latin American countries, they *are* the executive), large government consulting contracts, and a dominant role in economic development policy in the International Monetary Fund, World Bank, and the World Trade Organization.

If this were not enough, economic thought during the immediate post World War II era works at the psychological level, providing a sense of formal simplicity, systemic order, and benevolence in a world that often appears random, volatile, and unjust. In a well known passage from his *Essays in Astronomy*, published in 1758, Adam Smith wrote: "[T]he repose and tranquility of the imagination is the ultimate end of philosophy ... Philosophy, by representing the invisible chains which bind together all these disjointed objects, endeavours to introduce order into this chaos of jarring and discordant appearances, to allay this tumult of the imagination" (Heilbroner 1986: 16). The first fundamental theorem serves to allay the tumult, by providing a coherent picture of order and justice.[4]

THE NEW ECONOMICS

Given its great sources of strength, the dominance of competitive general equilibrium analysis was surprisingly short-lived. One problem was technical, specifically the inability to prove the uniqueness and stability of the general equilibrium. Mark Blaug (2001: 160) sums up the frustration with these internal limitations of the competitive model:

> [T]he most rigorous solution of the existence problem by Arrow and Debreu turns general equilibrium theory into a mathematical puzzle, applied to a virtual economy that can be imagined but could not possibly exist, while the extremely relevant "stability problem" has never been solved either rigorously or sloppily. General equilibrium theory is simply a research program that has run into the sands.

Another problem, hinted at by Blaug above, was the lack of compelling empirical validation of the model's implications. This brought into question the model's scientificity in a world dominated by Popperian concerns with theory falsification. It also brought uncertainty about the usefulness of the theory for policy formation. As Colander (2000) writes:

> In the 1950s and 1960s, it was hoped that practical models would be guided by general equilibrium theory. Thus, when Arrow/Debreu proved the existence of a general equilibrium in 1957, there was hope that the pure science of economics would progress in tandem with the practical application of that science. By the 1970s economists recognized that the Arrow/Debreu general equilibrium work was not going to get to the promised land.

Ultimately, these deficiencies were not the main causes of the internal revolt. It was the aridity, that is, the insulation from institutional and historical detail that brought a degree of self-questioning and rethinking. As early as 1975, Alan Coddington likened the contribution of general equilibrium theory to the understanding of actual economies as "the contribution of flatness to mountaineering." The limitations of its applicability to the world were already well recognized by economists, and around this time a small, internal response began. This move, which I term the "New Economics," did not abandon the primacy of rational economic man, but it did alter some of the fundamental assumptions of the previous framework. In the process, economists quietly abandoned the earlier methodology's powerful criterion for judging the progress of knowledge.

The New Economics arose in a series of subfields in the profession, including international economics, labor economics, industrial organization, and macroeconomics. In the New Economics, general equilibrium was not the core, guiding principle. As Colander (1999) writes, the new generation of economic models "freed economists to deal with practical policy models that were inconsistent with general equilibrium theory." At the same time, the robustness criterion for determining progress of knowledge was largely abandoned and an increasing reliance on induction entered into mainstream economics. Let us consider some of the basic insights from the New Economics in the areas of international trade and economic growth.

Strategic Trade Policy

The field of international trade theory was long viewed (proudly by its practitioners) as the most direct and relevant application of the neoclassical general equilibrium model. The various theorems derived from the factor endowments approach to trade gave dramatic results regarding the effects and merits of free trade. Despite early empirical evidence rejecting the basic trade theorem (the Leontief paradox), neoclassical trade theory continued to thrive and dominate the scholarly journals and the trade policy debates.

But the theory could not explain some simple and regularly observed phenomena. For example, why did France and Germany export automobiles to each other (in violation of the principle of comparative advantage)? Why were Japanese and Korean subsidies and protectionism successfully boosting exports and growth in those countries (distortions were supposed to reduce welfare)? Why did industrialized countries' state subsidies to research and development (R&D) seem to pay off in terms of private sector profits and export market growth (efficient capital markets were supposed to provide optimal financing of investment)? In some of these instances, the theory was not sufficiently open to allow even the posing of the question! A new approach was required if these relevant issues were to be addressed.

Beginning in the late 1970s, a new generation of trade theorists introduced increasing returns to scale, monopolistic competition, and strategic behavior by firms and governments into the model, seeking to provide a rational choice (although not perfect competition) basis for explaining the casually observed new tendencies in the world economy. By 1983, Paul Krugman, one of the pioneers in this area, was already summarizing the radical theoretical break of the "New International Economics" in an essay for the *American Economic Review* (Krugman 1983). Krugman admitted that the new models provided an alternative to comparative advantage to explain the pattern of international trade. The policy implications also diverged from the free trade mantra underpinned by the traditional trade model. For example, the new theory showed that government intervention in the form of a subsidy of R&D could promote technological progress by domestic firms, which would lead to the capture of exports and profits that would otherwise be lost to other countries.[5]

Increasing Returns and Endogenous Economic Growth

Another major focus of the New Economics was on the theory of growth. Traditional mainstream economic growth theory, based on papers by Robert Solow in 1956 and 1957, located economic growth in three basic factors: (1) technology, assumed to be given to the model and characterized by constant returns to scale; (2) capital intensity, that is, the amount of capital per worker in the economy; and (3) technological change, which was a catch-all for everything else not captured by (1) and (2). Solow's (1957) stunning empirical finding, based on evidence for the US economy for the period 1909–1949, was that 85 percent of US economic growth in this period was attributable to technological change. This was particularly striking because such technological change was considered by Solow to be exogenous, that is, externally *given*, to the economic model.

After a long reign of supremacy, and a sense within the profession that the question of economic growth had been solved, the Solow model came under scrutiny in the 1980s because of its prediction that over time all countries would converge to a common standard of living, as those countries with lower capital intensity would enjoy higher rates of economic growth than countries with high capital intensity achieved through investment. Cross-country evidence did not support convergence and a number of studies even showed divergence: over long periods of time, the rate of economic growth of the industrialized countries rose, while in many poor countries it remained relatively stagnant. The response was a series of growth models, which assumed increasing returns to scale. This rendered technology endogenous or internally generated in the sense that a higher level of output resulted in declining average production costs. The new models were consistent with the evidence of international growth rate divergence, but they did not have many of the nice properties of the Solow model. For example, many of the models gave numerous possible outcomes, otherwise known as "multiple equilibria."

Creeping Inductivism and the Retreat from Robustness

These new approaches all sought greater relevance, and had some common features across subfields, including an emphasis on imperfect market competition (rather than perfect competition), asymmetric information (rather than symmetric information), increasing returns to scale technology (rather than constant returns to scale), or on strategic behavior by firms and governments (as opposed to optimization independent of rival behavior). The mathematical functions that represented technology (i.e., the production functions) and preferences (i.e., utility functions) reflected these assumptions. Consider the completely general functional form of the utility function assumed in the general equilibrium tradition:

$$U = U(x_1, x_2, x_3, ..., x_n)$$
where U = utility
x_i = good i and i = 1,..., n

Now, consider the utility function that dominated theory in the New International Economics, the so-called Dixit-Stiglitz utility function:

$$U = (\Sigma x_i^\theta)^{1/\theta},$$

where U and x_i are defined as above and θ is a parameter reflecting the elasticity of substitution, that is, the consumer's willingness to substitute one good for another. The standard general equilibrium utility function was a general relation between utility and commodity consumption, while the new function assumed imperfect competition and multiple varieties of a good with equal cross-price elasticities for all varieties of goods.

The New Economics constituted an internally generated crack in the grand metanarrative in economics, that the general equilibrium (with all agents' preferences satisfied at market clearing and given prices) exists, is unique, stable, and Pareto optimal. Even the concern with Pareto optimality was often abandoned—too difficult to prove under the new assumptions—in favor of a "representative agent," whose utility became the focus of welfare assessment. The results were certainly more varied, contingent, explosive, and path dependent than those produced in the era of competitive general equilibrium. The New Economics shifted the focus away from competitive general equilibrium and toward the provision of a rational choice foundation with otherwise *ad hoc* hypotheses. Heilbroner and Milberg (1996) describe the changes in this period as an "inward turn." The goal appeared to be to explain in rational choice terms a variety of casually observed phenomena. Such an explanation was important mainly to render these phenomena persuasive to other economists: it had the advantage of formal simplicity.[6]

While these new sets of assumptions are typically identified as the chief characteristics of the New Economics, methodologically speaking the important shift was the move away from the strict hypothetico-deductivism of general equilibrium analysis and toward a vaguely construed inductivism. The New Economics did not cause an abandonment of rational choice mathematical modeling, and in the case of New Keynesianism, it actually increased its role. But the New Economics constituted the beginning of a reversal of the direction of the relation between observation and hypothesis, that is to say, a shift in the accepted rhetorical conventions for producing economic knowledge.

In the New Economics, theories were often derived in a way so as to give a particular result or they were constructed in a way that led to instability or path dependence. Results were not only not unique—multiple equilibria were now the norm rather than the exception—they were not robust, that is, the results were highly sensitive to the choice of assumptions, parameter values, and functional forms.[7] In the most recent developments, the new economics has given way to a variety of techniques, including experimentalism, behaviorism, complexity, and agent-based approaches, that in some cases involve the abandonment of the assumption of individual rationality.[8]

The least noticed, but perhaps most important aspect of this shift for our purposes, was the abandonment of the criterion for assessing the progress of knowledge. In the era of competitive general equilibrium analysis, as I noted above, an economic model was understood to generate new knowledge if it provided a proof of a known result, but required weaker, that is, more general, assumptions than did existing proofs of that same result. The great strength of this methodology was the clarity and simplicity of its criterion for establishing the progress of knowledge—increased mathematical generality, or robustness, of its proofs. In the era of New Economics, robustness was thus inadvertently abandoned as a methodological principle.

The Empirical Turn

If the lack of robustness posed a problem for identifying progress of knowledge, it was also an obstacle for those interested in drawing policy recommendations based on the theory. There was a feeling that the models were *ad hoc* and could be used to model *any* pre-determined outcome. Moreover, the models were difficult to operationalize and thus, were difficult to assess with traditional tools of empirical analysis.

The response to the weaknesses of the New Economics in the late 1990s has been an empirical turn, a further distancing of economics from the hypothetico-deductivism of the competitive general equilibrium era. In this era, hypotheses are often rooted in simple economic logic, intuition, or even as a response to current events, and emphasis is no longer placed on the deductive model, but instead on the sophistication of the measurement of variables and correlations among them. A new mode of persuasion emerged. Some examples are Rodrick's (1998) study of the relation between wages and democracy, Krueger and Whitmore's (2000) analysis of the relation between class size and student performance, Krueger and Card's (2000) study of the employment effects of a minimum wage increase, and Edmonds and Pavcnik's (2005) study of the effect of trade liberalization on child labor. None of these papers contains a formal mathematical model and, thus, they do not depend in a significant way on the assumption of utility or profit maximization.

Consider Edmonds and Pavcnik's (2005) study.[9] The paper begins with a verbal argument for why liberalization of rice exports raises the price of these exports. Two effects of this price increase are possible: if the trade liberalization raises the income of rice farmers sufficiently, it can induce higher rates of school attendance by Vietnamese children, who are no longer needed on the farm to generate basic family revenue. It could also lead families to demand more use of child labor if the attainment of higher production for higher income required it. The relation between trade liberalization and child labor is thus "an empirical question," and the authors adopt fairly standard econometric practice to draw a conclusion.

The central result is reprinted in Table 1 below. At first glance, the table is unremarkable. It is based on a simple econometric model (six independent variables plus a constant term) that includes price, income (price times quantity), and controls for other variables that might be important, mostly demographics on household composition, season, age, and gender. Most of the coefficients are labeled as "significant at 5 percent," implying a relatively low degree of chance that the "real" coefficients are zero. The R-squared, measuring the percentage of variation in the dependent variable explained by the model, is at acceptable levels for panel studies of between 0.54 and 0.61, and the small range across models is reassuring.

Table 1. Child Labor Participation, Rice Prices, and Net Production
Children 6–15 in rural panel households

	(1) Child Labor	(2) Child Labor	(3) Work in Agriculture
Ln(Rice Price)	−0.291 [0.085]**	−0.234 [0.087]	0.07 [0.083]*
Ln(Rice Price)*Net Production		−0.054 [0.015]**	−0.035 [0.009]**
Time = 1998	−0.175 [0.025]**	−0.174 [0.026]*	−0.134 [0.031]**
Household Fixed Effects	Yes	Yes	Yes
Season Effects	Yes	Yes	Yes
Age*Gender Series	Yes	Yes	Yes
Observations	9027	9027	9027
R-squared	0.61	0.61	0.58

Notes: All regressions also include a constant. Robust standard errors, corrected for community/year clustering, in brackets. * significant at 10 percent; ** significant at 5 percent. 6 children that participate in agricultural work have missing data on work in household production and are omitted from column 4.
Source: Edmonds, E. and N. Pavcnik, "The Effect of Trade Liberalization on Child Labor," *Journal of International Economics* vol. 65, no. 2, March (2005): 401–19.

At second look, however, the table reflects many of the trends we have identified in contemporary economics, including the abandonment of both the old general equilibrium economics and the New Economics and instead the move to careful empiricism. For starters, the article is published in the *Journal of International Economics,* the leading mainstream journal in the field, traditionally a journal of theory and certainly a journal of mathematical rigor. But times have changed. This study gets a clear result without an explicit rational choice premise. The paper contains no general equilibrium model and no utility or production functions. There is not even a deductive model of international trade, much less one of labor supply or of time allocation in the household.

The larger point is that the old and the New Economics would have had difficulty even considering the issue of child labor. Moreover, the results of the study as presented in the table confirm the free market version of the "theory," specifically, that trade liberalization is associated with a lower incidence of child labor and even of child work in household production. Would the paper have been published if the estimated coefficients on the rice price variable had been positive (indicating a higher price is associated with higher child labor supply) or insignificant? This is hard to know. Note that sometimes the new empiricism provides an effective challenge to conventional wisdom, such as the Card and Krueger (1995) study refuting the negative employment effects of a minimum wage increase.

The gradual erosion of the narrow deductivist criterion for the generation of hypotheses has created a broadening of the acceptable criteria for hypothesis generation in mainstream economics. There is a longstanding tension between deduction ("pure theory") and induction ("applied analysis") in economics, but in past epochs, it was the deductivists who won out, in both the classical and the neoclassical epochs. In the present case, not only does it appear that inductivists may win out, but also many of the same economists involved with the New Economics have switched over to the new empiricism

Figure 4.1, "Three Modes of Economic Persuasion," depicts the three methodologies applied to the study of international trade in mainstream US economics, beginning with competitive general equilibrium analysis from the early part of the twentieth century. General equilibrium trade theory was built on axioms, which generate hypotheses about the direction and welfare effects of trade with liberalization. The New International Economics began by positing a phenomenon to be explained and then proceeded to establish the functional forms and assumptions on agency that, with rational behavior, produced the posited outcome. In the new empiricism, there is even less stringency over the choice of hypotheses and the emphasis is on the empirical test of the hypothesis. In sum, a creeping inductivism replaced the strict

Figure 4.1 Three Modes of Economic Persuasion

A. General Equilibrium Trade

1. Axioms ⟶

comparative advantage
interindustry trade
factor price equalization

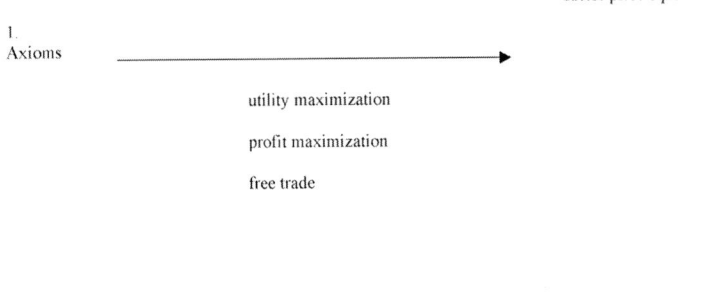

utility maximization

profit maximization

free trade

B. New International Economics

intra-industry trade ⟶

assumptions:
imperfect competition
product variety
increasing returns

⟵

utility maximization

profit maximization

strategic trade policy

game theory

C. New Empiricism

Trade liberalization
reduces child labor

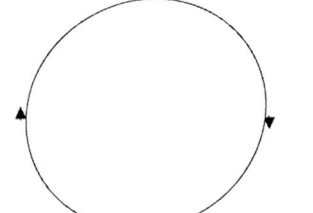

data set
with controls;
econometric
model
estimation

hypothetico-deductivisim of competitive general equilibrium analysis. What constitutes the proper scope of the field of economics, that is, what questions mainstream economists should appropriately pursue, is no longer as self-evident today as it had been under previous methodologies.

The recent bestseller *Freakonomics* (Levitt and Dubner 2005) is a popular version of the new empiricism. The book contains two types of essays. One is the very loose application of rational choice thinking to spin implausible hypotheses on causality. This is exemplified by the infamous hypothesis that *Roe vs. Wade* led to reduced crime rates some years later.[10] The second is the focus on aberrant behavior (cheating teachers, drug dealers) to show how even cheaters and criminals can be understood as behaving rationally (that is, if the expected utility of crime is greater than zero). In *Freakonomics,* the methodology can be described as a very loose use of rational choice logic and very clever use of data and statistics. The title of the book reflects the effort to glorify the randomness of its "context of discovery." The lack of a clear criterion for the progress of this type of knowledge makes its sustainability in scholarly circles problematic.[11] But *Freakonomics* is a popular reflection of the broad paradigm shift in the field of economics generally.

Knowing Econometrically

The reemergence of the centrality of induction in economics circumvented the problem of the *ad hoc* nature of the models that characterized the New Economics. It also established a new type of beachhead for economic research across the social sciences, which was no longer rooted in rational choice, but rather in statistics and econometrics. But the move to full-fledged inductivism is problematic. The first issue is the problem of induction itself. The second is the theoretical void left by the move away from rational choice. I deal briefly with the first issue in this section and take up the second in the next, and concluding, section.

If deduction can never overcome its "sausage problem" (that no *new* knowledge can be generated deductively since any result from mathematical reasoning is already contained in the initial formulation of the problem itself), induction will never surmount its "swan issue" (that just because all observed swans are white does not make it impossible to rule out that the next swan observed may be black). This is the nagging Humean "problem of induction," namely, that empirical observation can never provide universal or general knowledge since it is always based on a particular, non-universal sample.

An aspect of the problem of induction more specific to social phenomena is the near-impossibility of performing repeated experiments. This issue was addressed in economics with the adoption of Neyman-Pearson techniques of statistical inference, beginning in the 1920s. While the multivariate regression model does not constitute repeat experiments (other than replication), it involves the next best thing: isolating the relation between two variables, while "controlling" for variation in other variables deemed relevant to influencing variation in the dependent variable. Such near-experimental conditions also allow for (in fact, assume) a certain amount of random movement around the real relations among variables, which further justifies the use of "noisy," real-world observations to test otherwise deterministic models of economic interaction.[12]

Econometrics is used to answer two types of questions. The first is about the validity of a particular refutable hypothesis. For example, are wages higher in countries with more democratic political arrangements? The second type of question is about the size of a particular relation between variables. For example, what is the magnitude of the effect on wages of a payroll tax increase? There are difficulties with each of these empirical exercises; some surmountable, others not.

The "Con" in Econometrics

Since scholarly journals generally publish only positive results—that is, results that support rather than reject the hypothesis—economists, who have strong professional incentives to publish in these journals, will alter the model specification until the best possible result is attained. Leamer (1983) labeled this the "con" in econometrics. His concern was that this bias had greatly diminished the legitimacy and credibility of published econometric studies; in effect he was saying that econometrics is also a rhetorical form, that is, a means of persuasion:

> There is a growing cynicism among economists towards empirical work. Regression equations are regarded by many as mere stylistic devices, not unlike footnotes referencing obscure scholarly papers ... The econometric art ... involves fitting many, perhaps thousands, of statistical models. One or several that the researcher finds pleasing are selected for reporting purpose.... The concepts of unbiasedness, consistency, efficiency, maximum-likelihood estimation, in fact all the concepts of traditional theory, utterly lose their meaning by the time an applied researcher pulls from the bramble of computer output the one thorn of a model he likes best, the one he portrays as a rose. The consuming public is hardly fooled by this chicanery. (Leamer 1983: 36–37)

Mayer (2000) surveyed 278 economists on their belief in published econometric studies and found that about 30 percent were either quite skeptical or distrustful of most or all econometric results. Leamer suggested that journals publish *all* of the model estimations for each final estimation cited in an article. He noted that with increasing computing power and falling computing costs, the number of runs was only rising and could be in the thousands for a given article.

Economic Constants?

Economics has resisted the Humean curse by seeking to establish the existence of certain stable relations among economic variables and between economic change and social welfare. An example is the quantity theory of money relating changes in the price level to changes in the supply of money. The presumed stability of this relation has led many to support a rule for a constant and low rate of growth of the money supply. But Mirowski (1994) found the establishment of empirical constants to be particularly problematic in economics. He calculates the birge ratio (a measure of variation across a sample) in estimates of particular economic relations. This measure has been used in similar meta-analysis done in other fields, including the natural sciences and public health. Mirowski found that estimates of such concepts as the US interest rate elasticity of money demand, the US import price elasticity, and the US output elasticity of employment varied widely across samples, model specifications, and estimation techniques. The problem of wide variation in the estimate of theoretically stable parameters, while not often acknowledged among practitioners, has no doubt contributed to the difficulty of resolving economic debates using empirical observation. There is no clear criterion for establishing whose constant is the right one. Persuasion via empirical analysis becomes more problematic in this context.

The Kletzer Effect

But what if there is no debate over model specification or choice of sample? Then the con of econometrics and the problem of high variation across estimates disappears ... almost. It turns out that a given result can support various theories or be given radically different interpretations. I call this the "Kletzer effect" after a recent debate in the interpretation of a study by University of California-Santa Cruz economist Lori Kletzer (2001). Kletzer's study is used to support both sides in the debate over the effects of rising international outsourcing by US firms, one side that claims international trade benefits US workers, the other arguing that it is harmful to the interests of American workers.

Kletzer (2005) summarized her results as follows:

> Import competition is associated with low reemployment rates (on the order of 63 percent for the period 1979–2001) ... Two-thirds of reemployed work-

ers earn less on their new job than they did on their old job, and one-quarter experience earnings losses in excess of 30 percent. The average earnings loss is more modest, but still sizable at 13 percent. The distribution of earnings losses is very similar to that found for all workers displaced from manufacturing jobs for other reasons. (Kletzer 2005: 43)

No one debates the quality of Kletzer's empirical work and it is published with a well-respected research institute, the Institute for International Economics. Also, her results are eminently plausible: not too high and not too low. People on both sides of the issue are comfortable using Kletzer's results in support of their views. Consider some recent examples. Agrawal and Farrell cite the Kletzer study and conclude that the results "substantiate very high expectations of redeployment for the economy as a whole ... [T]hese levels of re-employment and recapture translate into an additional 45 to 47 cents of value recapture for the economy ... What has made this possible is the flexibility in the job market and the mobility of workers across the country" (2003: 11). Amiti and Wei (2005) note that the McKinsey findings indicated that more than 69% of workers who lost jobs due to imports in the United States between 1979 and 1999 were re-employed implies that 31% were not re-employed, and they interpret this as an indication of rigidities in the labor market. Apparently, one's person's flexible market is another's rigid market. Bhagwati et al. (2004), in their defense of the general benefits of US offshoring, claim that the findings of the Kletzer study show that there are no special labor market effects of outsourcing as separate from technological change. They write that, "the rate of reemployment and wage changes for workers that Kletzer characterizes as trade displaced are quite similar to those for other workers. In other words, a common factor, most likely technological change, is behind the displacement in all categories" (Bhagwati et al. 2004: 111–12). Levy (2005), who is skeptical of the beneficial effects of US services offshoring, writes that "the [Kletzer] data are mixed at best ... The fact that this study [the Kletzer study] was cited by Agrawal and Farrel in support of their claims about worker mobility again suggests the ideological nature of these beliefs" (Levy 2005: 687).[13]

At the heart of the Kletzer effect is the issue of the problem of establishing conventions for assessing the merits of an empirically based argument. Even when such conventions exist, there is nothing objective about them. Why does a ten percent probability of error constitute a significant result, and not 15 percent or .0001 percent? And of course there is no reason why such conventions should not change over time (as they have with the introduction of co-integration analysis into time series econometrics over the past 20 years). The presumption of an objective standard has given enhanced status to the statistical definition of significance. McCloskey calls this the "abuse of significance," whereby economists *use* the statistical concept of significance—rooted in probability theory—for broader notions of significance for economy or society (McCloskey 1983, 1996; McCloskey and Zjiliac 2000). As Blaug (1980: 22) has written, "Whenever the predictions of a theory are probabilistic in nature (and what predictions are not ...) the notion of assessing evidence without invoking normative methodological principles is an absurdity." The Kletzer effect arises when norms are indeterminate to the point where the same empirical finding gets marshaled by opposing sides of a debate. It is not obvious to me that more discussion among social scientists about statistical norms will make the Kletzer effect go away. At issue is the much bigger question of the moral judgments often required in the interpretation of empirical analysis.

Conclusion

Economist Jack Hirshleifer wrote in 1985 that, "There is only one social science ... What gives economics its imperialist invasive power is that our analytical categories—scarcity, cost, preferences, opportunities, etc.—are truly universal in applicability ... Thus economics really does constitute the universal grammar of social science" (Hershleifer 1985: 53). Today the move by economists into nontraditional areas of study that are normally the focus of political science, anthropology, and sociology has been furthered precisely by the abandonment of its "universal grammar." I have argued that it is econometrics and induction, not rational individual choice analysis and its hypothetico-deductivism, that provides the new tools for imperialism of economics in the social sciences. This is ironic since it was the rational choice paradigm that was said to be the source of this intellectual imperialism.

In the absence of such foundations, the important debate will be over how research questions will be selected—that is, what will be the likely trajectory of this new intellectual imperialism? If recent scholarly research is any indication, the organizing principle will revolve around the role of "institutions." Institutions will provide the shell within which the new imperialism of economic proceeds. It is through institutional models that economics in its newest methodological phase can explore outcomes outside the traditional purview of economics. And it is with institutions as the central category of analysis that empirical regularities can continue to dominate over rigorous rational choice deductivism in the explanation of outcomes.

The issue becomes more contentious when we see the type of institutions on which economists have begun to focus. The important institutions for the new empirical economists appear to be those that establish and protect property rights, having to do with land ownership regulation, corruption, transparency, intellectual property protection, the likelihood of property expropriation, and generally those rights related to the private appropriation of revenue from economic activity. This research is driven by the insights of the new institutionalism (for example, North 1990), which sees social organizations (e.g., firms) as the result of the inefficiency of markets and which are often rooted in inadequate property rights regulation. With this guiding principle, economists have sought to explain issues such as child labor (Edmonds and Pavcnick 2005), civil war (Collier and Hoeffler 2004, technological innovation (Mokyr 2004), political formation (Acemoglou and Robinson 2004), and the failure of international aid to developing countries (Easterly 2006). Recent research along these lines captures culture (Guiso et al. 2006), religion (McLeary and Barro 2006), politics (Rodrik et al. 2002), and the sociology of business (Langlois 2003). Working against the imperialistic tendency is that in their work on institutions, these economists are also drawing on research in other social sciences and even engaging in interdisciplinary research projects.[14]

In sum, there has been a demotion of *homo economicus* and a promotion of the role for institutions in the explanation of social outcomes. The gaping void left by the atheoretical nature of the new economics has been filled by efforts to understand the role of institutions. Does this mean the end of any general equilibrium analysis in economics, the collapse of that unifying object of inquiry in economics for much of its history? Recent developments indicate that this is not necessarily the case. Temporarily kicked out of the house, *homo economicus* in the guise of the new institutionalism is slipping in through the back door, as Gudeman argues in this volume. The battle for control of the terrain in generating new knowledge about society will not be fought over the acceptable level for statistical significance of an estimated regression coefficient. The debate will be over how institutions are theorized and contextualized in a broader conception of society, as Swedberg intimates in this volume. The challenge to social scientists, who value other approaches to knowledge and who are suspicious of the ideological bias of the economists, is to build a more compelling theory of institutions and institutional change, to widen the scope of our understanding of institutions beyond the narrow focus on property rights enforcement and towards a broader conception of regulatory regimes and social groupings that give meaning to economic life.

Notes

I am grateful to Jennifer Bair, Stephen Gudeman, Ivo Strecker, and participants in the conference on "Rhetoric, Politics and Economics" at University of Mainz for comments on a previous version of this chapter.

1. The synchronicity in the development of this idea in various guises by Jevons, Menger, Walras, and Gossens around 1870 has never been fully explained.
2. McCloskey (1985: 71) puts it concisely: "Relaxation of assumptions is the essay-maker of modern economics."
3. See, for example, Myrdal (1928).
4. In Milberg (2007), I link this emotional dimension to the fantasy of ethnic assimilation in post-War US society.
5. This result and many others like it led to discomfort bordering on schizophrenia in the field, where proponents of the new models denied the policy relevance of their own models! For a discussion, see Milberg (2001).
6. In a telling anecdote, Warsh (2006: 318) reports that when Krugman discussed his New Economics insights related to economic geography with a "noneconomist friend," the reply was "Isn't that all kind of obvious?"
7. The lack of robustness was identified early on in the development of this paradigm and was used to downplay the significance of its policy implications. See, for example, Grossman (1986).
8. Surveys of these recent technical innovations include Colander et al. (2004), Colander (2005), Hodgson (2007), and Davis (2008).
9. For a more detailed review of other examples, see Milberg (2004).
10. I say infamous because the work has come under much critical scrutiny for the construction of some of the variables. See, for example, Foote (2006).
11. The inevitable spinoffs of *Freakonomics* have begun, and not surprisingly for the male-dominated field of economics, the subject is professional sports. See Berri et al. (2006).
12. Mirowki (1988) shows that it was precisely this application of stochastic concepts to economics that saved economics at the time from the criticism of the limited applicability of its determinate models to explain (noisy) social outcomes.
13. Given the diversity of interpretations of Kletzer's work among scholars, it is not surprising that a similar divide occurs in popular discussion of the impact of international trade on US workers. Friedman (2005) cites the study as providing reassurance that adjustment to expanded international trade is relatively smooth. Dobbs (2004: 104) writes with alarm that those who lose jobs to outsourcing are "finding new jobs that pay only about 80 percent of their original wages."
14. Examples are the joint research by Feenstra and Hamilton (2006), by Benhabib and Przeworski (2004), and the friendly citations of anthropological research in Easterly (2006). For a methodological assessment of this new wave of "institutionalism," see Spiegler and Milberg (2008).

CHAPTER 5

THE PERSUASIONS OF ECONOMICS[1]

Stephen Gudeman

■ ■ ■ ■ ■ ■

SINCE THE BEGINNING OF MODERN ethnography, anthropology and economics have had an uneasy relationship. There has been poaching (W.E. Armstrong (1924,1928) once tried to demonstrate that Rossel Island [Yela] money was like our "modern" currency), quarrels (Frank Knight famously attacked Melville Herskovits (1941)), and abrupt dismissals. But for long intervals, we had few border fights because each of us studied different peoples (or so we thought): anthropologists were experts about "primitive," small scale, simpler societies; economists knew about market societies. The situation was never that simple, but we lived with the fiction, kept to our own, and did not confront each other. In the last forty years, however, the crosscurrents have thickened and the tension has grown as each discipline's knowledge claims have expanded. When anthropologists began to erase the division between "us" and "the others," studied the effects of market expansion and capitalism on other economies, and began to look at our own, we encountered import barriers preventing entry of our goods. At the same time, economists were extending their analytical armature, such as rational choice theory, into domains that once "belonged" to us (Becker's (1976) work on the family is a well known example). Perhaps anthropologists should have been cheered by this extension, already presaged by our "formalists," because economists were assuming that all people are equally "rational," as Carrier has observed. But these breaches and invasions, as well as developments in studies of science, have brought our differences to the fore. Some (but not all) economists deploy a specific notion of human reason, build models that do not require local meanings, and offer prescriptions for economic behavior. Let us call this a formal or universal rhetoric. It is closely related to the form, style or expressive side of rhetoric. In contrast, many anthropologists record local voices and provide descriptions of people's practices and representations to build a content-filled view, and do not offer predictions and normative advice. I label this a local persuasion, because it is related to the content, specific, or substance aspect of rhetoric. If one side has tended to be axiomatic, prescriptive, and deductive, the other has been interpretative and contextual; if one side focuses on form, the other considers meaning. For example, if a people say they must "wash" or "cook" cash before using it for household purposes, or claim that yams are people, some economists see the response as irrational (it is a metaphor, "noise," or a transaction cost) to be eliminated through development and modernization, whereas anthropologists try to understand and illuminate the context of the statements and practices. Caught between the two sides, economic anthropologists always face a problem: how can we relate diverse modes of economic life to our dominant, market notion of rational choice without disparaging a people's customs and cultural arrangements?

Today, neither anthropology nor economics is a unified discipline. Economics has many variations including neoclassical, Austrian, post-Keynesian, institutionalist, new institutionalist, and heterodox forms. Anthropologists, facing an invasion by other fields seeking to use its methodology, have increasingly turned to historical and literary perspectives. But each discipline remains persuasive; if anthropologists stay rooted to the idea of ethnography, or of what people say and do, much of economics offers the lure of simplicity, closure, and abstract models. These are different modes of persuasion. I want to explore these different rhetorical styles and epistemologies by focusing on the concept of property and some of the ways the two disciplines approach it. If I am not fully satisfied with the rhetoric of economics, it has much to do with the way I see economy itself.

In my view, economy includes two interpenetrating ways of making a livelihood. In part, individuals live from the trade of goods and services that are separated, parted or alienated from enduring relationships. I term this mode, *impersonal trade* or *market*. For example, trade in which goods are parted from their holders and impersonally and competitively exchanged with others occurs in all historical and ethnographic situations, though varying in importance. Through the impact of anonymous competition, the central value in this realm is efficiency in exchange and consequently in production and consumption, where rational choice is exercised to be efficient. This realm of economy has become prominent in many contemporary societies, and it dominates most economic discourses. But people also live from goods and services that mediate and make social relationships. I term this mode, *mutuality* or *community*, in which goods and services are secured and allocated through continuing ties according to heterogeneous values, such as age, gender, position, need, equality or equity as locally defined. By "community" I mean an association of people who share common beliefs or interests, as Swedberg explains in this volume. Communities may be small and territorial or large, dispersed, and even imagined as in the case of a nation, religion, or global interest group. They also may overlap and be embedded one within another.

The shared interests of a people, which connect them and make up part of their identity, often have a material form that I call the "base." I use this word to cover an incommensurable collection of goods and services mediating relationships between people, and connecting them to things and intangibles. A base provides conditions for sustaining locally constituted life. Access to it is gained in accord with socially shared norms and practices. Always in the making, a base is unfinished and specified by situation, and it varies in prominence across economies. But it is more than a material object or service, for it is a heritage that lies outside the person as material resources, tools, information, and symbols, and within as sediments from others that partly create a social identity. Through a base, a person is the product of others from the past and in the present. For example, respect for the ancestors, their accomplishments and effect on contemporary life, whether manifested through lineage rituals or by making a weekly visit and placing flowers in a Swedish graveyard, expresses this social dependence on the past.

These two value realms of mutuality and market are dialectically related; their relative importance varies over space and time, and they are intermixed in many ways, because impersonal trade is always framed by mutuality, as Rousseau ([1762] 1913), among many others, observed. Trade occupies an arena within a constituted form of mutuality, beginning with the sociality of communication and continuing with formal rules and the informal protocols about it. For example, regular trade requires shared, political agreements, such as peace pacts or written laws enforced by commissions. This mutual arena for trade has many changing forms and scales, from a political order and laws to civic associations, family ties, ethnic identity, friendship, and fictive kinship. Impersonal trade is played out against a constitution and the "non-contractual." Conversely, allocations within a community are not the whole of material life, because a degree of impersonal trade is always encountered. The scale and combination of mutuality and trade shifts, but both realms make up economy. In contrast to my dialectical view of economy, most of modern economics imagines material life only through the perspective of prices or trade-offs that are reached through impersonal exchange. (For a related formulation of value realms, see Klamer in this volume.)

In both discourse and practice, a market's borders seem to be firm, but *cascading* continuously expands them. Cascading occurs when market participants, through the search for profit, extend their reach to noncommoditized things and services, such as forest preserves and domestic work—as observed by anthropologists and feminist economists. When markets expand, local constructions of economy are fragmented as calculated relationships replace mutuality. In market rhetoric as well, most economists try to create a seamless economic totality by cascading the limits of their model. For example, *exogenous* variables not included in the model are separated from *endogenous* ones that are: unpredictable events, such as innovations that create new value, may be excluded from the formal model (Solow 1997). In addition, *externalities* are separated from *internalities*. Externalities are effects of market acts that fall outside the market arena: they are not traded, as in the case of uncosted pollution, whereas internalities are transacted. But events and acts categorized as externalities or exogenous variables do not make up a local model, because they are constituted as the remainders of a competitive market model. To include this larger range of behaviors and effects, economists often cascade the borders of their model in order to internalize the externalities (through calculations of benefit and cost) or to convert exogenous variables to endogenous ones. Through this rhetorical process of cascading or encompassing content by form, they derive local meanings and actions as products of market behavior. I call the effects of this cascading process "debasement," because it converts socially shared benefits and relationships to market transactions; it might also be termed "colonization," to invoke the expression of Habermas ([1981] 1987: 318).

Property and Base

Drawing on this dialectical and rhetorical perspective about economy, I want to explore how it illuminates formal and local stories about property and base. Both holdings have material and conceptual forms; both have narratives that explain their presence and use. But they are not mirror images. A base is legitimated through narratives that are built around figurative devices such as metaphor, metonymy, and other forms of reason. Private property seems to persist without such origin stories. For example, in a market, participants arrive with rights to resources, such as land, labor, goods, money or ideas; the rights are transferred through bidding, regardless of their earlier acquisition by trade, inheritance, robbery, purchase, or the remaking of materials.[2] The history or memory of a property is irrelevant, because anonymous trade involves quitclaims: after a good is sold, the seller has no legal or ideological connection to the possession unless by contract, such as a warranty. But the question remains: how is private property explained? What makes this holding legitimate?

Justifying market possessions has become increasingly challenging because new forms of property are continually being devised, such as books, phrases, goods, technologies, medicines, and derivatives, which do not fit into a single category. Property rights also are divisible in continually new ways as proportional claims to the same thing or as claims to different features of it: for example, a building's owner may lease space to a corporation that is owned by shareholders and that rents its equipment from still others. Rights to the building may be held by the owner, but also by the person who gave the owner a personal loan secured by secondary rights to the building, by a bank that provided his mortgage, and by others to whom parts of the mortgage are sold and resold until ultimate ownership with its credits and liabilities spreads through markets, shifts by the day, and becomes nearly untraceable. Yet, the formation of a transparent system of property rights and markets in which they can be traded, it is said, hastens economic development. Because it clarifies incentives that lead to the efficient allocation of resources, creating and enforcing a property rights system has become common sense among policy institutions, such as the International Monetary Fund and the World Bank, neoliberal market advocates (de Soto 1989), new institutional economists (North 2005), and other standard economists.

Legitimating or explaining the presence of property rights, however, remains a point of discussion in Western philosophical and political thought. For example, Hobbes, Locke, and Rousseau all recognized the need to justify a state or sovereign order before individual property rights could be established. Rousseau observed that "the right of the first occupier, though more real than the right of the strongest, becomes a real right only when the right of property has already been established" (Rousseau [1762] 1913: 17). Property rights require that a people share a prior understanding, or rules and norms that legitimate them. But how are a system of property rights and their arena of trade justified, and what is the relation between the shared framework that is created by persons-in-community, or "conjoint" persons, and the individualized or "disjoint" holdings it supports?[3] If local stories provide a relatively seamless connection among a base, allocations from it, and the conjoint person, do market narratives encounter a breach between the shared system and the private holdings it supports? This disjuncture is often covered over by veiling local models through cascading the market one.

Local Narratives

In many ethnographic situations, social agreements, expressed through narratives and practices, justify the holdings. Spirits or ancestors of the living may be said to animate and offer a fertile resource. This connection between the living and the dead legitimates use of the possession, because access to it may be conditioned on communal participation, with the collected goods allocated through kinship or other relationships. To create these stories that connect them to the world they use, people often draw on local images, such as the experiences of touch, smell, cohabitation, a powerful event or physical labor. The narratives usually have a phenomenological touchstone and draw on figurative projections or metaphors. For example, original connections as they appear in ethnography and other written work may be explained as:[4]

- a covenant with God,[5]
- a gift of God,
- a gift of the spirits,
- a gift of royal authority,
- a transaction between human and supernatural forces,[6]
- choice of the object itself,[7]
- a gift of nature,
- first come, first serve,
- theft,
- labor embodied,
- knowledge or skills deployed,[8]
- a pact with the devil,
- devolution from the ancestors who first arrived,
- devolution from the ancestors who first emerged from the earth,[9] or
- a gift from parents.

The Bemba of East Africa say that they occupy their land and have the right to use it as descendants from the ancestors who are connected to the land by having arrived there first, using it, inventing agriculture, being buried there, and offering continued fertility. The ancestors created agriculture and opened the land.[10] Present day users are matrilineal descendants of the ancestors, born in a succession of wombs, which ensures the spirit presence of the ancestors in them. This narrative, which employs images of first come, first served, innovation, corporeal embodiment, and spirit power, legitimates the Bemba holdings and is part of their economic model. For example, tribute is sent to a chief or maternal uncle because he embodies the ancestors and makes offerings to ensure their goodwill that helps provide ample harvests. This allocation process from the base is part of its justification for use. The Bemba act as conjoint persons and do not trade their land nor explain their connection to it as a product of market or calculative reason.

Market Narratives

In economics, the problem of justifying private property has been variously handled. Broadly, classical economists, such as Smith and Ricardo, when building their models of economy, assumed a prior class structure of property holders, such as rentiers, capitalists, and laborers; neoclassical economists omit this social and historical datum and start with market trade; new institutional economists, who accept the assumption of *homo economicus,* try to show how a property rights system evolves. Macpherson (1979) has usefully distinguished two ways of justifying property in economic and philosophical writing. He argues that from Aristotle through Aquinas, Hegel, Rousseau, and Marx, private property was justified as a means for achieving human welfare and well being. But after the writings of Bentham, the development of utilitarian thought, and the rise of capitalism, the accumulation of property was validated as an end of activity (see also Macpherson 1962). In one case, holding property serves social purposes; in the other, private accretion becomes the goal.

Marx offered one of the most memorable and persuasive narratives about market property. Proudhon, said Marx ([1865] 1995: 195–96]), had claimed that property is theft, to which Marx wryly responded: from whom was it taken except another property holder? Marx himself drew on the arguments of John Locke in the *Two Treatises* ([1690] 1960). Locke had proposed a kind of imprinting and annexation story about property. His account was based on the misguided idea that the Americas were open territories, ready for taking through individual labor, because the existing inhabitants had not improved the land by applying their labor.[11] According to Locke, a person projected or extended himself to land and materials through his labor; by mixing this self-property (the possessive individual) with an object in the world and by improving it, the entity became his property.

> Every Man has a *Property* in his own *Person.* This no Body has any Right to but himself. The *Labour* of his Body, and the *Work* of his Hands, we may say, are properly his. Whatsoever then he removes out of the State that Nature hath provided, and left it in, he hath mixed his *Labour* with, and joyned to it something that is his own, and thereby makes it his *Property.* It being by him removed from the common state Nature placed it in, it hath by this *labour* something annexed to it, that excludes the common right of other Men. For this *Labour* being the unquestionable Property of the Labourer, no Man but he can have a right to what this is once joyned to, at least where there is enough, and as good left in common for others. (Locke 1960: 287–89)

Locke's narrative employed synecdoche, or part for all (labor for human), as well as metaphor (the projection of human on objects); and he presumed the presence of separated or self-possessed individuals rather than persons constituted in community. His assertion, that the means to ends or calculated act of laboring creates property, was successively elaborated by Adam Smith (1776) and David Ricardo ([1817] 1951). But Marx provided the most complete labor value story, beginning in the *Manuscripts of 1844* (1988), where he set forth the idea that property is objectified labor: through the activity of work, labor is congealed in objects and so confronts the human as an estranged part of the self. This thingification of labor in objects is a consequence of human work, but it leads to alienation when capitalists appropriate the objectified labor and separate the worker from the product of his activity.[12] Following Marx, profit is an extraction from the laborer.

Some people might reply that Marx was describing property rights not as they are, but as they should be. Marx certainly used his narrative to offer a critique of market distribution. But why not—if property accounts are stories with moral messages? More pointedly, Marx assumed, with Locke, that an individual has rights to his own labor prior to working and trading with others. But property in the self is a social entitlement; and the individual laborer is locally skilled or capacitated through a base of language, know-how, and habits (which many now reduce to human or social capital). Still, the labor right story, devolving from Locke and his successors, provides a justification today for claiming many forms of property. It legitimates rights to intellectual property, such as a song, dance or book; it encompasses claims to material or nonmaterial discoveries; it covers rights to an innovation, such as a product, the reorganization of a production system or the refashioning of a managerial structure; and it can be used to justify the appropriation of property held mutually by others, from oil, to land, to traditional medicines. More broadly, according to this individualistic story, property rights protect the labor and capital an individual invests and provide the incentive to improve the holdings: one works harder on personal property than on common holdings due to the certainty of claiming the product and its betterments.

Preferences

Recently, Carol Rose explored the issue of property justification to argue that it represents a "glitch" (1994: 27) in the neoclassical conception of economic behavior, because people must cooperate to set up a system of rights before the self-interested actor can enter the scene and trade property rights. "There is a gap," she observes, "between the kind of self-interested individual who needs exclusive property to induce him to labor and the kind of individual who has to be there to create, maintain, and protect a property regime" (Rose

1994: 38). (I might refer to her distinction as the gap between the conjoint, person-in-community, and the disjoint individual.) Rose concludes that classic theorists of property had to employ stories to explicate the beginnings of property regimes: "their narrative stories allowed them to slide smoothly over the cooperative gap in their systematic analyses of self-interest" (1994: 32). In my terms, property theorists invented local models, but the difference between the two realms of mutuality and market remains.

Some economists might deny the existence of a gap between initial mutuality and current self-interest on the grounds that shared property systems emerge to avoid a war of all against all that could lead to the destruction of a resource, as in the "tragedy of the commons" (Hardin 1968). This explanation of property law as derived from self-interest requires that cooperation or mutuality be an effective preference within individuals, a theme that has been developed by Gary Becker, who claims that his economic approach does not assume self-interest. Instead, Becker claims to offer a *"method* of analysis [and] not an assumption about motivation." He wants to shift the emphasis away from "narrow assumptions about self-interest" (Becker 1993: 385). Becker urges that in their separate utility functions, "individuals maximize welfare as *they conceive it,* whether they be selfish, altruistic, loyal, spiteful, or masochistic" (Becker 1993: 386). He argues that preferences may include benevolence (Becker 1976: 5) and sees both altruism in the family and selfishness in the market as means-to-ends behaviors (Becker 1981: 194). Becker thus claims that self-interest—like the taste for altruism, cooperation, or music—is a preference and separates self-interest as a motivation from its embodiment in the human calculator who maximizes preferences. But the idea that self-interest is only a preference, which the utility-maximizing individual may or may not entertain, seems like a fudge, for Becker concedes that there are wants in an individual's utility function that always remain unsatisfied. Can self-interest be seen as an optional preference (or substance) that is separate and different from an individual's ever-present desire (or form) to maximize his personal welfare? Is not individual welfare maximization the same as self-interest? Becker isolates the maximizing actor from his enabling social context and fills him with the preferences needed to explain his social choices. Ben Fine (1998) also argues that Becker turns both accumulated personal and social capital into things by including them within a person's extended utility function, which allows Becker to keep to his methodological individualism while denying the existence of moral commitments. In different terms, Becker abstracts several levels of form—preferences plus a utility function plus an outcome—to create a derivational model with the rational actor at its foundation (Gudeman 2008). He then cascades his model by explaining all social commitments as individual preferences. In effect, Becker turns mutuality into a private property of the self.

By his neoclassical account, the presence of a mutual context uniquely constituting the self-possessed, self-interested individual remains unexplained. A breach remains between the cultural agreements that a property paradigm first requires, and the rational choices within it. In many respect, this breach replays the formalist-substantivist debate discussed by Carrier.

Cascading in Theory and Practice

New institutionalists offer a different story about the emergence of property rights. They agree that economics is a theory of choice given the problem of scarcity, but add that the structure of constraints (or non-constraints) determines the way the competitive game is played. This structure can lead to (Pareto) efficiency as in the standard account, to stagnation, or to a position in between, given the "path dependence" (or cultural history) of institutions (North 2005). In order for the competitive structure to lead to efficiency, a clear and enforceable property rights system is needed. For the New Institutional Economics (NIE), a principal empirical and theoretical concern is to show how a property rights system develops in different ways.

I shall focus on an early and almost canonical account of property by Harold Demsetz (1967). Demsetz's article was an important forerunner of the New Institutionalism because it suggested how rational choice leads to or informs the central institution in markets: property. As Milberg (this volume) argues, NIE presumes the existence of *homo economicus*. Demsetz's story is especially relevant because it is one of the few occasions in which an economist used ethnography to justify his claims. I think it displays the breach between formal and local models, or between market and mutuality—but let us turn first to the economist's account.

In his frequently cited article written two score years ago, Demsetz drew on a market model to explain the beginning or "emergence" of property rights (1967). They "arise," he argued, by matching benefits against costs.[13] He claimed that property rights emerge to internalize externalities. In an unusual turn for an economist, Demsetz tried to lend realism to his formal argument by applying it to the origin of private property among the "aboriginal" Montagnais-Naskapi of Labrador. But with his turn to ethnography, Demsetz encountered the breach between formal and local narratives; in fact, Demsetz did not provide an origin account, but showed how the market realm of private property cascades into and debases mutuality. He assumed that the Montagnais-Naskapi were imbued with calculative reason prior to constructing a system of private property, which had emerged in response to their innate reasoning, although the Montagnais had long held a shared story about their base, its productivity, and how it was to be used. Demsetz's narrative did not close the gap between how a mutual system of rights arises and the way a market arena is expanded, except to say that market players make the market that constitutes them. Being designed to explain what it presumed, his tale turned solipsistic, while his suggestion that ethnographic realism provided his narrative's proof was a sham, because he silenced the extant Naskapi economy—so go anthropology's lessons.

Actors, Rights, Morality, and Externalities

Demsetz' story revolves around market actors who compete, aggrandize, and achieve economic efficiency. He imagines a world of socially unconnected individuals who nonetheless are endowed with language, expectations, and preferences. To justify this position, he refers to another tale often cited by neoclassical economists to charter their model: "In the world of Robinson Crusoe," says Demsetz, "property rights play no role" (1967: 347). This anchor thrown to the realm of literature and a Victorian story about shipwrecks, race, power, class, virtue, and capitalist discipline provides an image of origins, if not autochthony and a tone of realism. In the Crusoe world, property rights do not exist, because there are no "others" competing for scarce goods; mutuality also does not exist—but rational man does. According to Demsetz, property rights concern the extent to which one person can act in benefiting or harming himself or others. They specify the realm an individual controls. Demsetz allows that these "expectations" are expressed through custom and mores as well as law (1967: 347), but *homo economicus* precedes and impels their construction.

To this plotline based on the rational actor, Demsetz adds the subplot of externalities and internalities, which have to do with the interactions of market actors, and the extent to which their products and services are commoditized. Externalities, to recall, occur when one person's actions have a beneficial or harmful effect on another. For example, farmers who are upslope may unintentionally waste or lose some of their irrigation water that becomes a benefit to farmers who are downslope; the water is a free resource or positive externality (also known as a spillover). Conversely, sediment and waste from upslope farmers may fall on crops downslope, which is an unwanted harm or negative externality. An externality is neither bought nor sold, but it can be measured against (or commensurated with) other goods and services, and assigned a price. In contrast, internalities are transacted or bought and sold in the market.

The dividing line between externalities and internalities changes in accord with "transaction" costs. Transaction cost refers to all of the expenses of trading, such as contract and setup costs, insurance, and the risk of exchange failure. For example, if the upslope farmer can sell his extra water for more than the cost of channeling it, he will do so. But if his transaction cost is more than the gain, the spillover remains an externality. Demsetz expands this idea to argue that a "primary function of property rights is that of guiding incentives to achieve a greater internalization of externalities" (1967: 348). He adds, "property rights develop to internalize externalities when the gains of internalization become larger than the cost of internalization" (Demsetz 1967: 350).[14] The relation between externalities and internalities alters with technological change (Demsetz 1967: 350), but the dynamic in the internalization of externalities and the growth of private property is the search for profit, which is property itself. The expansion of property rights need not be consciously achieved, so long as the teleology of efficiency pulls the development. "Legal and moral experiments [with property rights] may be hit-and-miss procedures to some extent but in a society that weights the achievement of efficiency heavily their viability in the long run will depend on how well they modify behavior to accommodate to the externalities associated with important changes in technology or market values" (1967: 350). Demsetz's actors exist in a world of teleological Darwinism in which efficiency defines fitness, and the fittest property systems survive.

Enter Ethnography

Demsetz draws on Eleanor Leacock's (1954) study of the Montagnais-Naskapi to cloak his tale in ethnographic realism.[15] Leacock's account, based on fieldwork in 1950 and the use of earlier studies, revolves about the transition from production for use to production for exchange. Originally, groups in Labrador trapped animals for domestic consumption of meat, as well as hunting and fishing. But with the colonization by Europeans, spatial encroachment, and the arrival of French and British traders, fur trading (principally in beaver) increased. When groups in Labrador shifted from hunting for meat to hunting for salable fur, exclusive rights to trapping territories developed (Leacock 1954: 2, 6); command of a hunting territory gave control over its animal population and exclusive rights to the furs that could be secured.

Before the fur trade, people had cooperative patterns of use: "Formerly the Montagnais hunted co-operatively and shared their game" (Leacock 1954: 7). Evidence of individual territories showed up in the 1700s, when people began to blaze trees as markers of separate areas (Leacock 1954: 15, 16). But even after the advent of the fur trade, individuals could enter the territory of others to gather berries and bark, to fish or to hunt game; and, in cases of need, Montagnais could take what was needed within the area of another without payment or permission, because these products were communally possessed (Leacock 1954: 2). Among some groups, game caught for consumption was also communally shared, and even fur-bearing animals shot with a gun were divided on the basis of need and a person's debt at the store. The fur of muskrats that were trapped was shared as well (this fur had a low market value), and when a beaver dam was collectively raided, the fur was shared (Leacock 1954: 33, 34). Leacock observes that the Montagnais showed "considerable resistance to giving up communal for individualized patterns of living ... there was a *conflict* [italics added] between their desire to increase their incomes ... and their resistance to changing basic patterns of everyday existence" (1954: 9).

Demsetz's recounting of the changes follows Leacock's account, but his Montagnais have market motivations from the outset, even if they lack property rights. Before the fur trade, says Demsetz, hunting was carried out to secure food; however, "the externality was clearly present" (1967: 351), meaning that one person's hunt affected another's, although it was not cost efficient to establish property rights. Demsetz does not recognize the existence of a prior economy based on mutuality with local leaders and fails to see the later tension or conflict between the two, because *the presence of an earlier sharing economy provides evidence of other than market motivations.* For Demsetz, the inception of the fur trade changed only the cost/benefit ratio of trapping, making it "economic to encourage the husbanding of fur-bearing animals" and to establish property rights (Demsetz 1967: 352).

When rights are open or under communal ownership, says Demsetz, animals will be overhunted, because the effect will be borne by others. The community could meet and negotiate rights, but the transaction costs of doing so are high. Thus, "the effects of a person's activities on his neighbors and on subsequent generations will not be taken into account fully. Communal property results in great externalities" (Demsetz 1967: 355). In contrast, the owner of private property takes the future into account because it affects the present value of his holding: the cost of over-hunting is imposed on the hunter alone. As Demsetz moralizes, "We all know that this means that he will attempt to take into account the supply and demand conditions that he thinks will exist after his death" (1967: 355). The owner of private property also can count on others not to invade his holding, and so making his efforts at husbanding effective. "Forest animals confine their territories to relatively small areas, so that the cost of internalizing the effects of husbanding these animals is considerably reduced [as compared to plains hunting]. This reduced cost, together with the higher commercial value of fur-bearing forest animals, made it productive to establish private hunting lands" (Demsetz 1967: 353). Finally, because the cost of negotiating externalities is lower when done one-to-one between Montaignais, more externalities can be internalized, with the result that resources are even more efficiently utilized.

But What Did Leacock Argue?

Demsetz stays reasonably close to Leacock's account as a series of historical events, but a very different perspective emerges if one includes the ethnohistorical material and local voices that she adduces. Leacock observes, for example, that colonization, European expansion, and the placing of trading posts, as well as the arrival of new traps that could be purchased, all had an effect on the Montagnais. She emphasizes the impact of trade and consumption.

Leacock observes that even as early as the 1670s, with their desire for goods, the Indians had become partly dependent on traders' supplies and had learned to play the traders one against another (1954: 12). Later, in the 1800s, the Hudson Bay Company tried to induce the Indians to hunt fur by creating artificial wants. According to one trader cited by Leacock, "as trading posts, however, are now established on their lands, I doubt not but artificial wants will, in time, be created. They may become as indispensable to their comfort as their present real wants. All the arts of the trader are exercised to produce such a result, and those arts never fail of ultimate success. Even during the last two years of my management, the demand for certain articles of European manufacture has greatly increased" (McLean 1932: 262). Leacock adds that the more furs a person collected, the more material comforts he could obtain. In contrast to the aboriginal situation in which sufficiency was the aim, material wants had become possibly limitless (1954: 7). As she observes, the relatively early displacement of native equipment by tools secured from the traders indicates the importance of trade for the Montaignais (Leacock 1954: 11). And there was a close connection between this dependence on fur-trading and individualized hunting (Leacock 1954: 17). Leacock even begins her story by saying, "Private ownership of specific resources as exists has developed in response to the introduction of sale and exchange into Indian economy which accompanied the fur trade" (1954: 2).

Leacock presents ample evidence, as I mentioned, that the pattern of individual holdings did not develop smoothly and that the Indians showed "considerable resistance" to giving up their communal mode of existence. Aware of this conflict between the desire to augment income to acquire goods, and changing their mode of existence, they resisted full-time trapping (Leacock 1954: 9). With trade, local identities also changed: "the individual's most important ties, economically speaking, were transferred from within the band to without, and his objective relation to other band members changed from the co-operative to the competitive" (Leacock 1954: 7). According to Bailey, whom she cites, "the French were always desirous of dealing with individuals rather than with groups, the members of which were not thought by them to be responsible for each other's actions. Moreover, the actual pelts were owned by individuals. Thus personal ownership might by easy transference have been extended to the hunting lands" (Bailey 1937: 88). In other words, consumption desires and the art of trading, which demanded the use of calculative reason, were the origins of this dramatic change. Through them, market reason and practices cascaded into and colonized the Montaignais economy.

Derivations and Local Models

This is not the end of my counterargument, because Demsetz's account is not only devoid of local meanings or content, but it is also formally circular or solipsistic. He started with the purpose of showing how private property rights arise, which he says occurs through the internalization of externalities. The unsaid part of this tale is that externalities exist in advance of private property; they existed in Labrador before the fur trade and will exist whenever a resource is held mutually or in commons. For externalities to exist, however, *they must be measured and made commensurate or matched against other benefits and costs,* which means that there are market exchanges. And if there are market exchanges, then private property also exists, because it is the substance of anonymous trade. In contrast to Leacock's description of the prior economy, Demsetz assumes a world in which actors compete for wealth and private property, because if externalities are to be internalized, rational actors, markets, and property rights must be on the stage. The outcome is presumed at the start. Demsetz diverts attention from the solipsism of his story, however, by his claim of realism and beginnings, as if the Montagnais represented an original moment before economy.

I might contrast our arguments in shorthand. For Demsetz, given the universality of *homo economicus,* then

Scarcity (the economic problem) → Competition → Private Property.

For me, given norms of exchange, then

Trade → Competition → Scarcity → Calculative Reason (*homo economicus*) → Private Property.

Demsetz has no account for how people come together to constitute shared rules for the trade of private property. Stable property rights for use in trade presume shared rules for trade, which involves property. Property institutions embody more than the use, winnowing, and refining of formal reason, they embody mutuality, which is missing in Demsetz's account.

Thus, Demsetz is not describing the origins of private property rights but how—once given—they cascade into or colonize the realm of mutuality. He tells a story about the extension of private property and the expansion of commoditization, but not about their inception. By metaphorically projecting inception on expansion, Demsetz implies that the causes of expansion are the same as the causes of origin; in doing so, he elides the local situation as well as the shifting conditions of conquest, military power, and the state that helped bring the traders to Labrador. The persuasiveness of his argument depends on the reader's belief in a deductive model with levels and derivations that are powered by *homo economicus* (Gudeman 2008).

So What?

We might confine this argument between anthropologist and economist to the dustbin of their other peevish disagreements, except that it emblemizes a theoretical difference, for the Montagnais experience has been replicated countless times around the globe. In fact, it is very similar to what I observed in my Panama fieldwork, where I witnessed the shift from subsistence farming to cash cropping sugar cane (Gudeman 1978). Precisely as this change occurred, market reason was spreading and claims to private property were being made.

At the beginning of this fieldwork, I tried to elicit the choices and trade-offs people were making in the subsistence crops, such as rice, maize, and beans. This decision tree analysis did not work because the people knew what they needed to feed a family for a year, and, by rule of thumb, they cut down sufficient forest in the swidden (slash-and-burn) cycle to plant the needed amount. The forest was not conceived to be scarce. Traditionally, the people were squatters on land held by a set of absentee siblings who used the territory for grazing cattle. (The family had inherited their possession from a general who fought in the 1840 war of independence and seized the land afterward.) The siblings and earlier owners permitted the people to live and work on the land because their swidden farming created pasture in a rotating cycle: after two years of use, the land was left to regenerate for ten to fifteen years while the cattle grazed in the cleared areas. Then, after the Cuban revolution, the Panama sugar cane quota was increased, and two relatively nearby sugar cane mills began to augment their production. At roughly the same time, the aging absentee owners sold their land, and, after a series of events, it ended up in the hands of the agrarian reform agency, which did little for many years. Shortly before my arrival, this world began to change. Enticed by the possibility of trading for cash, the people began to raise sugar cane, especially because they thought they could raise it in the off time from their subsistence work. Increasingly, they supplied sugar cane to the mills and, with the receipts, became dependent on market goods, from radios and batteries, to kerosene lamps, and finally to rice, the subsistence food. Two changes followed. First, midway through my fieldwork, as I was trying to grasp the work flows and subsistence returns, I was struck by a difference in the use of measuring rods, or more exactly the use and absence of a measuring rod. The subsistence crops were "measured" in a variety of traditional units, from irregular gourds that held quantities of seed, to different ways of measuring work in a field, to how many days a harvest would last. But in the same conversation when I switched to discussion of the cash crop, money was the unique measure. (The mills would walk a field, determine the production volume it would support, and then advance a sum to pay for seed and labor. At the harvest, a mill would pay the supplier for the weight and purity of his sugar cane, less the advances.) When I asked a person about his sugar cane harvest, he would tell me about its weight and the money it provided. I also learned about the many calculated ways the people could enhance their returns at the expense of the mills. For this crop, formal market reason was used.

The second change was equally dramatic. During the time of the absentee owners, the people had constructed temporary wooden fences around their plots, not to mark them as private property, but to protect the crops from cattle. When the sugar cane arrived, the people began to fence the land with barbed wire, aiming to hang onto it as a possession and keep out other croppers. The opportunity to trade for cash and goods produced competition for land to raise sugar cane, which led to fencing. The rural folk tried to maintain their subsistence cycle of raising rice and maize by integrating it with the sugar cane that was raised in the same field. But sugar cane is a perennial, which wears out the soil, and as the domestic harvests diminished, the people began to ask whether the inception of the cash crop helped or hurt their existence. The sugar cane helped us and ruined us, they would explain, especially since the cash earnings never covered subsistence costs. Their narrative about their connection to the land, which provided sustenance and yielded strength for living with others, was debased. As in the case of the Montagnais, trade produced self-interested calculation that led to property claims and debasement of the community. Once again, the sequence ran

> Trade → Competition → Scarcity → Claims to property for trade → Debasement.

But so what? That is modernization. In the absence of compelling market narratives that justify private property, however, the local stories that people have about connections among themselves and to their world cannot always be silenced. These narratives have continuous hold, as today's events in countries shifting from socialism to markets illustrate.[16] For example, who has legitimate claims to a state's former possessions? Is it global capitalists who have purchasing power, national capitalists who offer a lower purchase price but keep local control, former government administrators who have managerial experience, party officials who have the social connections to make the acquisition, or workers who previously used the property? In Israel, where there are long-held, conflicting claims to the same land, who has rights to it? And which rights should be recognized—those based on the Bible, on historical use, on colonial occupation, or on present power? This allocation problem cannot be resolved by replacing local stories of justification with the narrative of market efficiency and Pareto improvements, for it erases the problem. With persuasions about property, the market model reaches one of its limits: it does not describe a total economy, while calculated trade contradicts the shared system by which individual possessions are constituted.

Conclusion

We thus return to our beginning topic: the difference between anthropology and formal economics—different epistemologies, different models, and different rhetorics. These orientations are not alternatives between which we can rationally choose as the occasion demands, our preferences dictate, or our training teaches, because there are moral and value differences between approaches. Many models in economics are abstractions in relation to local ones.[17] The issue revolves not only about some economists failed attempts at realism, as well as their solipsism, assumptions about the human as self-interested, eclipsing of sociality, and various conflations, but about ways of representing the economic world. Everything—including the natural world—is seen through a culturally and historically produced prism. Its supposed realism is presumed to apply to all social situations, while failures in its application are ascribed to insufficient analysis (the new institutionalists) or to social rules that inhibit rational expression (neoclassical economics). In contrast, I think these rhetorical expressions are incomplete and mask the necessary presence of local, substantive conversations, as Cosgel explains in this volume. They assert the universality of a knowledge form with its practices, which may be consoling in the face of uncertainty, but the totalization is achieved by retroactively transforming contingencies into necessities (Zizek 2000: 225), and transforming local constructions into a particular rhetorical form. If we find a breach between the two modes of persuasion, and on the ground tension between sociality and anonymous trade, I conclude that economies themselves are built on a dialectic of persuasions that must be the subject of continuing political conversations.

Note

1. A different version of this chapter, "The Persuasions of Economics," appeared in *Economy's Tension (2008)*, which was published by Berghahn Books.
2. I consider property to be a "bundle of rights" or social entitlements among people, as do most anthropologists (Hann 1995). Other definitions are used. Humphrey and Verdery (2004: 1) observe that property has been considered to be a thing, a relation between person and thing, person to person relations mediated by things, as well as a bundle of rights.
3. I use the terms "conjoint" person and "disjoint" person to denote the person-in-community and the individual (Markus and Kitayama 1998; 2003). In a related way, Strathern (1988) speaks of the "dividual" and the "individual."
4. Except as noted, I have discussed these connections in Gudeman (1986), (2001), and Gudeman and Rivera (1990), drawing on reported ethnography and on my own.
5. As in the Mishnah (Neusner 1990).
6. Sneath 2004: 168.
7. Among the Even of Siberia, land and reindeer, both of whom have spiritual force, may choose persons with whom they want to form relationships, a choice that is expressed in various ways (Vitebsky 2001).
8. Anderson 1998.
9. Malinowski 1978 [1935]: 341–44.
10. I discussed this ethnography from Audrey Richards (1939) in Gudeman (1986). For a different example in which the fertility of crops depends on the goodwill of ancestors, see Firth (1936).
11. By some estimates, there were over 100 million inhabitants when the Europeans arrived.
12. The argument is developed in many of Marx's other writings, for example the *Grundrisse* (1973) and *Capital*, vol. 1 (1967).
13. Alchian and Demsetz (1973) subsequently expanded the argument.
14. Demsetz states and restates his central theme: "The emergence of property rights can be understood best by their association with the emergence of new or different beneficial and harmful effects" (1967: 350). "The emergence of new property rights takes place in response to the desires of the interacting persons for adjustment to new benefit-cost possibilities" (Demsetz 1967: 350).
15. See also Speck (1926).
16. Verdery offers a detailed account from Transylvania (Romania). She notes that land reform involved the contradictory issues of historical justice, political expediency, distributive effects, ethnic empowerment, economic efficiency, paying off the losers, equality, and accumulating political capital (Verdery 2003: 80). Even historical justice was ambiguous: did it mean restoring land to its owners before socialism or to the laborers who farmed it collectively (Verdery 2003: 158)?
17. I think they are initially incited by the attempt to understand and give meaning to the practice of anonymous trade (Gudeman 2006).

CHAPTER 6

CONVERSATIONS BETWEEN ANTHROPOLOGISTS AND ECONOMISTS

Metin M. Cosgel

■ ■ ■ ■ ■ ■

ECONOMISTS AND ANTHROPOLOGISTS DO NOT seem to talk systematically to each other. The evidence on the flow and sharing of academic knowledge suggests that they have little interest in regularly exchanging ideas or joining interdisciplinary efforts with each other. Studies of citation patterns show that economists rarely cite the works of anthropologists, and anthropologists similarly do not find much inspiration in the works of economists (Rigney and Barnes 1980; Pearson 2002; Pieters and Baumgartner 2002). No formal channels of communication have been established to facilitate a sustained conversation between the two disciplines. No journals regularly publish contributions from both disciplines, and no professional associations exist with significant membership from both groups.

The broken relationship between economics and anthropology cannot simply be attributed to the continual fragmentation of social sciences into narrower disciplines since the nineteenth century and the general difficulty of communicating across fragmented disciplines. Although economists and anthropologists have failed to sustain conversations with each other, they were able to maintain them with others. Patterns of interdisciplinary citations and formal networks show various active communication flows between these disciplines and others. Economists have been able to meet regularly with their colleagues in law, business, history, political science, and others at the annual meetings of various interdisciplinary professional associations (such as the Economic History Association, Public Choice Society, and American Law and Economics Association) and read each other's work in the publications of these associations. Anthropologists have been able to do the same with their colleagues in medicine, biology, psychology, and history. The broken flow of communication between economics and anthropology stands out as an exception to the trend. Although there may have been economists and anthropologists continuing the conversation individually, their efforts have remained for the most part as isolated attempts, not systematic movements.

Although the puzzling relationship between economics and anthropology has attracted significant attention, the problem has typically been studied as a matter of methodological differences resulting from the division of labor. Economists are said to subscribe to the assumption of rationality, in sharp contrast to the anthropologists' broader view on human behavior. The two disciplines are also said to differ significantly in their use of abstract models, organization and classification of knowledge, and methods of gathering and processing data. Although these differences may be accurate and important, they could not have been solely responsible for preventing economists and anthropologists from talking to each other. Given that economists and anthropologists have been able to overcome similar differences in cross-fertilizations with psychology, sociology, political science, and other social sciences, the source of the problem appears to lie elsewhere.

Recent developments in the rhetoric of inquiry provide a unique opportunity to break free from previous tendencies and approach the problem with a fresh perspective, viewing it not as a matter of methodological conviction, but rhetoric culture. One of the recent productive approaches within the rhetorical tradition has been to view the economy and culture as consisting of conversations (Cosgel 1992, 1994, 1997; Cosgel and Klamer 1990; Cosgel and Minkler 2004; Gudeman and Rivera 1990; McCloskey and Klamer 1995; Strecker 1988). Adopting such an approach, this chapter will take not the firms, households, or tribes as the principal objective of analysis in both disciplines, but instead will focus on the conversations *between* these units. I view conversation as a purposeful activity, aimed at solving a problem. Dividing conversations into two groups based on the type of problems they aim to solve, I examine how economists and anthropologists differ systematically in their preferences and capabilities in studying these conversations and what consequences this difference has had for their own conversations across disciplines.

Specialization and Cross-fertilization

A fundamental principle of economics with which Adam Smith begins *The Wealth of Nations* is the division of labor. Specialization and the division of labor increase the productivity of workers by allowing them to concentrate on simple, narrowly defined tasks. The division of labor is implied by the specialization of workers not just by distinct types of employment, but even within each employment, a process observed not only in the town market or on the factory floor, but also in the production of knowledge in the academic world. Just as Smith saw a division of labor between the baker and the butcher, the academic world has experienced a similar proliferation of specialties since his time, philosophy being divided into the smaller domains of economics, psychology, sociology, anthropology, and other social sciences and humanities.[1] Specialization has certainly been a key component of progress in the academic world. By specializing in narrow areas of teaching and research, each academic has been able to increase his or her contribution to the stock of knowledge.

The benefits of specialization ultimately reach beyond a discipline. In addition to the direct benefits received by the immediate consumers of knowledge, there are also external benefits, which are realized as new ideas and methods are cross-fertilized into other disciplines. Such cross-fertilizations have been the genesis of some of the most innovative recent developments in the social sciences. As Dogan and Pahre (1990: 1) argue, "innovation in the social sciences occurs more often and with more important results at the intersections of disciplines." Scholars have spread the benefits of specialization across disciplinary boundaries by exporting their own refined ideas, methods, and perspectives to other disciplines and by importing useful developments from others.

Economists and anthropologists have variously borrowed the products and technologies of other disciplines for cross-fertilization. Economists have always followed developments in mathematics and statistics closely, and borrowed freely to improve their techniques of mathematical proofs and quantitative analysis. Mirowski (1988) has even argued that it was developments in physics that inspired the marginal revolution of the 1870s in economics—one of the most significant turning points in the history of economic thought. Economists have also borrowed from business and social sciences, developing such subfields as financial economics, demographic economics, and political economy. Anthropologists have similarly followed developments in other disciplines closely for inspiration. Viewing this as indispensable for the field, Belshaw (1989: 17) remarked: "interdisciplinary connections are essential corpuscles in the lifeblood of anthropology, without which it would cease to be effective." Originating from a number of separate fields, anthropology has borrowed heavily from sociology, biology, linguistics, psychology, medicine, and various other fields, throughout its history.

Specialization has also led to various sorts of lending from economics and anthropology to other disciplines. To extend the benefits of specialization, economists and anthropologists have crossed disciplinary boundaries to contribute to developments in other disciplines or to create new subspecialties at the cross-sections of two or more disciplines (Dogan and Pahre 1990). This type of cross-fertilization has allowed disciplines to extend their conventional boundaries by identifying fertile areas where narrow applications of the traditional tools and concepts of other disciplines have proven inadequate or incomplete. Economics has extended into law, history, and sociology, leading to the establishment and development of various subdisciplines, such as economics of the law, economic history, and rational choice sociology. Developments in anthropology have similarly had widespread influence in sociology, psychology, philosophy, and other disciplines.

To see the direction of borrowing and lending between disciplines, we can examine citation patterns between them. In a recent study, Pieters and Baumgartner (2002) used citation analysis to document "who talks to whom" between economics, other social sciences (anthropology, political science, psychology, sociology), and business (accounting, finance, management, marketing, and MIS/operations research). Using the citations of the five most influential journals in each of these disciplines between 1995 and 1997 for analysis, they aggregated citations by discipline and determined the percentage of intra- and interdisciplinary communication flows between these disciplines. The results show that articles in economics journals cite and receive citations from those in business, political science, and sociology. Journals in (general and cultural) anthropology, on the other hand, cite only the journals in sociology and receive citations from those in sociology and psychology. One has to be careful, however, in appropriately interpreting these results. Anthropology is a diverse field with several semi-autonomous subfields, making it difficult to compare citation patterns directly with other disciplines. Moreover, this study was based on citations by a limited set of journals within a limited set of disciplines, rather than all citations to all types of scholarly publications, including books, conference proceedings, and other journals. Despite these limitations, the results are sufficiently robust to show some of the general tendencies in interdisciplinary communication.

The Puzzle: Lack of Conversation Between Anthropologists and Economists

One of the most striking observations of Pieters and Baumgartner is the conspicuous lack of a single citation between the economics and anthropology journals during this period. It is also striking that a similar study of citation patterns (based on random samples of articles in a single journal in each discipline) by Rigney and Barnes (1980) had found essentially the same result, that is, almost no citations between economics and anthropology about two decades earlier. The implication that the two disciplines may not have talked systematically for some time is supported by other recent studies of citation patterns. Analyzing citations in all economics journals (tracked by citation reports), during the period of 1955 to 2000, to a carefully selected group of twenty three publications "relevant to the broad themes of economic anthropology," Pearson (2002) has found that only a small proportion of the citations to these works have come from economists. Economists have paid much greater attention to the works of their own colleagues than those of anthropologists, even to those generally considered to be monumental in this field. Citation studies thus variously lead to the same unfortunate conclusion. While specializing, economists and anthropologists have continued the conversation with other disciplines, but somehow failed to sustain it with each other.

The lack of a systematic conversation between economics and anthropology is surprising, because the two disciplines appear to share numerous areas of common interest. At a basic level, both disciplines are interested in human behavior and institutions. Judging by the types of behavior and institutions that appear in their textbooks and journals, economists and anthropologists appear to teach and research in parallel areas. The subjects that have traditionally been of widespread interest in both disciplines include work, poverty, religion, race, gender, education, urbanization, and economic systems. Despite these commonalities, there must have been substantial differences between economics and anthropology in other areas to prevent them from continuing the conversation and exploiting opportunities for cross-fertilization.

The puzzling relationship between economics and anthropology has attracted significant enough attention to generate a literature of its own. The puzzle has been at the core of numerous professional gatherings and scholarly publications, with the phrase "economics and anthropology" variously appearing in the titles of conferences and essays devoted exclusively to discussing the general relationship between these disciplines.[2] Leading journals have hosted famous exchanges and discussions on the subject, such as the Knight-Herskovits exchange published in the *Journal of Political Economy,* the conference session "Economics and Anthropology: Developing and Primitive Economies" published in the *American Economic Review,* and the minisymposium on the history of economic anthropology published in the *History of Political Economy.* There was also the well-known debate between "formalists" and "substantivists" surrounding the applicability of economic models to anthropological phenomena.[3] These debates and controversies have, of course, attracted further attention from those focused on specific dimensions of the relationship between these disciplines or in the subdiscipline of economic anthropology.[4]

Despite devoting significant attention to the problem, previous studies have generally approached it from a narrow angle, searching for methodological differences between the two disciplines. The differences that have received the most attention in this literature are those in behavioral assumptions and modes of inquiry. Behavioral assumptions are said to differ significantly because economists subscribe to the assumption of rationality, in sharp contrast to the anthropologist's more holistic approach to human behavior. Whereas economists build models featuring only the profit or utility maximizing *homo economicus*, anthropologists consider a plurality of motives and objectives, including various cultural, social, and moral influences on behavior (Dowling 1982; Lodewijks 1994; Wilk 1996).

Modes of inquiry are also said to differ significantly. Economists rely on models and theories to hypothesize about reality, approach it from a macro perspective, construct general categories and stylized facts, remain detached from actual events and subjects, focus on outcomes, and use secondary sources to gather quantitative data. Anthropologists, on the other hand, observe reality up close, maintain a micro perspective, attend particulars, consider actual people and events, focus on the process leading to outcomes, and use field research to gather qualitative data (Bardhan 1989; Cooter 2000; Epstein 1975; Gudeman and Rivera 1990; Lipton 1992; Mayhew 1994; Pearson 2000; Wallerstein 2003; Wilk 1996).

By focusing on methodological differences, previous studies have basically attributed the problem to specialization, viewing it as an unintended consequence of the division of labor between the two disciplines. Focusing on the consequence rather than the cause of disciplinary specialization is consistent with Smith's approach to the division of labor. As a member of the Enlightenment, Smith believed that "all men are created equal" and neglected the possibility that the division of labor might be based on differences in inherent abilities and comparative advantages between individuals. He focused instead on the benefits of simplicity and repetition. He argued that the division of labor increased productivity "owing to three different circumstances; first, to the increase of dexterity in every particular workman; secondly, to the saving of the time which is commonly lost in passing from one species of work to another; and lastly, to the invention of a great number of machines which facilitate and abridge labor, and enable one man to do the work of many" (Smith 1976: book I, chap. I). The invention of machinery in an industry is analogous to the development of disciplinary "capital" in academia.[5] By specializing in narrow fields, not only has each academic been able to increase his or her own "dexterity" and saved resources that would have been wasted in passing from one sort of task to another, but he or she has contributed to building the field's capital by introducing or developing labor-saving tools, concepts, theories, and research methods used in the production of knowledge. The scenario based on methodological differences and a Smithian approach to division of labor would thus suggest that, during the process of specialization, these disciplines must have somehow drifted apart from each other and developed in isolation different modes of inquiry and behavioral assumptions. These differences must have then prevented them from cross-fertilizing the tools, concepts, theories, and research methods with each other.

While these observations may be accurate in general terms, they do not get to the root of the problem. Methodologies are human creations, and they adjust to the changing needs of a discipline. Economists and anthropologists typically learn about the methodologies of their own discipline during professional training and follow them in research at varying levels of commitment. Emphasizing methodological differences to explain the lack of cross-fertilization, therefore, begs the question. It does not explain, for example, why economists would refuse to learn field methods to be able to study the preferences of individuals or the behavior of the businessmen up close (Lavoie 1990). Similarly, it is not clear why anthropologists would not learn the tools of mathematical analysis to build mathematical models of a primitive economy if it was desirable to do so. Previous studies of the problem thus show only the consequences of the problem, without explaining what caused it and why it persisted for so long.

Similar methodological differences that exist between these disciplines and others do not seem to have prevented their conversations. Economists and sociologists, for example, despite their historically different views on rationality, have continued the conversation, helping to shape each other's views on the matter. Similarly, economists' general distaste for survey data does not seem to have prevented their conversation with political scientists. The source of the problem appears to lie elsewhere.

The problem is not merely a matter of formal boundaries between disciplines. Economists have shown no respect for traditional boundaries, maintaining that their models and theories apply to all times and societies. Given the natural accusation for being imperialistic economists have thus far received, it would be ironic to accuse them of not exporting their approach to anthropology out of respect for disciplinary boundaries. But on their part, anthropologists have not shown much respect for these boundaries either, as can be seen from the recent anthropological analysis of issues pertinent to modern economies traditionally studied by economists.

The problem persists even in subfields where economists and anthropologists would be expected to work closely. There are subfields of economics and anthropology that share similar interests, such as "economic anthropology" and "economic development." Despite the common ground, however, these have remained as separate subfields, with little interaction between the two disciplines. Economic anthropology has remained primarily a subdiscipline of anthropology, failing to attract economists in the same way as some of the other interdisciplinary subfields, such as "economic history" or "law and economics," have achieved. As a parallel development, economic development has remained a subfield of economics, dominated by economists interacting only occasionally, if at all, with anthropologists. Another field where one would have expected close interactions between the two fields is the study of religion. Contrary to this expectation, recent economic analysis of religion has established close ties with sociology and political science, but not with anthropology. There appears to be a deep-rooted difference between the approaches of economists and anthropologists that is preventing their conversations, a problem more fundamental than the methodological differences identified by previous studies.

Specialization by Conversation Genre

For a more satisfactory analysis of the problem, we need to adopt a different view of specialization, one that emphasizes not just the consequences of the division of labor, but also its causes and its advantages due not just to mere repetition, but to the accommodation of natural differences between individuals. This requires us to move beyond Smith's approach to the division of labor as influenced by the Enlightenment and to consider a different tradition, representing the views of Plato and many others prior to Smith, which emphasized nature over nurture and attributed the advantages of the division of labor to differences in inherent capabilities. This tradition gained strength after Smith, with the emphasis, as placed by Ricardo, on comparative advantage. The nineteenth-century writer well known for his views on the division of labor within this tradition was Charles Babbage, who criticized Smith for overlooking a key advantage of the division of labor and leaving the analysis seriously incomplete. Babbage argued that in the absence of specialization, each worker would be required to perform a number of tasks involving a variety of skills and capabilities. Because the supply of these skills and capabilities varies considerably in every society, the great virtue of the division of labor is to unbundle them and allow workers to specialize in tasks for which they are best suited (Babbage 1835).

To identify the capabilities relevant to the problem, I follow a rhetorical approach and choose the conversation as the appropriate unit of analysis. Rather than follow the conventional procedure of distinguishing between economics and anthropology by the subject matter, I distinguish by the type of conversations that cuts across these disciplines. Although the distinction between the two has often been drawn in terms of differences in geography (for example, eastern versus western societies), culture (peasant versus civilized), and time (primitive versus modern), economists and anthropologists have frequently crossed these boundaries, which suggests that subject matter has not been the basis for the division of labor between them. The relevant basis may have been the difference in the types of conversations primarily studied in the two disciplines and in the capabilities required to study these conversations.

Conversations have been a primary object of study in the rhetorical tradition. In parallel development in the two disciplines, economics and anthropology have recently joined this tradition, variously showing the centrality of conversations not just in scholarly inquiry, but within a culture and an economy as well. Gudeman and Rivera (1990: 4) have proposed "the model of conversation as the practice of anthropology and as the activity of other cultures." McCloskey (1994: 367) has similarly argued that "the economy, like economics itself, is a conversation."[6] Conversations within an economy and culture include both verbal and nonverbal forms of communication. We engage in conversations not just when we talk at the dinner table, but every time we consume goods, go to work, and participate in exchange. We express our identities through consumption, our abilities and interests at work, our passions and incomes at the marketplace, and in our conversational form.

To distinguish between the different forms of conversations, we can use the concept of the genre. Though primarily pertinent to the analysis of the narrative text, genre theory has been useful when examining the ethnography of speaking (Carbaugh 1988). It can also be helpful when distinguishing among groups of conversations in the economy and culture that share distinct features. Adapting the terms and definitions of the theory to the analysis of conversations, genre would refer to a classification based on the routines and expectations about the setting, time/place, medium, participants, or the purpose of the conversation. Although the classified sets may overlap with one another and vary according to the system of generic classification, genre is a useful concept because it articulates the boundaries of the sets and provides a way to interpret single acts of speech within a network of conversations.[7]

To maintain focus on the problem of communication between economists and anthropologists, let us classify conversations according to their purpose or the type of problem they aim to solve. Classifying conversations by their purpose rather than by their setting, time/place, medium, or participants is consistent with the position adopted earlier of deviating from the conventional procedure of distinguishing between economics and anthropology by the subject matter. Although not all conversations may aim to solve a problem, considering them as purposeful activities for solving problems helps to focus on those that are of primary interest to economists and anthropologists. It also helps to construct an analytical procedure to distinguish between the two disciplines.

Based on the type of problem they aim to solve, conversations in the economy and culture can be grouped into two genres. Those in the first genre aim to solve the problem of interest, that is, how to align the incentives of the participants. The problem arises within this conversation because people have their own interests, which often conflict with the interests of others. In situations where people's actions may create a conflict with others, conversations may resolve the conflict by allowing participants to recognize their mutual interests and by generating agreements that will ensure mutually beneficial behavior (see Swedberg's discussion in this volume).

Conversations in the second genre deal with the problem of knowledge or content, that is, how to align or interpret localized, dispersed information. In some situations, a person's actions depend on information about the preferences, beliefs, plans, and behavior of others, which is information about how they will act and what they know or care about. This problem occurs because such information may not be available readily to everyone. Note that although the unavailability of information may be a problem in both genres, the nature of the problem is categorically distinct between them. In the first genre, the availability of information becomes a problem when individuals strategically withhold or reveal inaccurate information because of conflicting interests, as seen in the type of problems known in economics as "hidden information" or "adverse selection" (Akerlof 1970). The focus in the second genre is not on the desire to withhold information, but on the inability to put it coherently together. The problem remains even if interests do not conflict and individuals are willing to share the information voluntarily, because the information is dispersed and needs to be gathered through conversation.

To see the difference between the two genres, suppose you were able to hear some of the conversations taking place in a restaurant. At some tables you might hear conversations of the first genre between two friends contemplating whether to start a new business and who should be responsible for what, between an engaged couple discussing where to live after getting married or whether one of them should change jobs to accommodate the other, and between a job candidate and the head of the search committee for an academic position discussing the qualifications of the candidate or the match between their interests. In the same setting and even between the same types of characters, conversations of the second genre could be taking place at other tables. You might hear two old friends talking about their recent accomplishments to catch up with each other, a couple on a first date sharing with each other their religious beliefs or preferences in music and movies, or two academics discussing recent research in their own fields to learn about new developments. The examples can easily be extended to other settings and characters. Whereas a conversation between two businessmen working out a merger between their companies would be an example of the first genre, their conversation to learn about each other's families, hobbies, or worldviews would be of the second genre. In the entirely different setting of a meeting between the chiefs of two primitive tribes, they would be engaged in conversations of the first genre when resolving disputes about hunting grounds or deciding the exchange rates between bartered goods, and they would be engaged in conversations of the second genre while learning about each other's food, dance, gods, or tribal traditions. It is not the differences in participants or time or setting that determines the genre of these conversations, but their purpose. If one concerns the terms of an exchange or the procedures of trade, the other concerns knowing or understanding them. (See Carrier's chapter in this volume.)

This does not mean, of course, that there are no other ways of classifying the conversations in the economy and culture. There may be various other genres or other bases for differentiating between them. The objective here is not to contribute to the theory of genre or the theory of conversations, but to find a way to distinguish analytically between economics and anthropology that will help to understand the problem of the lack of communication between the two disciplines. Given the enormity of the task and the limitations of previous approaches to it, even though the problem may have other dimensions worth studying, I am simply proposing to start a new avenue for exploration by making a simple division between two genres that I think are sufficiently broad to cover the possibilities most interesting to economists and anthropologists.

Economists and Anthropologists Study Rhetoric Culture Differently

The emphasis on conversations suggests a definition of rhetoric culture as the set of institutions that assist in conversations. Participants in these conversations do not start from scratch; they rely on a variety of rules, norms, customs, traditions, and other institutions that assist communication by guiding and constraining an individual's choice of "words" and his or her interpretations of the choices of others. The distinction between the two genres of conversations helps to identify two subcategories of rhetoric culture. The first category consists of institutions that assist in the alignment of interests, and the second consists of those assisting in the alignment of knowledge.

Individuals have different preferences and capabilities for studying conversations and rhetoric culture. Just as two individuals may differ significantly in their preferences for music, literature, and sports, they may have different preferences for conversations, one preferring conversations of the first genre and the other the second. They may similarly have different capabilities for studying these conversations. Just as some individuals might excel in playing the clarinet, writing novels, playing football, or studying conversations of the first genre, others might excel in singing, poetry, swimming, or studying conversations of the second genre. Based on these preferences and capabilities, individuals would be expected to self-select into different types of occupations in music, literature, sports, and conversation analysis in the division of labor in a society.

Anthropologists and economists presumably differ systematically in their preferences and capabilities for studying conversations and rhetoric culture. Although economists and anthropologists have shared a general interest in studying the institutions of conversation, they have specialized in genres that require different types of skills. Economists have preferred the first genre and have acquired capabilities that are better suited to studying it than the second genre. By specializing in the first genre and improving these capabilities, they have collectively studied the rhetoric culture surrounding the genre, variously showing how the law, markets, firms, contracts, and other institutions have helped to solve the problem of differing interests. As scholars with preferences and capabilities better suited to studying the problem of organizing and understanding the knowledge of others, anthropologists have specialized in the second genre and have studied how the art, language, rituals, customs, and other institutions provide a meaningful world.

The division of labor observed between economists and anthropologists is the outcome of a process of self-selection and professional training, a process best understood by combining the insights of Smith and Babbage on the division of labor. Recall that whereas Smith emphasized the benefits of professional training and repetition to explain the division of labor, Babbage emphasized the differences in inherent skills and capabilities. Smith is right because the division of labor has allowed economists and anthropologists to improve their individual capabilities and acquire the common skills developed in their disciplines through doctoral training and professional growth. Babbage is right because those who have become economists have presumably had an inherent special capability to notice and study the misalignment of incentives in a conversation that other scholars might have failed to notice or study adequately. Otherwise they would not have pursued graduate education in economics, their application would not have been accepted, or they would not have been able to graduate and become professional economists. Similarly, others have become anthropologists because they have better capabilities for solving the problem of knowledge organization. Whereas an economist would have a capability for studying how religious rituals help align interests in a society, an anthropologist would have the capability for studying how distribution and exchange of goods help transmit information.[8]

But it is also possible for the process to generate the "wrong" outcome for some economists or anthropologists. Individuals are not always the best judges of their own preferences and capabilities, and various imperfections and rigidities in the screening, training, and placement of academics may have caused some to end up in the wrong specialization by mistake. Someone with preferences and capabilities better suited to studying the problem of knowledge might turn out to be in a department of economics, and someone else with a comparative advantage in being an economist might instead end up being an anthropologist. Moreover, preferences and capabilities may have changed over time, causing some to find themselves in the wrong specialization at some point in their careers.

Although some economists have been interested in the problem of knowledge, research on the problem has primarily remained outside of the mainstream, confined mostly to showing the role of prices in conveying information about supply and demand conditions. Mainstream economists have typically either assumed away this information problem based on the assumption of perfect information, or they have restricted it to the problem of individuals witholding unobservable information strategically from others. The Austrian School of Economics has always taken a deep interest in the role of knowledge (Knudsen 2004; Langlois 1992; O'Driscoll 1977). For example, in his famous 1937 article titled, "Economics and Knowledge," Hayek (1937: 33) argued that "the empirical element in economic theory … consists of propositions about the acquisition of knowledge." As O'Driscoll (1977: 21) has argued, however, "Hayek's early diagnosis of the problem has been largely ignored." I would argue that this is not because economists have failed to realize the importance of knowledge or somehow decided collectively to forego research and publication opportunities on the subject, but because their preferences and capabilities have been inadequate to deal with it properly. As Lavoie (1990: 169) has also urged, economists interested in the problem of knowledge need to "become more like anthropologists, in the sense that they should do more of their empirical work 'up close' through participant observation rather than only from the distance required for statistical work."[9] They may also need to conceptualize knowledge as anthropologists do, more as information about meaning that leads to understanding than merely as information about price.

Similarly, although some anthropologists have studied the problem of diverse interests, research in the field has been confined primarily to the field of economic anthropology. Some of the debates and controversies that have plagued the field might be attributed to the mismatch between the specializations and the preferences and capabilities of some anthropologists. It is quite telling, for example, that the formalists in the famous formalist-substantivist debate were almost all anthropologists and several of the substantivists were economists (Mayhew 1994: 302). In what appears to be a confusing twist of positions, they seem to have chosen sides not according to their specialization and professional training within disciplinary boundaries, but based on their preferences and capabilities for studying rhetoric culture across these boundaries.

Concluding Remarks

Where does all of this leave us? It may be possible to proceed from here in two opposite directions. The first is the pessimistic and protectionist direction, supporting the views of those who consider the approaches of economists and anthropologists to be incompatible with each other and to reject one of the approaches as wrong. If studying the conversations and rhetoric culture of the first genre is incompatible with studying those of the second genre, then one might be justified to discourage cross-fertilizations between the two disciplines for fear of complications from the mismatch. Similarly, if one vehemently opposes some elements in another discipline, then one might seek to protect his or her discipline by discouraging cross-fertilizations for fear of contagion of those elements. Variations on these positions may also be used to support unorthodox approaches in their opposition to the mainstream. An unorthodox approach in economics might seek to form alliances with anthropologists or to extend its applicability by identifying its similarities with anthropology and highlighting the mistakes of mainstream economics and the differences between anthropology and mainstream economics. Various synergies have been found, for example, between anthropology and institutional economics, along with predictions for the continuance of the bleak relationship between anthropology and mainstream economics.[10]

The second is the optimistic and tolerant direction about the future of the relationship between economics and anthropology. Given the troubled history of this relationship, it may seem ironic and even contradictory to maintain an optimistic attitude toward its future. But if we can see the previous areas of difficulty as sources of challenge and change rather than frustration and fortification, the future need not seem so bleak. The optimism lies in the fluidity of disciplinary boundaries, the mobility of academics across these boundaries, and the rewards of cross-fertilization in research and teaching.

The optimistic position clearly indicates to those who have found themselves in the wrong discipline to take advantage of this unique opportunity. The task of cross-fertilization may fall initially, if not primarily or exclusively, on those in the wrong discipline, who may need to improve their capabilities before being engaged in full-fledged cross-fertilization. If they have somehow escaped the forces of specialization outlined by Babbage in their choices of disciplinary affiliation, they can ignore formal affiliations and disciplinary boundaries and take advantage of the benefits outlined by Smith by building on their comparative advantage in capabilities. Someone interested in studying conversations solving the problem of knowledge, but who somehow became an "economist," may thus learn anthropology and field methods to be able to better study these conversations and to cross-fertilize between the two disciplines. This capability may equip such a person with skills ideally suited for the analysis of preferences, entrepreneurship, technology or other "black-box" phenomena of conversations typically ignored or inadequately explored in economics. Similarly, an "anthropologist" who wishes to study the problem of diverse individual interests may learn the appropriate economic theory and the methods of modeling and quantitative analysis to be ideally suited to studying how marriage, religion, kinship groups, and other social and cultural institutions align incentives. Although this would clearly be a costly procedure because of the time required to make the overhead investment in acquiring the knowledge and skills, the benefits of the investment would also be expected to be high in personal reputation and social knowledge, as the outcomes of previous episodes of cross-fertilization in other disciplines would indicate.

Given that the conversations between the two disciplines have not thrived under the status quo, a different type of action may be required to recharge the relationship with new energy and to set it on a new course. One way to reduce the cost of the investment required for cross-fertilization is for economists and anthropologists to collaborate across disciplines. Interdisciplinary collaboration would also facilitate better appreciation of the different genres of conversation by colleagues and better marketing and placement of joint research products. Another possibility is to go beyond the old-fashioned ideas that have failed to provide sufficient fuel to interdisciplinary conversations and look for new developments in one of the disciplines for inspiration. An example of a recent development in economics instrumental in generating interdisciplinary conversation is the New Institutional Economics. By replacing some of the narrow and controversial assumptions of economics (such as rationality) with broader ones (bounded rationality) admitting a wider range of observed reasonable behavior, this approach has developed a strong track record for extending the applicability of economics to other disciplines and generating interdisciplinary research and cross-fertilizations. More tolerant and curious of the multiplicity of human motivations, complexity of behavioral patterns, and path-dependence of history, New Institutionalism has rapidly reached beyond economics and found acceptance in sociology, political science, and business disciplines, recently being promoted for application in anthropology

(Ensminger 2002), although both Milberg and Gudeman in this volume express reservations. There may, of course, be other developments currently taking place in economics or anthropology that might better stimulate the stalled conversations. What is clear is that economists and anthropologists need to cross disciplinary boundaries to find the right set of stimulants.

Notes

1. For a brief history of academic specialization in the United States, see Dogan and Pahre (1990: 53–62).
2. See, for example, Bardhan (1989), Booyens (1998), Buckley and Chapman (1996), Casson (1996), Cooter (2000), Dowling (1982), Epstein (1975), Grossbard (1978), Lipton (1992), Lodewijks (1994), Mayhew (1999), and Posner (1980).
3. For brief accounts of the debate, see Lodewijks (1994), Mayhew (1999), Posner (1980), and Wilk (1996).
4. For example, see Billig (2000), Ensminger (2002), Gudeman (2001), Lavoie (1990), and Mirowski (1994).
5. On the nature and benefits of division of labor within "philosophy," Smith (1976: book I, chap. I) writes:
    In the progress of society, philosophy or speculation becomes, like every other employment, the principal or sole trade and occupation of a particular class of citizens. Like every other employment, too, it is subdivided into a great number of different branches, each of which affords occupation to a peculiar tribe or class of philosophers; and this subdivision of employment in philosophy, as well as in every other business, improves dexterity, and saves time. Each individual becomes more expert in his own peculiar branch, more work is done upon the whole, and the quantity of science is considerably increased by it.
6. For examples of variations on this approach, see also Brown (1994), Cosgel (1992; 1994; 1997), Cosgel and Klamer (1990), Farrell (1995), Klamer (1983), Shiller (1995), and Zeitlyn (2004). See also Rosaldo (1987) for a rhetorical analysis of the anthropological literature.
7. For theories of genre and narrative form, see Fishelov (1993), Keen (2003), and Martin (1986).
8. For the capabilities of economists and anthropologists and the process of self-selection and professional training, see Chun (2000), Geertz (2002), Goldschmidt (2000), Goodenough (2002), Keane (2003), Klamer (1983), Leach (1982), Klamer and Colander (1989), and Swedberg (1990).
9. A related area of interest in economics originating from the problem of knowledge and similarly neglected in most economics textbooks and mainstream approaches is the theory of coordination games or the problem of coordination in the theory of organization. For the relevant literature, see Milgrom and Roberts (1992), O'Driscoll (1977), and Schotter (1981). See also Chwe (2001) for applications in other disciplines and Langlois and Foss (1999) on the theory of the firm.
10. For example, see Billig (2000), Greenfield (1982), Lodewijks (1994: 84–86), Mayhew (1994), and Mirowski (2000).

CHAPTER 7

"The Craving for Intelligibility"
Speech and Silence on the Economy under Structural Adjustment and Military Rule in Nigeria

Jane I. Guyer with LaRay Denzer

■ ■ ■ ■ ■ ■

Rhetoric and Intelligibility

This chapter focuses on what Friedrich von Hayek considered the grave dangers of "the craving for intelligibility" (1944: 204) with respect to economic life. Hayek published *The Road to Serfdom* toward the end of a war that he saw as having profoundly entrenched centralized economic management in the state and in the hands of ideologues, with disastrous results for Germany and for the world. He argued not only against National Socialism, but also against the Keynesian formula for selective state intervention, and was in favor of a return to markets as soon as the war was over. To "submit" to markets was by far the lesser of evils, as "the refusal to submit to anything we cannot understand must lead to the destruction of our civilization" (Hayek 1944: 204).

In the new era of the post–1989 world, voices in the public sphere, both in the West and in countries such as Nigeria, are again searching for one or another set of terms that can offer intellectual and political traction on the state-people-economy relationship. How do economic and political leaders talk to their people? For what aspects of collective life are they technically and morally responsible? Are the people subjects or constituents with respect to those aspects? In what form can they or should they answer back? The theories and methods that are invoked at such times are compelling creations of their moment in history. And yet they also work out over time. It is to this working out of one economic theory and rhetoric over time, in one political-economic context, namely, Nigeria under structural adjustment and military rule (1983–99), which I address in this chapter. I draw on the remarkable coverage provided by the Nigerian newspapers over this period. Their journalists consistently reported on pronouncements and responses, mounted their own investigations, and raised their own critiques in spite of intermittent repression. What emerges is an example of the ongoing battle involved in bringing together a specific economic situation and a particular economic theory, in a public rhetoric in which everything is at issue and the stakes are high: the type of intelligibility that is communicable, its relationship to unfolding events in the world, and the ways in which it can be sustained over time.

Hayek is very interestingly and complexly fundamental to posing these questions for modern Nigeria, and, eventually, far beyond. Structural adjustment policies that downsized the state and opened African economies to more deregulated market forces were a descendant of his theoretical orientation. At the time that structural adjustment policies were implemented in Africa, there were observers from a different theoretical persuasion who saw potential good in this implementation. The African state was beginning to look like a class affair of revolving military and civilian elites, who used its infrastructures to establish their own power and consolidate capital accumulation in the midst of economic crisis for the masses. Basil Davidson, for example, supporter of the populist liberation movements throughout the mid twentieth century, referred to the "curse of the nation state" in one of his last books as *The Black Man's Burden* (1992). Much earlier, Frantz Fanon (1963) had seen the relationship between the African bourgeoisie and the state as ominous for the political future. Hayek had also seen the demands of the German middle class for government favor in the face of economic troubles—in his case, the hyperinflation of the Weimar period—as the ground upon which the rhetoric and practice of totalitarianism took hold.

From a pragmatic standpoint as well as a theoretical one, Nigeria might be seen as actually quite well situated for greater market freedom and the formation of the kind of spontaneous order, which Hayek advocated, if one looks with a positive theoretical eye on its vast "informal sector," already recalcitrant to regulation and taxation. Most people probably did not "crave" articulated centralized solutions and might well have been positively disposed to a rhetoric that acknowledged a gap of ignorance between the power of human knowledge and the power of the world. Market uncertainty is a well-established expectation. It is much less clear, however, that either the informal sector or the formal sector in Nigeria would accept what Hayek repeatedly refers to as "submission," since local philosophies of life entail active intervention through divination and sacrifice (see Guyer 2005). Hayek writes:

> It is men's submission to the impersonal forces of the market that in the past made possible the growth of a civilization … it is by thus submitting that we are every day helping to build something that is greater than any one of us can fully comprehend … it is infinitely more difficult rationally to comprehend the necessity of submitting to forces whose operation we cannot follow in detail than to do so out of the humble awe which religion, or even the respect for the doctrines of economics, did inspire. (1944: 204–205)

How such submission might work in public life in various political contexts would depend fundamentally on what people can learn to accept as ignorance, and what dispensation they can acquire for "awe" and "respect" for the domains of power that rightly belong beyond full human comprehension. In the event, as I discuss in detail later, Nigerian commentators sought out "fuller comprehension" on some issues that turned out to be not ignorance, but intractable incoherence (or deliberate maskings) in the application of the theory to particular conditions. Their struggles thereby illuminate fault lines in theory and practice that may be more widely relevant in a world where this same theory meet experiences of life.

Most current attention in economic debate, both for and against present policies, has been devoted to the concepts that are used to "connect the dots," which theorists *can* claim to have confidence in—freedom, growth, reduced taxation—and *do* therefore produce an intelligible policy and informed rhetoric to convey to citizens. These concepts have been deployed to support all kinds of novel adventures in the service of visions of the future. But what about the domains of *ignorance* implied in monetarist theory and neoliberal ideology? It is to Hayek's enormous credit, I think, that he does not side-step this question. Rather, he expresses steely resolve: "It is the price of democracy that the possibilities of conscious control are restricted to the fields where true agreement exists and that in some fields things must be left to chance" (Hayek 1944: 69). His argument is full of warnings about "illusions," "deceiving ourselves," and the necessity to "re-learn frankly to face the fact that freedom can only be had at a price and that as individuals we must be prepared to make severe material sacrifices to preserve our liberty" (Hayek 1944: 133). Because his book of 1944, *The Road to Serfdom,* re-inspires the phase of liberal thought that we now experience (at least in the United States), its message offers a beacon of clarity for triangulating the conditions and the rhetoric in which we are all immersed.

The line I explore here, through the lens of Nigeria, is the particular political and rhetorical *burden* of a theoretical position that embraces fluctuation as a necessary condition of the market system, but that is bereft of concepts to convey this in positive terms at the time that fluctuation happens. According to Hayek and followers, market fluctuations are not controllable or even always understandable, but they are an essential and positive component of the long-term process of growth. In the classical tradition of rhetoric, the rhetorical utterance extended and transcended truth by taming the zone of ignorance into an encompassing logic. It served the purpose of persuasion in three major arenas—the legal court, the legislative assembly, and the public forum—under conditions where incontrovertible truth could not be ascertained. As Bizzell and Hertzberg write, "In civil disputes, persuasion established claims where no clear truth was available" (1990: 2).[1] Partial truths still provided basic landmarks in the argument. The skill of rhetorical performance extended the partial truths to create a coherent and motivating interpretation of a whole that brought the listeners from their various positions of skepticism to a point of convergence. The idea of "persuasion" implies a convergence of interpretation and thereby of motivation in favor of concerted action. Hayek's theory, however, would imply a converse rhetorical move: a felt collective condition is addressed by actually enlarging rather than contracting the area of shared ignorance and by promoting the felicity of people submitting to conditions in—presumably—their own private and varied ways.

One needs to ask where exactly the burdens of a rhetorical rendition of this theory are likely to fall, because a call to "submission" to "conditions" is not a politically simple one to make. On the one hand, the near-sighted view of *imminent* minute movements in the markets can advocate that actors respond; on the other, there is a far-sighted view of *future* growth.[2] But the practical politics of *large* shifts over the *short* run are hard to grasp. Being called on to address painful fluctuation and outright crises at the time of their occurrence presents the need to contend explicitly with contextual pressures, whereas the context falls outside of the theory. Explaining crisis under Hayek's theory, either as an elected official or a disciplinary expert, must pose both scientific and political challenges. How can the concepts be made to match the occurrences? How can fluctuation and disorder/re-ordering be alluded to, as they happen, in terms of a theory that extols them as "creative in the long run"?

The lack of contextual concepts and mid-range temporal frames leaves a vacuum of meanings available for rhetorical mobilization. At the high level, there are large abstractions such as freedom, chance, sacrifice, democracy, or (unspecified) forces one cannot comprehend, "the price" one has to pay, the "humble awe" one has to mobilize, and, of course, "the market." At the very specific level, there are financial instruments and markets developed in the finest of numerical and conceptual detail. Left out of the terms of this rhetoric are precisely those domains of life and temporal horizons that are most awkward for which to make a consistently positive claim, namely, the multiplicity of the entailments within any real economy (as understood by its participants) and the near-future temporal frame that "fluctuation" somehow invokes. This, of course, is where people live. When all boats are rising, it might be persuasive to focus on the "now" of demand and on the "distant horizon" of our common fate. But finding a consistent monetarist rhetoric in bad or confusing times is surely much more difficult, especially when the "sacrifices" asked of citizens seem "both unbearable and unnecessary," as Hayek (1944: 19) noted that they certainly would be.

In his day, Hayek was critiqued on exactly this point, and not from the classic left or the Keynesians. Mirowski paraphrases Michael Polanyi's review of Hayek as "apparently not willing to describe the interplay between the inarticulate and rationalizable aspects of practice, be they in the marketplace or elsewhere, and therefore had effectively reneged on the promise to theorize the role of knowledge in economics" (Mirowski 2004: 79). Polanyi worried that "(I)n an era obsessed by the fear of mass unemployment (he turned) an indifferent eye on this problem" (Mirowski 2004: 80, quoting Polanyi 1949: 267). There are two problems of intelligibility that Polanyi is pointing to: "the role of knowledge" in the scientific sense (what does the scientific expertise tell us about the situation?) and the role of communication (what can and should be communicated to a population "obsessed by fear"?). Bad times pose real and unavoidable dilemmas for both scientific knowledge and political rhetoric about the economy. The very idea of "the economy" is based implicitly on an assumption of "nation," that is, a collectivity (see Mitchell 2003). So, what options open up, face-to-face with a national population: a rhetoric that preserves theoretical consistency about the ultimate direction of "growth" at the price of public anger and suffering? Or one that addresses the near future in its own terms, at the cost of abandoning in theory or in practice the principle of singularity and direction? Perhaps there are historically specific resolutions, rather than a principled one: holding off the great wave of the public's "craving for intelligibility" by stalling for time, or encouraging a one-time historic bail-out into the "freedom to choose" (Friedman and Friedman 1980), which eventually entails removing "the economy" from the public forum of debate altogether.

The following alternatives do offer solutions that may be principled as well as pragmatic, although they are certainly fragile. Monetarist public speech does sometimes follow the persuasion and coherence of classic rhetorical form: in this case, however, not by completing present evidence by projecting its logic forward, but by creating a complete model of the future and projecting its terms back onto the present. This "virtualism" draws attention away from present confusion, as experienced, and imposes on it the categories of the coherent model (Carrier and Miller 1998; Baxstrom, Khan, Singh, and Poole 2005). Persuasion then amounts to acceptance of the relevance of futuristic categories for recognizing the present. This argument is a brilliant one, but not necessarily easy to sustain in the kind of hard or confusing times that the theory itself predicts, because the gap between the categories of the future and those of people's experience in the present may diverge beyond any suspension of disbelief. Radical uncertainty in the world and radical skepticism amongst the citizenry can recast this rhetorical tactic as "spin" or just plain lies.

The strategy of virtualism is quite different from its alternative: facing the fluctuations of the present head on, including the extreme detail of the specialist's calculations, and so directly advocating the public's recognition of the limits of knowledge and the importance of submission, as Hayek's position would imply. People must just relearn how to leave things to "chance." The political downsides of this position include offering so much information about the situation of crisis or major fluctuation that an alternative interpretation can emerge. Those who cannot get even into the foothills of an understanding of the financial system are likely to revolt against it, and those who do understand it realize that experts are buffering their own situations, and perhaps even making profits from arbitrage of the spatial and temporal disjunctures entailed in instability. People will demand an explanation, and their own worries and suspicions can come to dominate the public debate. Experts then back off into an attitude of "humble awe" (Hayek). Leonhardt (2003) exemplifies a version of this last strategy of emphasizing that "it's beyond us," but with a dash of the allegorical virtualism of the first, seemingly to head off the public from latching onto real accounting (and accountability) with respect to what he calls the "dark side." He argues that "today's economy has escaped definition" and has "flummoxed political strategists" (Leonhardt 2003: 1); it can best be denoted as a "Goldilocks Economy," with a "dark side" represented by people's concerns not about "the here and now," but about "the big costs down the road" (Leonhardt 2003: 6). Commentators admit confusion: "Federal Reserve officials, who meet this week, are beginning to suspect that the perplexing decline in long-term interest rates is more than a temporary aberration" (Andrews 2005: C1).

A final possibility for rhetoric leads in a similar direction, but to a more radical end. It involves acting strictly on the letter of the theory that government does not manage "the economy," only the money supply, therefore saying as little as possible about anything economic other than money.

Each approach is more-or-less feasible, so how are political rhetorics managed in an actual event of crisis or wide and incoherent fluctuation? In the United States we have not—or had not when this paper was first written—yet confronted extreme friction between monetarist theory and popular experience. But outside the West, there have been places living under monetarist policy whose populations have already seen the kind of unbearable conditions that Hayek alluded to as dangers. Writing of fluctuations in the world currency market, Eichengreen warns that such places and historical periods should be expected: "Large economies, relatively closed, can pursue domestic objectives without suffering intolerable pain from currency swings. For the majority of smaller, open economies ... the costs of floating are difficult to bear ... Volatile exchange rate swings impose almost unbearable costs..." (1996: 196). Several economies experienced major fluctuations in their currency's exchange rates and in consequent conditions of life during the 1980s and 1990s. Africa was amongst the first, under what was intended to be a controlled process of "structural adjustment" of the place of government in economic life. Nigeria started down this path in 1985. With an ancient commercial culture, a high level of expertise and vibrant economic organizations, Nigerians turned very rapidly to informal and extra-formal modes of operation as world markets loosened up. By 1992, a shift had taken place, from expectations placed on government to recognition of the sheer necessity of keeping goods, provisions, employment, and finance moving in spite of economic policy (see Guyer, Denzer, and Agbaje 2002). Yet at the same time, the sheer power and wealth of the federal government constituted both a threat and a resource that would never be ignored. People still made claims and criticisms. Over the twenty years since the particular combination of instability and central power came into focus, the search for a rhetoric of intelligibility has had time to go through several iterations, playing across a repertoire of possibilities as conditions of life and of skepticism shifted. It is to that sequence of iterations that we turn.

Using an archive of newspaper articles collected by LaRay Denzer, myself, and students at the University of Ibadan over the 1990s, and with some notable recuperations for the 1980s, we are able to trace out some of the unfolding rhetoric and response as first a populist military president (Babangida, 1985–93) and then a repressive one (Abacha 1993–98) tried to represent some version of a neoliberal national budget to the Nigerian people. Throughout this period, the government continued to present an annual budget accompanied by a speech of explanation, which was followed by various published commentaries and critiques. Ultimately, the exercise degenerated into enormous confusion. The most common reasons given from the outside are the transparent "greed" of those in power, and the pervasive "cynicism" of the powerless. But the debate in the press was not a brawl of symbolic slings and arrows; it was reasoned seriously in economic terms. By tracing out this extreme case, in its own terms, one can point out the extraordinary delicacy of *any* rhetorical claim to uncertainty by those who are closest to the power of both science and the state under monetarist policy, as Hayek predicted. This volume devoted to economic rhetoric allows us to pause longer over the public space and public speech of economic indeterminacy than a dismissive explanation in terms of a third world dictatorship would allow.

Nigeria

The Nigerian economy under structural adjustment and military rule (1984–98) was increasingly presented as unintelligible. Until recently, I—like others—assumed that this was a function of the *military mismanagement,* which all observers agreed upon. Under autocratic rule, there may be no need for government to bother with persuasive rhetoric from benchmarks in truth, because the public cannot answer back. In any case, the official record—on the trade balance, revenue by source, employment trends, and so on—can be either neglected altogether or kept secret, so that there are no "objective" landmarks on which to center the debate. Following Mbembe (2001) and others, Andrew Apter (2005) has made a strong and fascinating argument about the performative—rather than persuasive—nature of Nigerian military rhetoric. I am persuaded by his demonstrations, but no longer to the exclusion of other levels and dynamics of engagement between government and people. The Nigerian government did present the standard economic indicators in the annual budget speech; ministers did comment on economic events and policy directions; and economic journalists did analyze the logic of their statements. My change of mind, to foreground what presents itself as argument over what presents itself as a performance, came from hearing some of the same terminology surfacing in our own public life a decade after it surfaced in Nigeria. The replication seems uncanny. On the side of advocacy, people then and now, there and here, talk about the *very long-run future* and *growth* as benchmark for policy success, the centrality of *control of inflation through the national money supply (interest rates, control of excess liquidity, savings)*, and the importance of staying *steadfast, staying the course,* and the wisdom of *individual* leadership. On the critical side, they talk about a "faith-based economy," an economic culture of greed, the resurgence of class warfare, the leaders as "magicians," and the inscrutability of their official pronouncements. In the very last week before the conference for which this paper was written, the New York Times ran an op-ed by Paul Krugman (2005) devoted to the "spin" on the US deficit, which shadows almost exactly the debate I discuss below. It would not be difficult to take the cartoon of the 1991 Nigerian budget, showing popular consternation and confusion, and redraw it about the U.S. budgets—with their deficits, belt-tightening, and massive off-budget expenditures—over ten years later. It is called: The People's View, and includes speech bubbles saying: "Who can help me now?" "I'm not sure I understand," "Now kerosene done cost," and "We need to pray more."[3] I am not taking cheap shots by drawing this parallel, but rather am opening up a serious question. How do monetarists in fact create an intelligible argument about the near future in bad circumstances?

I do not reject the self-serving, performative, and culturally specific interpretation of Nigerian military rhetoric about state and economy, but there was always a recognizable seriously engaged "rational" economic debate in Nigeria as well. The public rhetorical engagement about a monetarist and structural adjustment policy had many years to play out, over what I will describe as three distinct phases: a collective public debate about the meaning of economic terms under rapidly changing conditions (1984–87); an effort to wrench the nation and the market into a single identity (1987–93); and a retreat into cacophony and silence (1994–98). It is doubtless that it could have worked differently, but the three phases I present here have sequential plausibility to them, as both government and people ran the gamut of available rhetorical strategies about the plausibility of long-term growth one after the other, starting with a struggle over definitional categories for relating actual life in the present and near future to the model, followed by abandonment of claims to intelligibility, and subsequently, an interplay of cacophony and silence.

"Deficits," "Contingencies," and "Subsidies": The debate of 1984–87

The realistic difficulty for Nigerian economic policy in the structural adjustment era was that every variable was moving at once. All modern governments are aware of prices, not in "the market" in a generic sense, but in the specific market that keeps their particular national economies moving and populations compliant: the price of capital in the financial markets in some, the price of staple foods in the commodity markets in others, or the producer or consumer price of oil and gas in the energy markets in still others. This means using policy instruments to benchmark that price to something fairly stable or amenable to stabilization in people's real lives. For Nigeria, the key market is the world market in crude oil, denominated in dollars, which is markedly unpredictable. The annual budget projection is necessarily based on informed speculation about the dollar price of oil on world markets. If the oil price and the exchange rate for the dollar are changing at once, even contingency calculations are no longer workable.

In the early phase of structural adjustment in Nigeria, the value of the naira was falling against the dollar as the world price of oil also plummeted to $10 in the late 1980s. By the end of the 1980s, there was also inflation, in retrospect from large amounts of off-budget government spending. When the budget for 1987 was announced, there was a huge debate over whether it was, or was not, a deficit budget, and how one would know. The Federal Director of the Budget, Omowale Kuye, explained that "revenue projections have an element of contingency ... built in to the tune of N4.513 billion[4] ... not a set-aside," but an "uncertainty," presumably and justifiably, about the price of oil and other home produced exports on world commodity and exchange markets that were changing rapidly and not necessarily in any coordinated or predictable fashion. Only this "contingency" of N4.5 billion on the revenue side made the budget appear balanced. This contingency was not an addition to the N17.9 billion total budgeted revenue, but had been included as part of that amount. So journalists argued that the terminology was being used to conceal what was in fact a deficit budget (Omokhodion with Iduwe 1987). There was no way of knowing whether such an amount was realistic or fantastic, and apparently there was no agreement about how it should be conceptualized. The same question—of whether a particular budget was balanced or not when it was presented—continued year after year. In 1988, the plan to reinflate the economy involved promising a deficit that would be "modest and reasonable" (*The Nigerian Economist* 1988: 13). Also a deficit budget year was 1989. By 1991, however, the budget was announced as a "surplus budget" (*West Africa* 1991: 12), and at least one newspaper commentator wrote that if one made exact comparisons of the categories included, it in fact represented a 70 percent *increase* in spending in comparison with 1990 (Imirhe 1991). By 1991, the critics were also writing of a consistent "over-estimation of the price of a barrel of oil" (Adeleye with Olatunde 1991: 52) in the projections on which the budget was calculated, and by 1993, they were writing of a "Budget of Deceit" laced with (to quote a former military governor) "gimmicks" (*Newbreed* 1993: 11). In 1991, the Nigerian government may—or may not—have kept to its budget projections, but at the same time it also hid the entire $12 billion in windfall revenues from the First Gulf War oil price hike. The Okigbo Commission was eventually empowered to investigate after the change of government in 1992, but the report was quickly confiscated (Agbese 2005).

By 1996, there was a rising tide of outrage against government manipulation of the budget numbers to produce these elusive qualities—"balanced budget," "low inflation," and so on—as I will come to later. But in the beginning, the question of definition was a real one. How *did* one know the referent of the concept of a "deficit" or "surplus" budget when the base price of oil and the exchange rate for the naira, on which all revenue projections crucially depended, could not be known? The budget was a kind of visionary exercise rather than a planning document, although it retained the categories and format of the latter. This sort of ignorance of the market is implied in what Hayek would have us submit to: not only ignorance of the reasons for the movement of conditions and indicators, but also ignorance of the origins and referents of the concepts that classify them. In economic policy, the "craving for intelligibility" can come down to scrutinizing the most banal of concepts and reexamining the most tedious of tables to see how the concepts and the numbers actually work together. Nigerian commentators tried to do this quite persistently.

The definition that aroused by far the most intense popular engagement was the so-called "subsidy" on domestic petrol prices. In Nigeria, the oil economy was launched under the rubric of national integration, and therefore was under a certain sense of national ownership, after the Civil War (1966–70). By the early 1980s, it was already clear that the revenues had been funding massive collective symbolic projects such as The Second World Black and African Festival of Arts and Culture (FESTAC '77; see Apter 2005), the new capital at Abuja (see Elleh 2002), the steel industry at Ajaokuta (see Forrest 1995), the proliferation of states and therefore capitals and administrations, and the spectacular enrichment of the military and upper classes. Behind this front was another revolution: the vast motorization of the artisanal economy and ordinary social life of the Nigerian people (Guyer 1997). Vehicle imports surged; mechanized farming expanded; dealerships and repair shops proliferated; expanding cities were fed from further and further away; national trade networks were extended and intensified; and people traveled more and more often to a rising tide of family celebrations, local meetings, chieftaincy installations, courses of study and apprenticeships, and so on and so on. In some quite inexplicit way, an affordable and predictable price of "our" petrol became a populist assumption of the national compact.

The idea that this constituted a "subsidy," and that a government subsidy was a negative thing, was a profound surprise when it was launched under the pressures of structural adjustment starting in 1982. The debate of that era culminated in a standoff about what "subsidy" even meant in the context of an oil-producing economy. A subsequent politicization of the whole issue has recurred with ferocity up to the present. The government was unable or unwilling to make a plausible argument for either knowledge or ignorance, and the population became increasingly unwilling to accept any of their explanations. I recount the first confrontation (1985) and briefly some of the rhetorics of the latest (2003) confrontation, in order to set the stage for subsequently grappling with the claim of ignorance in the face of "markets."

The most fascinating aspect of the interchange about petrol prices at the pump is the attempt to morally and practically benchmark them to various *different* other prices. Monetarism depends on abstractions of abstractions with respect to the management of the money supply and its ramifying effects throughout "the economy." But abstraction seems to be the first quality to fall under attack when prices fail to make sense to people. A price is not just a relationship between supply and demand in people's eyes, but is also a relationship between one good and another, a person's income and her standard of living, a seller and a buyer, and the state and the people (in the case of certain goods). In fact, one might even define the "craving for intelligibility" as the refusal to accept higher levels of market abstraction in favor of a concept that can be morally, politically, and intellectually pegged to something more or less tangible. And the experts can be drawn into this logic, whether or not it makes sense to them theoretically. For example, in the face of the economic crisis of 1981, the IMF compared the price of Nigerian petrol (pejoratively) to Coca-Cola, implying some just or sensible distance between the two prices. Domestic petrol prices were considered far too low relative to Coke; hence the concept of subsidy, since petrol prices were controlled. But there is no reason internal to market theory that would suggest a cultural or moral ratio between one price and another.

In the 1985 debate, the subsidy concept for oil prices was finally accepted by the Nigerian government, and announced to be at the exceptionally high level of 80 percent. In line with the reigning theory, the subsidy was removed on 1 January 1986 and petrol prices were fixed at a higher, but still controlled, price. Another simultaneous component of structural adjustment, however, was devaluation of the over-valued naira. In 1986, the naira value for trade was allowed to fall against the hard currencies of the world. From an international standpoint, the subsidy immediately "reappeared" as soon as the naira fell against the dollar, due to the fixed nominal price for petrol at the pump that was set in naira. It was even recalculated—this time at 60 percent. At this point, an economist (Ashwe 1987) redefined it as an "implicit subsidy," and therefore not a result of deliberate policy; however, that linking of "implicit" and "subsidy" would have to be explained to a population that had only just accepted the notion of subsidy at all. Ashwe tried to redefine the whole situation: "Starting from first principles … when the 'shouting match' started," going through a series of calculations of the price of crude, the cost of refining, the exchange rate, and the "cost at the pumps" to arrive at the conclusion (see below) that getting rid of the "subsidy" is highly "dubious," and in any case oil is a Nigerian endowment whose price is set by a world cartel (Ashwe 1987: 51). "Fuel Subsidy: To Be or Not To Be. Government perches on the horns of a dilemma as it weighs the economics and politics of petroleum subsidy" was a headline appearing at the time (*Newswatch* 1987). Strong voices questioned the subsidy concept altogether. They claimed that since Nigeria was a producing country, the price to consumers should reflect the costs of production and refining, and not the world price at all. Political scientist Claude Ake wrote that the petrol used in Nigeria was never on the international market, "so you cannot translate into dollars. The whole talk about oil subsidy is rubbish" (Akinrinade 1988: 19).

The battle over the standard for the "right price" was now fully engaged. Then, the world price of oil plummeted, and some commentators began to extend the subsidy logic to argue that the Nigerian consumer was actually being *taxed* by having to pay the fixed nominal price that was now *higher* than the world market price. By 1991, when the idea of withdrawing the subsidy came up again, commentators started arguing that, "the tape has been rewound. And the drama is starting all over again" (Adedoyin and Dike 1991). This condition of going in circles was immortalized by musician Fela Anikulapo-Kuti under the song title of Perambulation (see Olaniyan 2005). But some processes did progress. Since the franc Communaute Financiere Africaine (CFA) was stable and Nigeria is surrounded by franc zone countries, as world oil prices rose again, there also began a steadily expanding network of petrol smuggling. The conditions on the *regional* market now added themselves to those on the domestic and international markets, vying as the benchmark for judging whether indeed the Nigerian consumer was being subsidized or taxed, and by how much. The informal sector moneychangers quickly developed an acute sense of transborder profits under all kinds of fluctuating conditions, so there were surges and deficiencies in the domestic Nigerian supply. Eventually, those wealthy enough to run arbitrage during supply fluctuations added their own more or less deliberate interference, which added yet another criterion to estimate how much speculative profit was being made from the domestic market.[5] The whole domain became radically incoherent while also being radically essential to the entire flourishing informal economy and social life. The greater the withdrawal of the military government into laissez faire rhetoric (and self-serving arbitrage on the side), the greater the public's need to count on affordable petrol prices to run their do-it-yourself economy without the government at all.

The Nigerian press sources—particularly the tables in *Newswatch* of 30 November 1987, and repeated allusions of the kind quoted in Ashwe above—make arguments for what one can identify as six different ways of grounding the domestic petroleum price in some defensible matrix of intelligibility:

1. By comparison with domestic consumer prices in other oil producing countries: by this standard, Nigeria's price was low, but in part because tax regimes differ. Structural adjustment philosophy was certainly not advocating increasing taxes, so they did not dwell on this difference. But this difference was large. For example, Britain's price could be indexed at 277, while Nigeria's was 40, where the difference is partly due to much higher taxes in Britain.
2. By comparison with Nigerian incomes: in Nigeria the ratio of petrol prices to incomes is very high: 1:20, whereas in Britain it was 1:30 and in Kuwait 1: 14,480.

3. By comparison with regional consumer prices: the price was much higher in the franc zone neighboring countries, with only Cameroon being an oil producer at the time.
4. By comparison with the costs of production and therefore realistic margins: this was always a nightmare to calculate, since every aspect of production and distribution is managed by contractual terms and government guidelines.
5. In relation to government revenue needs: gaps in the budget could be used as a justification for claiming a subsidy and demanding its abolition. The press caught on to this argument early in the process, since it confirmed their skepticism about the budget.
6. As a simple national right: in an interview in 1992, the president himself vacillated. While complaining about the generally low level of patriotic respect for policy and law, Babangida also noted the Nigerian conviction of a collective moral claim over "their" oil. "(T)he Nigerian believes that this is his country, God has given him this (petroleum product) and therefore because God gave him, he must use it" (*Nigerian Hand Book Review* 1992). One government strategy of dealing with the whole moral rhetorical issue in the public sphere was eventually (1996) to define a special fund for development financed by oil revenues—the Petroleum Trust Fund (PTF)—to focus attention on at least some sort of gain that a suffering population was getting from "their" national oil. This, of course, was off-budget, but it intervened in the market for everything.

We all remember the rhetoric of "getting the prices right" during structural adjustment, but the Nigerian domestic oil subsidy debate (which continues to the present) shows several things about judgments of "rightness": a) intelligibility *is* demanded by the public, especially of those goods that manifestly and always pass through government hands and that affect the lives of everyone; there is no begging off to "chance" in this crucial case; b) the options for plausible arguments on the basis of "the market" are, in fact, multiple; there is quite obviously no singular coherent market, and no one standard by which to judge prices, so by concentrating on one argument an analyst reveals quite clearly the priorities he or she accords to key variables and thereby his or her political commitments; c) it is not possible, then, to prioritize one or other of the plausible arguments (of which we have six here) on supposedly "rational" grounds without revealing an obvious favor for a particular constituency; and d) by the time that massive arbitrage has set in and has been institutionalized, it is almost impossible to make any principled theoretical argument at all because—even under military rule and intermittent intimidation of the press—the basic facts of shortage, gain, smuggling, and so on are completely public knowledge.

Beyond Specific Concepts: The Nation and the Market

In the period between 1987 and the annulment of the elections in 1993, there was a great deal of discussion oriented toward the relationship of market to nation. Debate about terminological issues continued and expanded as various policy instruments were "manipulated." This word is not a judgment; it is Babangida's own: "So what we did was to instruct the Central Bank to keep on manipulating (the naira) without saying so" (*Nigerian Hand Book Review* 1992). Headlines asked not only "what is a subsidy?," but "what is the Nigerian debt?" (*Newswatch* 1988: 36), "what is profit?" in a "deregulated economy" (*Financial Guardian* 1992: 6), and "is our economy planned?" (*The Nigerian Economist* 1987: 10). Public anger boiled over in 1988 and 1989. In 1992, the government itself suggested that the economy was unruly, and in 1993 the World Bank Vice President for Africa, Edward Jaycox, was reported in the Nigerian press to have admitted that structural adjustment in Africa had been "a systematic destructive force" (*The African Guardian* 1993: 28).

I cover the public rhetoric of this period only briefly. What became clear was that the idea of a *national* economy was coming apart under the conditions of the structural adjustment program (SAP) era. Again, this was not necessarily, and from the outset, due to venality on the part of the governing elites. The conditions of monetarist theory departed radically from realities in places like Nigeria. Cagan writes, "Monetarist theory of aggregate expenditures is based on a demand function for monetary assets that is claimed to be stable in the sense that successive residual errors are generally offsetting and do not accumulate. Given the present inconvertible-money systems, the stock of money is treated as under the control of the government" (1987: 199). These two systemic conditions for monetarism were nowhere close to being fulfilled, so the burden of the idea of a system fell rather on the shifting sands of a rhetoric of economic nationalism. In 1989, in the wake of nationwide riots, the president made a major speech that was reported under the title, "SAP is not evil," to explain structural adjustment as a "well-thought-out program that aims at increased production in every sector of the economy in order to create more jobs, more goods and less foreign debts." Its enemies are detractors "bent on destroying the credibility of the military institution," whereas "we have a duty to the nation ... we shall do our duty to our country" (*Newswatch* 1989: 20). By 1992, he was reiterating the "unpatriotic" criticism, but to a much broader array of participants and in a much more resigned fashion: "The Nigerian is a very intriguing person ... there are at least 100 million opinions on any subject in Nigeria ... as long as you run a government in a society that is not docile, just like our own Nigerian society, it is not easy to take decisions ... It is a very difficult situation but it makes the Nigerian society tick. I like it" (*Nigerian Hand Book Review* 1992: 119, 120). A certain rhetoric of national character was setting in, that now embraced radical multiplicity and radical indeterminacy, with no clear theoretical framework in view at all, just a vacuous prediction that "the naira will rise again," largely because the Nigerian people are who they are.

Cacophony and Silence

By the mid 1990s, allusions to nationalism or national character had all but disappeared. Sani Abacha reinstated the neoliberal rhetoric about a national economy and a distant horizon of growth when he came to power in late 1993. Abacha's first budget speech was classic for its emphasis on moral values and implicit sacrifice for the country: "The Federal government ... reiterated that the success of the 1994 budget was contingent upon the commitment of all Nigerians to the ideals of patriotism and high moral standards" (Edemodu 1996: 18). In keeping with the economic rhetoric of the time, the budget was to be balanced and the Central Bank was mobilized to control inflation. In 1995, the Budget was dubbed "The Budget of Renewal," requiring "changes of direction, discipline, and the will to survive ... patience, hard work and perseverance. Nigerians must not expect miracles overnight in trying to revamp the economy." The goals were set in classic neoliberal terms: reduction of inflation, expansion of the economy's productive base and the level of capacity in the manufacturing sector, the creation of jobs, narrowing of the gap between the official and the parallel exchange rates, and reduction of the fiscal deficit by reducing wasteful government expenditure (*Business Times* 1994).

The claim of success came so fast as to be breathtaking. As early as March of the same year, the Finance Minister, the (eventually) notorious Anthony Ani, announced at a press briefing that these policies were working and that the government budget was now in surplus. He was also working to "articulate our debt profile, so as to determine the currencies in which they are denominated," to help "evolve a viable debt management strategy" (*Daily Times* 1995: 7, 15). In a replay of the subsidy "debate" of a decade earlier, and evoking the muddle of Babangida's early budgets, Ani was setting up conditions for the furor that eventually broke with a vengeance again in 1996 over what "deficit" meant. The conditions of life had by now utterly deteriorated. In December 1995, the newspaper, *Policy*, announced "Another Lost Year" (Uzor 1995). The 1996 budget, when it was finally released, was dubbed by the press, "the Budget of Faith" (*The Saturday Newspaper* 1996).

Episodes of complete silence now began, interspersed with contradictory claims, even from within the government itself. In 1996, the budget was not published until 16 February. On 15 February, *The Vanguard* published a cartoon showing a military man labeled "GOVERNMENT" stirring a giant pot labeled "BUDGET" while looking over his shoulder at a tiny miserable child labeled "NIGERIANS"; he is saying "Breakfast will soon be ready—don't worry, be happy." The eventual budget speech was entitled the "Budget of Consolidation," based on the idea that there are external "constraints" and that therefore "economic recovery can only be gradual and must be backed by consistency in policies … (which are) allowed to stand the test of time" (Abacha 1996). But behind the scenes, specificity and multiplicity were being fostered without any coverage of theory. Alongside the monetarist talk about certain aspects of the national budget, more and more spending was moved off-budget; reductions in government spending were applied mainly to the federal level, most notably by ceilings on public sector salaries, while at the state and local level governments expanded enormously. The two official exchange rates—one for debt service and one for all other transactions—were steadily diverging, and fuel, water, and electricity services became intermittent, at best. The new rhetorical option involved maintaining a sliver of the national budget that was intermittently indexed to "keeping a steady course towards a distant future," while, off-budget and off-the-air, the government was manipulating an expanding range of ad hoc-isms on the side.

After six weeks of anticipating the 1996 budget, when it finally appeared the commentaries in the press were a cacophony of views, depending on exactly which aspect people most focused on, since the whole idea of an economic *system* had already broken down. Within a single article in *The Vanguard*, economist Ibrahim Ayagi proclaimed that the budget had not "addressed the sufferings of the masses," while one Chief Briamoh pronounced it "a masterpiece, for the first time in the past 10 years, our budget is dedicated to the masses" (Iyeke 1996: 1, 2). Ayagi links his interpretation to control of inflation, while Briamoh is looking at whether "there might be increase in transportation fares, fuel etc." Both are completely inexplicit on how "their" indicator would work out in any general theory of systemic connections within the Nigerian national economy. Another commentary attacks the rhetorical attributes of the budget speech directly, with no pretense that the terms touch the Nigerian ground anywhere except the self-interest of the rulers. Dele Sobowale calls it "Much Ado about Nothing." Unresponsive repetition of the 1995 budget is at the heart of the critique. The persistence in policy is because "the authors have run out of ideas"; "what the public gets are fig-leaf excuses. That is, when the government cares to explain anything at all"; and "(k)een observers wonder why it took so long to produce … 'Xerox copies' of the 1994 and 1995 budgets." In fact, the government did not even *respond* to an IMF proposal for a grant to do one specific useful thing, namely, to develop cashew production. In sum, the budget is "mere tropes of words tossed on paper by people who care little about redeeming promises … any benefit to the citizenry at large is an unintended by-product of attempts aimed at maximizing the advantages of those in power." Sobowale's final reminder is that the six weeks of silence from 1 January to 16 February "speaks volumes" (Sobowale 1996: 19).

The habit of alternating cacophony and silence intensified over the year, evidenced in "Thrills and Spills of the '96 Budget" (Adewale et al. 1996); "The Budget of Faith" (*The Saturday Newspaper* 1996); "Antinomies of a Fiscal Policy" (*Post Express* 1996a); "Storm Over Budget Surplus" (*The Guardian* 1996b); "Mixed Reactions Trail Budget Performance" (*The Guardian* 1996c); "1996 Budget Still Off-Target" (*Post Express* 1996b). Analytical commentators juxtaposed the inconsistencies from within the government's own pronouncements:

> Nobody knows exactly how much was realized from oil last year. The CBN (Central Bank of Nigeria) put it at $10.35 billion. The 1996 budget says it was $7,957 billion. Nobody knows how much the country spent on oil imports last year. While Prof. Aluko (economic advisor) put it at $800 million, independent sources said it was as high as $1,924 billion. (Gahia 1996: 17)

Into the midst of this confusion, Finance Minister Anthony Ani threw out the news that the budget was now definitely in surplus, only to be contradicted by the Central Bank itself. As one commentator pointed out, one can show a budget surplus just by failing to fulfill budget provisions (*The Guardian* 1996a: 17); we "need much more information if the budget surplus announced is to make sense." Finally, "Nigerians cannot reconcile a monetary surplus with their present state of penury" (quoting Djebah in *The Guardian* 1996a).

The gap between the Finance Ministry and the CBN was never explained. By 1997, when I spent two months in field research, the fuel shortage was deep, chronic, and profoundly damaging. And it was barely explained. Commentators were all over the map trying to make sense of it. Every story had subplots and deviations. For example, the four refineries were out of order, but why? They had not been repaired; the money had not been allocated for repair; the money had been allocated, but had gone missing between one ministry and another; the fault was a particular official, to which the reply was no, it was not; members of the military government had interests in South American oil, and so they were profiting by importing their own oil to Nigeria to meet the crisis at high prices, and so on and so on. For almost the entire two months I was in Nigeria, in February and March there was no official statement on a crisis that was leaving crops rotting in rural markets, children dying at home for lack of transport to hospitals, industries folding for lack of fuel, and the patchwork efforts to make up for a collapse in electricity and water supply—through tanker delivery of water and home generators for electricity—grinding to a halt. I have never been more aware of the degree to which what we call "modern life" depends on these three commodities—oil, electricity, and clean water—of which the *sine qua non* is oil. Only after about six weeks was there any attention from the top, and then it was simply to promise a personal intervention in the delivery of a certain number of tankers of imports.

Withdrawal into Aso Rock (the fortified presidential palace) in Abuja became one of the distinctive features of Abacha's presidency. Of course, we can say that this is a result of incompetence and venality. It is. But the whole syndrome is one outcome of an inability to embrace the reality that "the national economy" cannot be represented consistently as an abstract process on the way to long-term growth. People search for intelligibility. The retreat from it by government rhetoric presents itself to the citizenry less as a humble submission before the awe inspiring might of the market than as a willful dereliction of attention to what is happening into the collective near future, which in turn inspires close public attention to the various immediate choices of the moment: their own, but also those in political and economic power. Everyone searches for points at which any number, thing, word or concept can be made to attach to any other in a meaningful way.

So what is to be said when there is no sense? It *is* a rhetorical problem. Babangida could be charming and could articulate about it. Abacha was personally incapable of populist dissembling. Nigeria became the poster-case for a rampant corruption that wove into all the fissures of arbitrage that opened up over this era. But the problem of intelligibility amid turbulence under monetarism is much larger than Nigeria, and even larger than the so-called developing world.

Note Toward a Conclusion

Amidst the turbulence, there is one rather surprising persistent fact. The terms of the rhetoric range rather narrowly across the spectrum I identified through logical derivation from monetarist theory. There is not much innovation. As Adedoyin and Dike wrote in 1987, "the tape has been rewound." The public feels as if reasoning is going in circles, reflected brilliantly in the popular song mentioned earlier: "Perambulation." In Nigeria, the rhetoric of a "national economy," of subsidy and deficit, and the arguments for meaningful reference points for anything from toothpaste prices to "sacrifice," were remarkably recurrent over this period, even though their meaningfulness fluctuated. The occasional referent echoes uncannily from one phase to the next, even in the western economic press. For example, when the petrol price changes of 2003 caused a national strike, the article about it in *The Economist* contains almost exactly the same terms as the rhetoric of twenty years previously in the same journal: "a litre of petrol cost less than a bottle of mineral water"; "fuel subsidies cost at least $1 billion a year"; "Nigerians suspect the government's motives for taking away cheap petrol and doubt that the money saved will be put to good use" (2003), and so on. *Déjà vu* all over again (in the famous words of Yogi Berra).

If we put this rhetoric into historical motion, what is one to think of its remarkable repetitive perambulation? It goes from debate about terms, to calls for nationalism (of varying kinds), to cacophony and silence, and then back again to the same old terms, that is, the circular argument about form and content. Does neoliberal rhetoric necessarily go through predictable cycles: starting with debate, attempts at imposition of implausible integrating ideas, surly disintegration into meaninglessness and silence, only to be revamped into another round of debate under new political management? Or is it the features of the Nigerian economy and society themselves that are persistent, and people are referring to them in the only stale terms available? Or are we all locked into truly useless myopias about a reality this is shifting so rapidly as to impede us from standing back, catching breath, and actually facing real questions that were posed by Nigerian critics and have gone without answers for decades? What *is* a deficit? What *is* a debt? What *is* a subsidy? Is it really possible to leave whatever they are, or what the "market" turns them into, to the creative power of "chance" and the "necessity of submitting to forces whose operation we cannot follow in detail" (following Hayek)? Possibly each iteration of the same old terms leaves more and more to the private inventiveness of disparate constituencies. The claims of a collective faith in the distant horizon, the singularity of "the market," rational choice rather than reasoning, become increasingly distant and implausible, leaving us gravely disconcerted that the "craving for intelligibility" within the economic lives that people actually live is increasingly generating no concerted answer at all from those charged by the political process and by expertise in the discipline of economics to account for them. If so, lengthening phases of silence—the retreat of the state into the Aso Rock fortresses of the world while the people invent their own analytics and pragmatics—would be one logical form of the "freedom" for whose sake Hayek advocates our sacrifice of intelligibility.

Notes

The Nigerian journalists responsible for the stories are, as far as possible, named in the text. Without their courageous work, no one could reconstruct the history of this period or of these debates. The collection of the newspaper sources was made possible by a Research and

Writing Grant from the John D. and Catherine T. MacArthur Foundation, for which we give thanks. We are particularly grateful to Olatunji Ojo, who did much of the clipping (in the days before on-line newspapers), and Wale Adebanwi, who wrote background histories of all of the newspapers for us. Justin Lee excerpted a series of files. William Milberg and Stephen Gudeman offered important suggestions on the paper. Guyer's study of these sources was supported by a fellowship at the Woodrow Wilson International Center for Scholars in Washington D.C. in the spring of 2003. Some items of the material were first presented in an unpublished paper by Guyer and Denzer entitled, "The Oil Economy of the Nigerian People,," presented to the Program of African Studies, Northwestern University, 1999. The present paper was written in 2005, so well before some of its arguments became directly applicable to the rhetoric of economic crisis in the United States in 2007–2008.

1. My limited critical knowledge of the vast literature on rhetoric means that I take the "student's" route of accessing compendia and textbooks for issues that seem pertinent to my own concerns.
2. The New Palgrave entry on monetarism states this succinctly: "Monetarist thought puts primary emphasis on the long-run consequences of policy actions and procedures. It rejects attempts to reduce short-run fluctuations…" (Cagan 1989: 203).
3. The convergence becomes stronger with each passing day. As I discuss in more detail below, President Babangida implied that he did not know how the Nigerian economy worked, largely because international investors had not responded as predicted to his policies. In spring and summer of 2005, the US Federal Reserve was puzzling over the persistent decline in long-term interest rates, "a new reality," "clearly international in origin," on which "Wall St. economists are as divided as Fed officials about the proper interpretation." Later in the summer, the press started to talk about excess liquidity: too much capital in the world in search of too few investment opportunities, which, however, is "good for growth—but risks are mounting" (Miller 2005: 49 and cover story). (Nigeria undertook a series of mop-up campaigns for excess liquidity in the 1990s). Alan Greenspan offered that when balance would be restored "people would know it when they saw it" (Andrews 2005: C1 and C9). The business pages of the New York Times redound with "culture," "charisma," "vision," "superstars," "brand names," and the idea that Greenspan's pronouncements are now considered "a strong fundamental for the stock market" (The Associated Press 2005). Also, see Kaplan (2003) for a discussion of Greenspan's rhetorics.
4. Nigerian currency is in naira (N); billions are British billions of one thousand million. The naira was originally at parity with the British pound sterling, but fell over this period to fifty or more to the pound.
5. The following rumor circulated in 1997: because members of the governing elite owned rights in oil in Venezuela, they deliberately ran shortages in Nigeria in order to make the economic and political rent on imports to meet the clamorous unmet demand at elevated prices. The veracity of the story is less important for my purposes than the popular vision.

CHAPTER 8

Mass-gifts
On Market Giving in Advanced Capitalist Societies

Nurit Bird-David and Asaf Darr

■ ■ ■ ■ ■ ■

Introduction

In this chapter, we focus on the rhetorical dimension of the classic anthropological distinction between "gifts" and "commodities" that goes back to Marcel Mauss' canonical essay "*The Gift.*" Anthropologists previously discussed "gifts" and "commodities" as two substantial types of exchange, each involving a different setup of relations between the two sides to the transaction and between them and the object being exchanged. The anthropological discourse does, naturally, involve a strong rhetorical dimension. Our concern here, however, is with rhetoric in its classic sense as the art of persuasion, drawing on emotions, shared understanding, etc. Having noted the rhetorical distinction between gift and commodity, we chose to focus specifically on the usage of the notion of "gift" to persuade buyers in the Israeli and US market economies to buy various commodities. The distinction that is drawn in rhetoric between substance and its expression and the concern over their relations, provides us with a perspective from which to examine such rhetorical uses of "gifts" and "commodities" by local actors at the hub of the Israeli and the US market economies.

The giving of "matanot" (gifts) as a method of encouraging sales is a common phenomenon in Israel. Advertisements in newspapers as well as commercial mail entice consumers to buy commodities with the promise of an accompanying "gift." In shops, prospective buyers are inundated by shelf advertisements as well as ceiling banners, to buy a product and get another as a "gift." The "gift" may be the exact article being purchased, an extra percentage thereof, or a closely related item. For example, "buy a bottle of liquid soap [of a particular brand] and get a sponge as a gift," or "buy a liquid soap, and get an added 30 percent as a gift," or "buy a bottle of liquid soap and get another as a gift." The "gift" may forge broader connections between organizations as, for example, when consumers in a supermarket are invited to "buy a coffee [of a certain brand] and get the second book as a present" when making a purchase at a nearby bookshop. This phenomenon is highly prominent in the Israeli consumer market, but is by no means limited to that particular market. Though in a much more restricted form, it can, for example, be found at cosmetics stands within department stores and in drug stores in the US. In this chapter, we focus on this phenomenon, which we suggest calling the giving of mass-gifts. We maintain that it lies at the very heart of advanced capitalist markets and raises questions relevant to the century-old and still vibrant debate begun by Marcel Mauss's seminal essay, "*The Gift*" (1954 [1925]).

Mauss's essay has been subjected to considerable comment and elaboration (e.g., Carrier 1990a, 1991, 1995; Durham 1995; Gregory 1980, 1982; Hyde 1983; Parry 1986; Sahlins 1972; Thomas 1991; Valeri 1994; Herrmann 1997; Darr, 2003; also see Bird-David 1997 for a review). The debate has essentially gone in two directions. One direction has been to maintain the gift-commodity distinction, but free it from both Mauss's evolutionary thesis as well as from the "softer" reading, which posited that the notion of the "gift" prevails in traditional or exotic cultures whilst the concept of the "commodity" is predominant in the industrial cultures of the West. A second and contrary direction in this debate has been to mute the distinction between gift and commodity and focus instead entirely on the notion of "commodity," while shifting the analysis from category to process and practice. Both directions have their fair share of strengths and weaknesses. In this chapter, we explore a synthesis: we maintain the gift-commodity distinction, and in line with Arjun Appadurai's fresh treatment of the "commodity" (1986), we approach "gift" as something that is situational. With respect to "gift," we also shift the analysis from category to process and practice. However, and more importantly, we also pay attention to the rhetoric as much as to the material aspects of this subject.

Observations in supermarkets inspire the model for our analysis, which is then applied to data obtained from a participant-observation study (1995–96)[1] among salespeople in an advanced industrial sector. In this chapter, we examine how some commodity-like shopping transactions are rhetorically framed by those involved as a "gift" and modelled on the metaphor of "gift"; how buyers and sellers in major mainstream venues of the economy fluidly construct and rhetorically shift between "purchases" and "gifts"; and how an implicit "commodity-gift" distinction is used manipulatively in core areas of advanced capitalist economies. We maintain that mass-gifts play on the (native) altruistic sense of "gift," and at the same time fall into the (scholarly) Maussian "gift" type, in that they seek to advance economic interests by subverting, and even disguising, market relations.

Gifts and Commodities: The Debate

Marcel Mauss distinguished between "gift" and "commodity" as substantial forms of circulating things among people. In the orthodox reading of his text, the distinction was made between commodities, as alienable things exchanged between aliens, and gifts, as inalienable things exchanged between non-aliens (see Gregory 1982: 43). Mauss also argued for an evolution from the gift, as characterizing "archaic" societies, to the commodity, which he viewed as the hallmark of modernity. In any event, he constructed "gift" and "commodity" exchanges as inherently opposed. As Appadurai put it, the two categories in Mauss's work are "fundamentally contrastive and mutually exclusive" (Appadurai 1986: 11).

Post-Mauss, the debate about gifts and commodities has taken various directions yet kept in focus the substantial dimension of these forms of exchange. One such direction was to explore "how the two types of exchange coexist in differing contexts within and on the border of the same society" (Herrmann 1997: 911). A number of studies have drawn attention to the practice of gifting within Western societies, for example, among groups of urban poor (Dow 1977; Lowenthal 1975; Stack 1974), in household economies (Carrier 1992b; Corrigan 1989), in offerings in the scientific community (Hyde 1983), in the exchange of presents between kin, friends, and neighbors (Cheal 1988; Davis 1972, 1992), and in systems of patronage (Campbell 1964; Holmes 1989). James Carrier (1992b) observed that Mauss's association of gift-exchanges and commodity-exchanges with exotic and Western societies respectively was only part of Occidentalizing the West, i.e., naturalizing and essentializing the West as a market economy. While such studies acknowledge the practice of gifting in Western societies, they still relegate it in advanced capitalist markets to domestic, private, or marginal arenas, are oblivious to its practice at the heart of these systems, as is apparent from a few pioneering studies (Darr 2003), and ignore the rhetorical usage of "gifts" and "gifting," which we describe below.

Another direction taken by the debate has been to mute altogether the differentiation between gift and commodity as representing any kind of substantive distinction. Herzfeld (2001: 104) observed that the association of the idea of the commodity with "the West" dies hard, not least because it has played such an important role for critics of Western models of the economy, especially critics with Marxist leanings. But some scholars have tried to go beyond this idea. John Davis (1992), for example, questioned the gift-commodity distinction by treating exchanges as multiple discrete forms, all of which are embedded in social relations. He categorized types of exchange into repertoires, derived from local perspectives. For example, in the British repertoire, he noted types of exchange that included altruism, barter, buying/selling, charity, donation giving, profiteering, reciprocity, shoplifting, shopping, swapping, theft, and trading. For all its usefulness, this "unwieldy laundry list" (in Herrmann's words, 1997: 912) makes comparisons difficult.

More influential in this direction of the debate has been the work of Arjun Appadurai (1986) and Igor Kopytoff (1986), who guided scholarly attention away from "the gift," and focused it entirely on "the commodity." They severed the identification between "commodity" and mass-manufactured industrial goods, and freshly reconstructed the commodity as "a phenomenon crossing historical sequences and economic types" (Bird-David 1997: 468). Furthermore, they overturned the previously commonly held assumption that an object's pre-existing value is what made it an object of exchange. Instead, Appadurai combined insights from Simmel and Marx, arguing that the "value in the commodity" lies in the act of exchange, whether actual or simply imagined. In Appadurai's terms, a thing can become but also un-become a "commodity." Its status is situational: the demand or the desire for it by someone else turns it into a commodity. In Appadurai's and Kopytoff's' work, the gift-commodity distinction is lost (see Thomas 1991; Herrmann 1997). Attention is directed away from the "gift" itself to the process through which material objects become and un-become "commodities." However, as our cursory vignette above shows, both the "gift" and the "gift-commodity" rhetorical distinctions are practiced and recognized, even at the heart of advanced capitalist markets, in retail shops, and as we shall show later, in industrial markets where firms sell to and buy from other firms.

As Gudeman (1986), Gudeman and Rivera (1990), Bird-David (1990, 1992, 1997), and, in a more restricted sense, Davis (1992), have observed, we should take seriously the theories of social actors about their economic actions. This courtesy, as Davis stresses, should be extended to the economic actors of our own societies as much as to those of exotic societies. Indeed, as Herzfeld (2001: 102) shrewdly observed, Mauss's own canonical essay cannot be read independently of contemporaneous Euro-American ideologies of gift giving, and gift-commodity distinctions. Mauss, like Durkheim, was principally concerned with exotic societies in which he hoped to discern the "archaic" principles underlying the fragmentation of the modern age; and, like Durkheim, he never himself experienced exotic ways of society through field research. As Herzfeld (2001: 103) put it, "we should recognize that [in generalizing the Maori sense of *hau*] he invoked an exotic model which exposes something of his own society's economic ideology." If we were to extend this point by dropping the "gift-commodity" distinction, it would mean, ironically, that we lose Mauss's insightful ethnographic observation as a native!

The "gift" is an undeniable emic construct, as much as an analytical one, with some interesting differences between the two. The "gift" is idealized in Western culture as something that is given altruistically. The giving is not motivated by self-interest, but by idealized love toward the receiver. The gift, in this cultural script, embodies affection and appreciation, and it expresses and regenerates both of these emotions. This native sense of "gift" is not identical to the scholarly sense of this term. Following Malinowski, Mauss construed the term "gift," as distinct from the term "commodity," as two forms of economic transactions and as two forms of reciprocity. The (scholarly) "gift," he stressed, is not unselfish; on the contrary, it is as much motivated by self-interest as is a commodity. The main difference between the (scholarly) "gift" and the commodity, in Mauss's terms, is the emphasis in the former on the "relations" between "giver" and "receiver" and, in the latter, on the object that is being exchanged. We will argue below that the mass-gift plays, if only rhetorically, on the (native) sense of "gift" as a means of subverting market relations. At the same time, it falls into the (scholarly) "gift" type in advancing economic interests by forging real or imaginary relations. In some ironic sense, mass-gifts exemplify the (scholarly) "gift" construct in Western societies far more than do domestic gifts in the West that hitherto attracted students' attention.

In her analysis of garage sales in the US, Gretchen Herrmann (1997) began to "complicate static models of exchange by demonstrating that garage sale transactions can fluctuate between gift and commodity, or partake of both at the same time, depending on the social relations of specific transactions' (1997: 910). Her work focused on an ethnographic site, which is partly situated in the privacy of the domestic realm and partly situated in the public domain of commerce. Herrmann shows how the actors fluidly construct the transactions as "more or less gift-like or commodity-like" (1997: 910), and how garage sale transactions are modeled by sellers and buyers on a market metaphor, even when they are gift-like, and involve extremely low priced personal possessions. While garage sales are trivial in terms of mainstream economists (Herzfeld 2001: 103), we want to describe the manipulative use of the "commodity-gift" distinction in core areas of advanced capitalist economies. We shall show (as does Herrmann) not only how buyers and sellers in major venues of the economy fluidly construct "gift" and "commodity," but also, complementary to Hermann, how some commodity-like shopping transactions are modeled by actors on the metaphor of "gift."

In the next section, we first try to highlight the special characteristics of what we call the "mass-gift." We then present a case study that allows us to look at the nuanced process in which the gift-commodity distinction is played out, with agents actively constructing and reconstructing material objects as "gift" or "commodity," or as something in between that can retrospectively even be constructed rhetorically as one or the other. We focus on sales interactions between sellers and buyers of mass-produced electronic components and the way in which samples are exchanged as one type of mass-gift. This gifting is not as overt as in the offering of gifts to consumers in the supermarket. But the nuanced ways in which "samples" are used in the process allows us to show another expression of mass-gifting which, together with the gifting that takes place in the supermarket, begins to outline the scope of the "mass-gift" concept and its applications. Additionally, as is the case with the notion of "commodity" as used by both Appadurai and Koytoff, this example helps us to see "the gift" not just as a category, but also as a practice and a process. The mass-gift, we shall argue, does not necessarily involve transactions between actors who are a priori related; in Gregory's words, it is not an "inalienable thing exchanged between non-aliens." Instead, we suggest seeing the "mass-gift" as a thing in a certain situation where, to paraphrase Appadurai, its socially relevant feature—be it real, imaginary or contrived—is to form social bonding, commitment, and belonging, or generally whatever can be cast as "non-market relations." Sometimes mass-gifts are underscored only by the implicit shared cultural understandings—or cultural scripts—of "the gift."

What is a Mass-Gift?

Our first objective is to try and define the "mass-gift" in relation to the more traditional notions of the "gift" and the "commodity." We shall begin by analyzing the methods employed by supermarkets as an illustration of the "ideal type" of mass-gift. Later, we shall extend and reexamine our definition, taking the more complex examples of the use of samples in a mass industrial market. We define mass-gifts as things that are given in conjunction with the past, present, or future purchase of a commodity. The purchase can be actual or expected by at least one side to the transaction. The mass-gift is constituted rhetorically or dramaturgically as an exchange that is external to idealized market exchange, in which money buys commodities. While the identity of the giver, typically a specific manufacturer or brand name, is clear, the receiver remains anonymous, and is constructed as a mass consumer.

How is the "mass-gift" manifested empirically? First, certain mass-produced products in mass-consumption settings such as department stores or supermarkets are explicitly presented to the shoppers as gifts. Here, the social setting and even the social relations of the exchange seem to be the same for commodities and gifts. The presentation of some artifacts in mass-consumption settings as gifts is clearly a rhetorical device, and its cultural and practical meaning for the giver and the receiver are worth exploring.

The first observation is that the "mass-gift" is an alienable thing exchanged between aliens, and thus conforms to Gregory's (1982: 43) definition of a commodity rather than a gift. The artifacts offered as mass-gifts are mass-produced and bear no personal link to a specific producer beyond the attachment to a general brand name. The receiver is also constructed as a mass entity. The gift is not tailored to any specific needs of the receiver, nor do the receiver's personality traits have any importance in this exchange. At most, the gift is made to suit the imagined needs of an imagined generalized consumer. In fact, and in contrast to traditional perceptions of gifts, the mass-gift is explicitly nonpersonal in nature and is meant to serve a mass-consumption market that involves mass producers and anonymous consumers. However, while the mass-gift is depersonalized, it is linked rhetorically, as well as by transaction, to a commodity. As we indicated above, it can be materially the same as the commodity, or related to the commodity in terms of usage (e.g., a second liquid soap, or the sponge for using the purchased liquid soap). It can also be seasonal (e.g., a honey cake given as a gift for Rosh Hashanah, the Jewish New Year, when it is traditional to eat honey during the family meal in the hope of a sweet year ahead; the gift is given by the supermarket on the purchase of any commodity, provided the overall expenditure is above a certain specified limit). The mass-gift, finally, can be related to the commodity in terms of complementary use in imaginary cultural scripts or actual everyday rituals—for example, a book with the purchase of a coffee.

Receiving the mass-gift depends on the purchase (past, present, or future) of identical or complementary products. The consumer receives the mass-gift upon buying a commodity or on the basis of a purchase in the future. The producer, as the giver of the gift, wishes the receiver to buy the commodity again in the future, thereby reciprocating, as it were, by paying money again sometime in the future. We could argue that the mass-gift retroactively reconstructs the buyer as a previous giver, saying in effect, "you, the buyer, bought from us and we reciprocate with a gift accompanying the commodity you purchased." In other words, in addition to a future-oriented moral obligation, the mass-gift reconstructs a previous transaction not only as an anonymous act of selling and buying, but also as an act involving a moral act.

Insofar as a thing "becomes" a commodity at the point at which there is a desire for it (in Appadurai's terms), the mass-gift helps to create that desire. The mass-gift can introduce a new product to the market, and thereby generate a "taste" and desire for it. It is in this context that samples of products, which we will be examining in detail further on, truly come into their own. The mass-gift can create a desire for a good purchase or a good deal, thereby implying a desire for the commodity itself. Thus, one buys a liquid soap because of the accompanying gift that one might otherwise not have bought, or perhaps one might have bought one of another brand. It can be said that mass-gifts and commodities mutually create one another, as much as they are in reciprocity to one another.

Zucker (1986: 61) notes that a gift economy is predicated on the existence of what she calls "trust" between the parties to the exchange, since a significant amount of time might pass between the gift and the counter-gift. Yet the mass-gift represents a gift economy that is not predicated on pre-existing trust or social obligation. One could argue that this form of transaction does not involve gifting, but is rather simply a substitute for a reduction in price. If so, why is the product in question presented as a gift and not simply presented as "Buy one get one free"—a common phrase in advertisements and far more commonplace than the description of the item as a "gift"? We believe that, by presenting extra value for the buyer as a gift, the giver, typically a mass-producer, demonstrates to the buyer by rhetorical means some of its power and economic wealth. The producer declares, through this mass-giving, that it can afford this gesture, and still remain powerful. Furthermore, one can even argue that by being presented with the extra 30 percent as a gift, the receiver comes to share some of the giver's wealth and, in an act of sharing, becomes temporarily part of the imagined community of the giving organization. Researchers have long noted the cultural role of gifts as producing and reproducing the social status of the giver, and we could argue that the rhetorical presentation of the commodity as a gift in a mass-consumption setting takes on some of this cultural meaning. Here, we do find a cultural meaning for the exchange of mass-gifts that is closer to the traditional depiction of a gift economy.

Despite its other deviations from traditional cultural perceptions of gifts, the rhetorical use of the term "gift" by the givers may suggest that they expect the receivers to react emotionally to the object as a gift. In fact, the givers of the mass-gift rely on normative scripts, which, via the process of socialization, have created in the receiver a sense of gratitude and limited obligation. This rhetorical use is even more surprising considering the blurring in physical terms of the boundaries between the commodity and the gift. We have already noted that artifacts can be defined as commodities and gifts depending on the social context of the transaction. But in the case of the mass-gift, the blurring of the boundaries between gifts and commodities increases. When a consumer is presented with two chocolate bars packaged together and is told that one of them is a gift, the question arises as to which one is a gift and which is the commodity just purchased? Even more confusing is a situation where a shopper is told that he or she has received 30 percent of the laundry detergent as a gift. How can one conceptualize the same artifact being constructed partly as a gift and partly as a commodity? The mass-gift rhetorically evokes associations of the (native) construct of "gift," as a means of subverting market relations, while at the same time it falls into the (scholarly) "gift" type in that it advances economic interests.

The category of the mass-gift that we present in this chapter is by no means monolithic. In fact, there are at least three distinct types of mass-gifts characterized by the different locus of the limited obligation they create—two of them appearing in the supermarket setting alone. The ideal type of the mass-gift is the one that is offered directly to the consumer by the producer of a brand named product. In this case, the shopper simply takes the commodity along with the gift off of the supermarket shelf and puts it straight into his or her shopping cart. The shopper pays at the counter and becomes at one and the same time the owner of the commodity and the receiver of the gift from a specific producer. The limited obligation constructed through gifting is nested in the imagined relationship between the shopper and the producer.

A second type of mass-gift involves, in addition to the producer, the specific shop or supermarket where the gift is offered. Here, when paying at the checkout counter, the shopper is told to go to the main customer service counter after payment to collect various gifts he has "earned" through purchasing different items. The gift or gifts are offered by supermarket employees behind the customer service counter, and the shopper may feel a certain sense of obligation not only to the brand name attached to the gift, but also to the supermarket, which is viewed as an additional giver. The apparent complexity of mass-gifting, even in the supermarket setting, led us to explore other types of mass-gifts in different situations. In fact, the third and most elusive form of mass-gift we identified involves the use of product samples in the exchange of mass-produced products in an industrial market, where firms trade with other firms. Here, the gift in the form of a product sample is supposed to create a three-layered obligation: to the specific producer of the sample; to a specific distributor supplying the sample; and to a specific salesperson as part of a package of services he or she offers the buying organization. For a better understanding of the use of samples as a form of mass-gift, we now describe the field study. In this study, we demonstrate the twofold nature of product samples as being both gift and commodity, and the way in which the two meanings of the same "thing" are constructed in the social negotiations that take place between market players. These market players constantly engage in the construction and maintenance of social networks of mutual obligation, a process in which mass-gifts perform an important role.

Product Samples as a Form of a Mass-Gift

To explore the complexity and dynamics of mass-gifting in the industrial heart of advanced capitalist markets, we draw on fieldwork done by Asaf Darr among USA salespeople, engineers, and purchasing agents of mass-produced and mass-consumed electronic components such as capacitors, resistors, and even different types of cables, all grouped under the industry title of "passive components." These commodities are used by almost all companies that deal in electronics, regardless of size, as part of their manufacturing operation. They are the bread and butter of the industry, sold in large quantities at prices that range from US$0.25 cents to a few dollars for each basic component. The field study was conducted in the northeastern United States (a leading Western economy) and included interviews and observations of interactions between buyers and sellers at local and regional trade shows.

The mass-manufacturing of capacitors and resistors is not only centralized, but is also part of a global production and consumption chain, where the actual manufacturing plants are located thousands of miles away from the point of distribution. Most sales of capacitors and resistors are not direct, but are conducted through local independent distributors. The latter act as mediators of exchange, and offer a variety of competing products to electronics firms in their sales "territory," and not just the products of a particular manufacturer. The manufacturing firms also have their own sales force, whose operatives have distinct titles. In accordance with certain rules the sales people (of both the manufacturers and the distributors) can approach prospective buyers.

The mass-produced commodities flow through an infrastructure consisting in part of social relationships among the sellers and between them and the buyers. The large manufacturers of capacitors and resistors employ "direct" salespeople in their sales branches. The direct salesperson works under a regional sales manager, supervising between five and fifteen other direct salespeople, depending on the size of the territory and its density in terms of potential clients. The direct salesperson is in charge of a smaller "territory," which typically includes a major city and its suburbs. The role of the direct salesperson is to sell directly to very large clients operating in his or her territory.

The sales force of the local distributors is composed of "inside" and "outside" sales people. The outside salespeople constantly roam their territory in search of new clients and new sales opportunities. More generally, they seek to maintain the strong social ties with the purchasing agents and the engineers they serve, based on mutual obligations. In contrast, the inside salespeople stay in the distributors' offices and manage the ongoing flow of orders and products to and from existing clients. They also provide existing and prospective clients with price quotations in response to the request of the direct salesperson.

Economists and a few economic anthropologists claim that a mass market is a location where sellers and buyers construct short-term ties with exchange partners, and where buyers tend to frequently switch to alternative sellers. However, for the people who make up the mass market for capacitors and resistors through their daily sales activities, the term "market" itself denotes a web of strong social relationships between sellers and buyers. The main asset of the "outside" salespeople is a dense network of interpersonal ties, which they develop with purchasing agents and engineers at their clients' plants. These relationships are predicated on an ongoing social interaction, in the form of weekly meetings and phone conversations with existing and prospective clients, which in every instance does not result in the conclusion of an actual sale. By constantly visiting the plants of prospective clients and having brief encounters with the purchasing agents, without necessarily getting an order, the outside salespeople start to develop a limited commitment to buy from them and not from their competitors. Referring to buyers during sales visits as "friends," and inquiring after family members, also assists sellers in building a rapport and in constructing and later cementing market ties. As Uzzi (1997: 52) notes, the multiplicity of market ties, in this case combining business and friendship, also promotes the ability of market players to access resources, such as information, regarding new business opportunities and lowers the risk associated with managing the relationship.

The direct and outside salespeople also establish a complex web of social ties among themselves that combines competition and cooperation and facilitates the ongoing flow of commodities from the manufacturer to the end user. Compared to outside sales people, direct sales personnel are often talented and highly experienced. They sometimes accompany outside salespeople in their daily rounds and assist them with advice and even demonstrate sales tactics when faced with difficult purchasing agents.

The direct, inside, and outside salespeople, as well as the purchasing agents and engineers, to whom they sell their products, are expected to give priority to the interests of their employers, which does not necessarily coincide with their own best interests. Thus, receiving gifts from a salesperson might be perceived by the purchasing agent's employers as a form of bribe. In the case study, in fact, a few electronics companies as well as labs operating in academic institutions in the territory studied, forbade their purchasing agents from accepting any form of gift, including invitations to lunch. Interestingly, there were certain rules governing the extensive gift economy in the mass market for passive components. For example, an invitation to lunch, could, in a different social context, be considered a legitimate business activity rather than a bribe. It was extremely uncommon for purchasing agents to accept luncheon invitations from salespeople with whom they had not yet done any business. Such an invitation was viewed as acceptable only some time after an order had been placed with a particular salesperson. It then became possible to disguise their acceptance by calling the engagement a business lunch, giving them the opportunity to go over the order that had been placed, rather than calling it a "gift lunch." The danger that one could be accused of offering or receiving a bribe may explain the lack of explicit reference in industrial markets to gifts, as opposed to the explicit use of the term in the supermarket setting. Yet, as we intend to demonstrate, free lunches, rounds of golf, and product samples—each disguised as a business activity—were all forms of mass-gifting in the setting of the industrial market for standard electronic components. Different types of gifts were offered at different junctures of the sales process, and their use and the shifting meaning between commodity and gift become clear in the following depiction of an idealized sales motion of standard electronic products.

Typical Sales Motions in the Mass Industrial Market

In order to become established in a new territory, outside salespeople first try to identify prospective clients who might be interested in buying capacitors and resistors. They use a variety of strategies, including "cold calls"—simply entering buildings in industrial parks and asking about the prospective buyer's line of business, as well as spying on the factory loading docks to see the range of products being shipped in and out. The physical identification of a potential client is only the first step on a long journey. What the salespeople must work against is a pre-existing network of robust sales ties between purchasing agents and competing sales people.

Our case study showed that it was not uncommon for outside salespeople to visit purchasing agents about once a week for a year or more, before getting any orders. During their initial sales visits, the salespeople were usually stopped at the reception desk, where they asked to see the purchasing agent. In many instances, the purchasing agents simply sent the salesperson away saying he or she did not need anything or was busy that day. In other cases, the outside salesperson and the purchasing agent engaged in a brief conversation in which the sales person would offer technical information about new components and product catalogues. Once some form of a business relationship began to develop, the purchasing agent allowed the salespeople to interact directly with the engineers. This meant that the salespeople could walk freely into the engineering department without being stopped at the reception desk. Now, the salesperson could offer to provide product samples to the client's engineers, an offer perceived by the salespeople as a very good investment in creating a limited obligation to order from them in the future. For their part, the purchasing agents were looking for dependable suppliers and perceived the persistent visits of certain salespeople, even without getting orders, as a sign of good character. Sometimes they did not agree to take product samples for their engineers during initial sales interactions; they probably viewed taking them, as did the salespersons, as a limited commitment to future purchases of commodities from those providing the samples.

As is customary in the electronics industry, capacitors and resistors used for building a product prototype had to be tested and approved by the engineering department before they could be used on a large scale as part of the ensuing mass-manufacturing process. Typically, the engineering department would test the components while building a product prototype, and only then put the parts on the "approved list," a step that allowed the purchasing department to place orders. This made direct interaction between the salespeople and the engineers in the plant of a potential client crucially important.

The flow of product samples was managed on a daily basis directly with the engineers. The salespeople kept a file of all of the samples they had supplied to particular engineers, and during their visits they would ask specific questions about the status of these samples and whether they had already been approved for use in the prototype, which is the basis for any future order. The sales visits were also an occasion to remind the engineers about the ongoing flow of samples, and to present the samples as a form of giving that was distinct from regular commercial exchange. For example, the salespeople talked about the samples they "gave" the engineers, implicitly referring to them as a gift. During a particular sales encounter with a group of engineers having lunch at a table in the engineering department of one of the firms he supplied, a salesperson offered them a new catalogue to help them choose a new resistor they needed. The engineers reciprocated immediately by telling the salesperson about a new design project, which might mean more business for the salesperson, but they were also quick to remind the salesperson that they had requested some samples of connectors a few weeks earlier. When the salesperson replied that he did not know what had happened with the samples, one of the engineers said loudly:

> Engineer: A guy was here [a different outside salesperson working for a different distributor] last week and he had them [*samples of connectors*] with him, but we told him to wait on it.
>
> [Short pause]
>
> Salesperson: [*self-deprecatorily*] OK. I will try again for you because you asked. I'll look it up for you.

Clearly, the engineer was aware of the moral obligation involved in the receipt of product samples, stating in fact that it was for this reason that he had refrained from accepting the samples from the second vendor. Interestingly, the salesperson quickly replied that he would try again to get the samples, as if acknowledging the engineers' pledge of loyalty to him, which required in turn a demonstration of commitment on his part. Once again we see how the exchange of samples as a form of a mass-gift is part of a larger barter economy.

One could argue that giving free samples was not a gift, but simply a necessary stage in the ongoing exchange of commodities, namely, familiarizing clients with the product and giving them the chance to test it as part of their prototype. In a practical sense this is true. However, once we consider this transaction within the social context in which it takes place, we can see that to a degree "sample" is a rhetorical gloss for gift both for the salesmen and the purchasing agents. The nature of the product samples as a form of a mass-gift in some social situations became clear in the instance above, but also during an interview with an outside salesperson, who talked about his involvement with the head of the engineering department of a prospective client: "I sampled him to death," the informant said, referring to the head of engineering,

> until I was finally asked to quote something. The whole order was about $150. I sent in my quote, and when I visited the guy the following week he told me another vendor sent in a quote that was a few dollars cheaper. I got real angry and when I returned home I called this head of engineering and reminded him of all the *free samples* I gave him. I then told him I thought it was unfair that he chose a different supplier in order to save a few dollars. (Italics added)

Note in particular how the term "samples," the common phrase used during sales interactions, turned into "free samples," a term much closer to the term gift, and possibly a term as close as the salesperson could use without being accused of offering bribes to the head of engineering. Here, the rhetoric employed by the salesperson exposes the use of the term samples, as an expressive form shaping the meaning of the exchange. This shaping allows the receiver to accept the items as part of the normal way of doing business. Also note that the salesperson presented the head of engineering with a moral argument, referring to his behavior as "unfair." Underlying the salesman's resentment was his sense of betrayal pitted against the implicit sense of a social relation that was forged by the giving of samples. The association between the "free samples," the moral argumentation, and the sense of betrayal echo unvoiced "gifting" scripts, and is yet another example of the usage of samples as a form of gift. In fact, the giving of samples formed part of a wider moral economy, whose existence conforms to our more traditional conceptions of gifting (for a more comprehensive analysis of the moral economy of the mass market for electronics components see Darr, 2006: 84–93). The role samples played in the moral economy of mass industrial markets highlights its twofold nature, as gifts and as commodities, depending on the social context of exchange, and at times even on the post hoc construction of the obligation created by the giving of free samples.

The samples were given in a more complex social context than the mass-gifts offered in the supermarket. There, the mass-gifts were given directly to individuals, whose own direct and personal needs they aimed to serve. In the industrial market, the sample as mass-gift is of no direct personal use to the individual recipient, who is merely the employee of a company with no personal interest at stake. Nonetheless, the nuanced act of giving transformed it into a personal act. The salespeople even tried to appeal to the recipients' aesthetic sensibilities. The samples were taken out of the salesperson's briefcase and given to the engineers in special plastic bags sorted according to color and size.

In some cases, even before business links had been established, salespeople offered samples to engineers and buyers to create an obligation, limited as it might be, for the buyer to reciprocate. Their nature as gifts was enhanced by the manner in which they were presented. For example, on one occasion one of the authors (A.D.) accompanied an outside and a direct salesperson on a sales visit to Central Outlet, the main electronics and tool store serving labs at a major university in the northeast of the United States. Bill, the outside salesperson working for a local distributor, had been visiting the buyer at Central Outlet for the past year, trying to have products he distributed displayed there, but his attempts had borne no fruit. He called George, a direct salesperson working for Electrocom, a large manufacturer of passive components, to help him build the sales relationships with the buyer. This was their second joint visit to Central Outlet. As we stepped into the store, we were greeted by Rich, who led us into his large office. We sat down and the direct salesperson smiled, and opened with his routine:

George: So how's everything here?

Rich: Good.

George: Remember what we spoke about last time?

Rich: Yes.

George: OK, so I brought you this. [*George hands Rich a thick catalogue*] It has everything in it, OK?

Rich: [*Rich puts the catalogue on the table*] OK, sure.

George: And we wanted to talk a little bit about ah terminals?

Rich: [*with a challenging smile, and speaking in a flat voice*] OK, Let us talk terminals.

George: [*smiles back*] Yes, let us talk terminals.

[*Instead of talking, George opens up his briefcase with a theatrical gesture and takes out three sample bags bearing the Electrocom logo. He hands the bags to Rich, who opens one of them and starts playing with the plastic terminals.*]

Rich: [*cheerfully, but with light sarcasm*] Oh, very nice!

George: Do you like the red ones or the blue ones or the yellow ones?

Rich: [*smiles*] Oh, well, I'm partial to blue.

George, the direct salesperson, employed a number of techniques to try and overcome Rich's resistance. He smiled a lot, was humorous, and tried, in saying that "we" wanted to talk about terminals, to create a feeling of a shared interest. But what broke the ice was the presentation of the samples that George took out of his briefcase. Here, as in other cases, the nature of samples as gifts was clear from the way they were presented to the buyers' representatives. Samples of resistors, capacitors, or terminals were often gift-wrapped in small plastic bags according to size and color, and were handed over by gestures typical of gift-giving. Rich's willingness to engage in a conversation about the colors of the terminals was the first sign of his willingness to establish a sales relationship with George.

This case can be seen as the extreme of the extreme, compared with the supermarket's mass-gifts. Not only were these samples of no personal use to the purchasing agent, it was, even for the company, a "passive" component, anonymous, banal, and indistinct, a part of the "nuts and bolts" of the industry with no special significance. Yet its presentation echoes an underlying script related to gifting. The salesperson wants to elicit the purchasing agent's personal satisfaction and pleasure. The word "gift" was not used at any point during the engagement between the salesperson and the purchasing agent of the store, who in this case was the recipient and who, at the retail end, was himself in the business of selling. Nevertheless, we argue, this exchange is not looked upon by the participants as a commodity-transaction. Nor is it viewed as such by the firm involved since samples are not reported for bookkeeping purposes. We suggest that despite the overt differences between sample-giving and "gifts" in the supermarket setting, which we take as our analytic prototype, they can be fruitfully compared under the umbrella concept of "mass-gifs."

Conclusions

The commonplace supermarket gifting in Israel is yet to be investigated as a field of research in its own right.[2] This observed phenomenon has served as a trigger and a template for an exploratory mapping of what we called mass-gifts. Its rhetorical clarity and apparent factual simplicity makes it "good to think with" about other more complex instances, such as the more nuanced and ambiguous sample-giving that we described. A comparison between the sample-giving and the supermarket "gifts," as two different varieties of mass-gifts, can help us appreciate the range, versatility, and dynamics of mass-gifts.

As Appaduari argues for the commodity, mass-gifts are situational. To an extent, mass-gifts are commodities that, metaphorically, are "wrapped" as gifts by rhetorical and behavioral means. As exemplified in the supermarket setting, some commodities are constructed verbally as gifts, within a transactional context that remains commodity-like. In an extreme example, a shopper takes the "gift" off the shelf and places it in the cart with his or her other purchases. He or she proceeds to the checkout counter, and places it along with all the other merchandise on the conveyor belt. The cashier, for his part, checks each item and prints the bill, which the customer pays. Only the cash register, a machine, deciphers the item called "gift" and deducts its price from the final bill. On the other hand, in the sample-giving situation, rhetorical construction of the samples as gifts is problematic for fear of being misconstrued as bribery. While the word "gift" is avoided, a gift-situation is created around the commodity-sample by constructing work relations as social and by insinuating, through gestures and indirect verbal means, free giving and moral obligations. Here, the overt rhetoric is one of commodity-exchange, but the context is gift-like, whereas in the prototype supermarket setting the overt rhetoric is one of gift-giving, but the context is commodity-like.

If we consider (with Gregory 1982) commodity/gift transactions in the dual terms of object/relations, in both these cases of mass-gifts, the object and the relations between receiver and giver are alienable, contrary to the classic gift characteristics. However, in the prototype supermarket setting, the object is "giftified" (to paraphrase commoditized), and, in the second, it is the social relations that are cast as gift-relations.

Time works differently in these hybrid gift/commodity exchanges. It has a crucial role in the sample-giving situation where the gifting-like element precedes the anticipated commodity-exchange. The gift-element is of the kind that Malinowski would have described as an opening-gift. It is supposed to start off relations of obligations that will result in commodity exchange. On the other hand, time is immaterial in the supermarket setting, where by and large the gifting-like element is the closure of the commodity transaction. As mentioned, the gift is given in an act of reciprocity, which marks the purchase. The consumer receives his or her gift on fulfilling the predetermined purchase condition. The gifting in this case succeeds the commodity, whereas in the first case it precedes it. Commodity and gift elements can thus be combined temporally, as well as in rhetoric and/or practice, in diverse ways.

These examples do not exhaust the various forms and contexts of mass-gifting in advanced industrial markets. But they suffice to pinpoint a continuum of possibilities. They show transactions at the heart of advanced capitalist markets that are modeled partly on gift metaphors. They show elements of gift and commodity exchanges—or, more specifically, elements of rhetoric and practice in gift and commodity exchanges—that are combined in diverse and dynamic ways at the hub of market activities, not just, as shown by Herrmann (1997), in peripheral garage sales. Altogether, they reveal a phenomenon deserving of attention. By identifying this phenomenon for further study, we support previous work, which shows the relevance of the gift concept across the board in Western societies, in public and private life, in domestic as well as in commercial situations. The mass-gift phenomenon, to which we draw attention in this chapter, in fact, echoes Mauss's sense of the "gift," far more than does the interpersonal gifting in the domestic settings that have been previously studied.

We support as well the argument that the gift/commodity distinction is an emic construct, not just an analytical formulation. We add that this distinction is a cultural resource. Its meanings and nuances are played on and utilized in advanced capitalist markets for subverting market relations.

Notes

1. Field excerpts and some of the analyses in the following section are part of a large comparative study focusing on sales work in mass and nonstandard markets published in *Selling Technology: The Changing Shape of Sales in an Information Economy*, by Asaf Darr (Copyright © 2006 by Cornell University). Used by permission of the publisher, Cornell University Press.
2. Topics of research include the scope and seasonality of using mass-gifts, organizational decision making and strategies regarding choice and use of mass-gifts, what mass-gifts mean symbolically to customers, and the cultural context that renders mass-gifts so popular in Israel.

CHAPTER 9

THE PERSUASIVE POWER OF MONEY

Keith Hart

■ ■ ■ ■ ■ ■

> Money talks, it'll tell you a story
> Money talks, says strange things
> Money talks very loudly
> You'd be surprised the friends you can buy
> with small change
> —J.J. Cale "Money Talks" (song)

IN THIS CHAPTER, I WILL try to account for money's power to influence our minds and social relations. It would be easy, but misleading, to argue that money's ability to persuade is a universal characteristic. The way money persuades is historically relative—very different for Adam Smith than for Maynard Keynes and even more for us who live in the digital revolution and the expansion of virtual society it entails. Moreover, the fetishism that grants money a quasi-independent role in human affairs needs to be exposed for what it is. People make and use money, not the other way round; but sometimes it feels like we are more acted upon than acting. Money conveys meanings at the same time as it negates them; it has—or is thought to have—both structure and agency at once.

As a symbolic medium of communication, money informs our subjectivity and gives concrete expression to our desires, releasing and fixing our imagination in many ways. It is a store of individual and collective memory, and is the stuff linking persons to their communities. It may be that money's chief function was once to persuade people to let go of what they already had;

but separating us from money has become the chief object of the engines of persuasion mobilized by capitalist economy. And the ideas we have of money were themselves disseminated by "worldly philosophers" (Heilbroner 1961), who devoted a significant part of their effort to persuading people to accept them. It is hard to separate money's unconscious influence on us through folk discourse from its characteristics as a social force *sui generis*. If the study of rhetoric makes much of the distinction between the content of a communication and how it is communicated, money's success as a rhetorical device and its persuasive power may lie in its seamless ability to synthesize the two.

Money Talks

Malcolm X's private archive was rescued from an e-Bay auction in 2002. Apparently, one of his children was behind on rental payments for a lock-up garage. The collection was saved for storage in New York's Schomburg Center for Research in Black Culture, giving rise to the following exchange in an interview:[1]

> *BBC reporter*: Presumably money played a part in appeasing all the parties.
>
> *Family lawyer*: That's true. Money always talks. When there's a gap in communication, you drop a dollar bill in there and all of a sudden everyone speaks the same language.
>
> *Reporter*: How much?
>
> *Lawyer*: We can't go into the details.

In my youth, the expression "money talks" was most often used in the context of horseracing. The connections of a likely winner would want to conceal its form in order to place bets on the longest odds possible. But the volume of their wagers would appear soon enough as reduced odds in the market. Others would then pile in, taking the evidence of their senses to be stronger than all of the forecasts of newspaper tipsters. If the horse won, those who took advantage of the market signs would say knowingly "Money talks." Or, as Deep Throat famously said at the time of Watergate, "Follow the money." Proverbial wisdom points to a persistent analogy between money and language. Here are some examples:

> The use of language resembles the exchange of coinage. Plutarch (Cribb 2005: 435)

> The two greatest inventions of the human mind are writing and money—the common language of intelligence and the common language of self-interest. Mirabeau (Innis 1951: 8)

> Just as my thoughts must take the form of a universally understood language so that I can attain my practical ends in this roundabout way, so must my activities and possessions take the form of money value in order to serve my more remote purposes. Money is the purest form of the tool…; it is an institution through which the individual concentrates his activity and possessions in order to attain goals that he could not attain directly. Simmel (1978: 210)

I wish to go beyond metaphor and ask how people communicate through money. What does money *do* and how?[2] Wherein lies its power to persuade?

In *The Wealth of Nations*, Adam Smith (1961: 26–33) imagined money's origins in a barter system as the supreme commodity whose usefulness lay in its function as a means of deferred exchange and payment. This theory or, perhaps better, myth has extraordinary tenacity in the modern consciousness.[3] He held that the chief function of money, as a natural simplification of barter, was to persuade owners of commodities to give them up, knowing that what they received could readily be converted later into whatever else they wanted. This was much more convenient than having to argue with them every time:

> If we should enquire into the principle in the human mind on which this disposition of trucking is founded, it is clearly the natural inclination every one has to persuade. The offering of a shilling, which to us appears to have so plain a meaning, is in reality offering an argument to persuade one to do so and so as it is for his interest.… Every one is practising oratory on others thro the whole of his life.… This being the constant employment or trade of every man, in the same manner as the artizans invent simple methods of doing their work, so will each one here endeavour to do his work in the simplest manner. That is bartering, by which they address themselves to the self interest of the person and seldom fail immediately to gain their end. (*Lectures on Jurisprudence*, 30th March 1763)

Here, I wish to explore money's role in the advanced capitalist economies, where if anything commodities dance to the tune of money. The chief effort of persuasion in market situations today consists in getting people to spend their money; and, as the Malcolm X example shows, to express something in money terms often seems to make it more amenable to social action. Indeed, as Marx argued (1970: 71–83), money is a means of communication so powerful that we often ascribe human or quasi-divine agency to it and what it buys. In some ways, Money is the God of capitalism and most of the inmates are believers.

That compounds the difficulty of accounting for money's persuasive power, since it is hard to distinguish between what we imagine it is and what it really does. As a step between fetishizing money and placing it more precisely in human purposes and actions, I will look at some theories of money that have entered folk wisdom. Keynes knew what he was talking about when he wrote:

> [T]he ideas of economists and political philosophers, both when they are right and when they are wrong, are more powerful than is commonly understood. Indeed the world is ruled by little else. Practical men, who believe themselves to be quite exempt from any intellectual influences, are usually the slaves of some defunct economist. (1936: 383)

It turns out that economists are not above employing the arts of persuasion too.

What then is money? It is a universal measure of value, but its specific form is not yet as universal as the method that humanity has devised to measure time all around the world. It is purchasing power, or a means of buying and selling in markets. It counts wealth and status. It is a store of memory linking individuals to their various communities, a kind of memory bank (Hart 2000), and thus a source of identity. As a symbolic medium, it conveys information through a system of signs that relies more on numbers than words. A lot more circulates with money than the goods and services it buys.

Huon Wardle has this to say about "drop pan," a Jamaican numbers game played daily for money:

> Under modern conditions, Simmel (1900) argues, money becomes the most objective gauge of human relationships; and control over money is the chief marker of the self's ability to validate its existence in a shared social framework of space and time... To play drop pan is to search for signs which connect the immediate and utterly contingent elements of Creole experience within an ordering of meaning which, nonetheless, is itself gauged against the shifting evaluations of money as a social principle. Lévi-Strauss describes totemism as a concrete vehicle for understanding abstract relational systems. Simmel's analysis of money reverses this. Money is a (relative) abstraction, which works because it is able to encompass concrete human connections. Drop pan is a game of concrete symbols played against the abstract master index, money. (2005: 88–89)

Money—the main device in capitalist societies for making social relations objective—is at the same time a benchmark for concrete narratives of subjective attachment. Money's persuasiveness lies in this synthesis of impersonal abstraction and personal meaning, objectification and subjectivity, analytical reason and synthetic narrative. Its seductive power comes from the fluency of its mediation between infinite potential and finite determination.[4] The parallel with rhetoric is obvious.

The Dialectics of Social Abstraction

In order for us to do things for each other in society, the services we perform have to be detached as commodities from what we do for ourselves within the confines of the small groups we live in. This process of social abstraction, "commoditization" (Hart 1982; Carrier 1998), draws us into ever-widening circles of interdependence, the most inclusive of which are calculated in terms of money. The classical political economists, from Smith to Marx, distinguished between a commodity's concrete value in use (quality) and its higher-order ability to enter into abstract relations of exchange with other commodities through money (quantity). They concentrated on the latter function, but there is a dialectic at work here. The commodity remains something useful and in that use lies its concrete realization. The reality of commoditization is thus not just universal abstraction, but this mutual determination of the abstract and the concrete; and our method must somehow reproduce that relationship. We now rely on the products of abstraction to engage with others in highly concrete ways. It can provoke considerable anxiety, when we do not understand the machines we depend on or lack the money necessary to take part. Nevertheless, the current wave of market expansion through the internet supports interactions at distances that were unimaginable a short time ago; and any discussion of money today has to address that development (Hart 2000, 2005b).

Both Marx (1867) and Simmel (1900) noted that social abstraction through capitalist markets went along with intellectual abstraction as philosophy and science in notable cases such as Ancient Athens, Renaissance Florence, England in the seventeenth century, and, we might say, the USA in the twentieth century.[5] This observation points to the use of words and numbers in ways that link language and money as systems of communication. At one level, they share what the Greeks called *logos*, the principle of reasoning, the aspiration to objectivity, the ideal order in all things. This contrasts with the material flux of life in all of its concrete complexity, a world of moving particulars of which each of us is the subjective personification. Plato and Aristotle (or Parmenides and Heraclitus before them) came to embody this contrast and we find it subsequently as a pervasive dualism in the history of western thought (Russell 1945). Of late, the opposition between quantity and quality seems to have reached critical proportions: the novelist/scientist, C.P. Snow, claimed in a 1959 lecture that the breakdown of communication between the "two cultures" of modern society—the sciences and the humanities—was a major obstacle to solving the world's problems. In the process, specialists in words and numbers have come to occupy separate castes, presumptively determined at birth. If money is like language, it seems to be strongly affiliated with the quantitative camp, for it relies on numbers to a high degree.

"Numerophobia," fear and rejection of rational techniques employing numbers (science and math for short), is well advanced in several sections of western societies, including the middle classes and perhaps more among women than men (Gigerenzer 2002). There does appear to be a sort of *schismogenesis* (Bateson 1958) in the education system that from an early age separates those who are happy to work with numbers from those who avoid them like the plague. Most social or cultural anthropologists fall into the latter category, preferring to deal in qualities rather than quantities. Numbers simplify by reducing to quantity, creating exactness in a world of uncertainties, and this is one reason why science (and money) is both loved and hated. Moral and cultural values are more easily handled by being reduced to what can be counted and this in turn generates varying degrees of polarization at different times and places. The dwindling reputation of scientific experts in the US and Europe today is in marked contrast with the situation in India and China, for example. No doubt it reflects a degree of popular estrangement from the system of mathematical relations as abstract functions.

This trend disguises another—the commonplace resort to number as a measure of magnitude in the everyday speech of some segments of Western society. This became clearer to me after I became a semi-detached member of francophone society a decade ago. Reduced to the unaccustomed role of being an observer more than a participant, I was amazed by how often numbers turned up in ordinary conversation. What year was that? How old is she? How much does the baby weigh? How tall is the toddler? How many gigabytes in that laptop? What size shoes do you take? How many liters to fill up the car? How long do you expect to be out? How many days of holiday do you get? What is the temperature outside? Not to mention, of course, how much does he make? How much does it cost? And so on and so on. Of all of the areas where quantity is ingrained in social life, money and time are the most important.

In addition to locating a phenomenon on a universal scale of measurement, number fixes description and narrative in a way that we often find compelling. Thus, when I speak to someone of my father's recent death, number helps to make the unfathomable concrete, yet comparable at the same time. ("How old was he?" "92." "Oh, he had a good life then…") Have you noticed how, when a lecturer says he is about to make a fixed number of points, people reach for their pens? Number gets our attention. I once read an article in *Scientific American* that said, "If transport technologies had developed at the rate of computers since 1945, we would now be able to fly round the world in 30 minutes for $5 on half a gallon of kerosene." This analogy is comprehensible and vividly memorable to all inmates of the culture. We certainly seem to "trust in numbers" (Porter 1996), not so much any more in the hands of economists and engineers, but as a crutch to understanding or a point of emphasis in our stories and conversations. If anthropologists could shake off their denial of being numerate, we might pose serious questions about how far this number fetish has penetrated other societies and how legitimate it is to impose the contrived quantities of experts on them. We might ask how the West's historical turn to abstraction relates to cultural variation in the resort to number as a way of demarcating phenomena perceptible to the senses.[6]

Most of these numbers, and certainly money prices, indicate "value" (Graeber 2001). The use of money to indicate personal worth cannot be underestimated, if we wish to understand its persuasiveness. Even if CEOs often exercise their power invisibly, they also award themselves huge salary increases as part of a latter-day potlatch competition.[7] They are less interested in their own purchasing power than in assigning magnitude to their rank in the league tables published by business magazines. With few rivals, money is the measure that endows the endless volatility of economic life with objectivity, with the finality of something that has become. This is so independently of its form. For, paradoxically, the dematerialization of money as a result of the rise of virtual economy seems not to have diminished its power to objectify.

Meaning, Memory, and Identity

Conventionally, money and meaning are an oxymoron. Money both is and is not like language. Language has words that have specific meanings, but money itself has no meaning or, let us say, because it is abstract, it can become any meaning. Money, unlike words, allows us to turn anything in particular into what is ours, so that personal identity can become anything through money. Money allows us to speak any language of meanings, but the reverse is not the case. Hence, anthropologists have often held that the introduction of western money into indigenous cultures destroys their distinctive local meanings, a claim that I and others have challenged (Hart 2005a; Guyer 2004). Here, I argue for a close historical relationship between money and meaning that links it to language in distinctive ways.

The word *money* comes from Moneta, a name by which the Roman queen of the gods, Juno, was known. It was in her temple that coins were struck, making it an early example of a *mint* (from Old English *mynet,* coin). Most European languages retain the word "money" for coinage, using another word for money in general. Moneta was a translation of the Greek Mnemosyne, the goddess of memory and mother of the Muses, each of whom presided over one of the nine arts and sciences. It was derived from the Latin verb *monere*, whose first meaning is "to remind, put in mind of, bring to one's recollection" (other meanings include: "to advise, warn, instruct or teach"; and later, "to tell, inform, point out, announce, predict").[8] For the Romans at least, money was an instrument of collective memory needing divine protection, like the arts. As such, it was both a memento of the past and a sign of the future.

Money conveys meanings and the meaning of money itself tells us a lot about the way we make the communities we live in. In *Frozen Desire*, James Buchan suggests that money is principally a vehicle for the expression of human wishes. In order to realize our limitless desires, they are trapped for a moment, frozen in money transactions that allow us to meet others in society who are capable of satisfying them.[9]

> Money is one of those human creations which make concrete a sensation, in this case a sensation of wanting... Quite early in its history, money ... passed from being a mere conveyance of desire to the object of all desire... For money is incarnate desire. Money takes wishes ... and broadcasts them to the world... [It] offers a reward that is not in any sense fixed or finite ... but that every person is free to imagine in the realm of his own desires. That process of wish and imagination, launched or completed a million times every second, is the engine of our civilization. (1997: 269)

This rhetorical framing of money as a vehicle for human subjectivity does not go far enough. Like the economists of our day, Buchan emphasizes the wants of individuals and the way these are made temporarily objective in acts of buying and selling. Money also expresses something social, about the way we belong to each other in communities. We need to understand better how we build the infrastructures of collective existence, money among them. How do meanings come to be shared and memory to transcend the minutiae of personal experience?

The eighteenth-century Neapolitan philosopher, Giambattista Vico (1984), pointed out that the Latin word *memoria* once meant not only remembering, but also imagination. Then, with the coming of the empire, a new word, *fantasia*, was coined by intellectuals and entertainers who claimed to make things up without benefit of the collective memory, thereby breaking the link between the two meanings of *memoria*. He asks us to recall the vivid memories of childhood. The child relies on remembered images to bring live experiences to mind and reshape them in a process that owes nothing to reasoning. Later, we learn to rely on rationalizations and on memory stored in containers outside the mind. The rules we have been taught to abide by supersede the act of remembering for ourselves. We pay entertainers to imagine for us. Money gives expression to the child in each of us, by venting our desires. It is also how we learn as adults to participate in normal society.

This was why memory played such an important part in John Locke's philosophy of money (Caffentzis 1989). When market transactions take place over time, as through the extension of credit, the abstract models of economics take on greater human and social complexity. Locke's theory of property rested on the idea of a *person* who, by performing labor on the things given to us in common by nature, made them his own.

> Man, by being master of himself and proprietor of his own person, and the actions and labour of it, has still in himself the great foundation of property. (Locke 1960: 2, 44)

But, in order to sustain a claim on his property through time, that person has to remain the same; and personal identity depends on consciousness:

> Since consciousness always accompanies thinking, and it is that which makes everyone to be what he calls self, ... in this alone consists personal identity, *i.e.*, the sameness of a rational being: and as far as this consciousness can be extended backwards to any past action or thought, so far reaches the identity of that person; it is the same self now it was then. (Locke, *An Essay on Human Understanding*, cited in Caffentzis 1989:53)

Property must endure in order to be property and that depends on memory.

> The great enemy of property is oblivion, since the loss of conscious mastery over time and succession leads inevitably to the breakdown of property. Thus the forces of oblivion are antagonistic to the self and property, while all the techniques of mnemonics are their essential allies. (Caffentzis 1989: 53–54)

What drove society from the state of nature to the social contract and civil government was the invention of money.

> Scarcity, for Locke, is not natural. It was only with the invention of money that wealth stopped being defined and bounded by use. With money a man could own more land and produce more than he needed for his own necessities. While still abiding by the natural law, he could accumulate wealth in a quasi-eternal form which he need not share with others.... Money trains its possessor, whether legal or illegal, in abstractness as well as in the potential infinity of satisfaction. The accumulation of money is thus the exercise of our power to suspend our determination, which is for Locke the highest expression of our liberty, before an infinity of choices. (Caffentzis 1989: 65–66)

Money thus expands the capacity of individuals to stabilize their own personal identity by holding something durable that embodies the desires and wealth of all of the other members of society. Money is a "memory bank" (Hart 2000), a store allowing individuals to keep track of those exchanges they wish to calculate, and, beyond that, a source of economic memory for the community. Memory banks are found in computers, of course, but the idea of a "bank" is the relatively stable deposit of fast-moving flows, whether of water, money or information.[10] The modern system of money provides individuals with a vast repertoire of instruments to keep track of their exchanges with the world and to calculate the current balance of their worth in the community. In this sense, one of money's chief functions is *remembering*.

People come to understand each other as members of communities; and money is an important vehicle for this. *Communities communicate common meanings*. These words share the Indo-European roots *kom* (with) and *mei*, which the *American Heritage Dictionary* glosses as "to change or move, with derivatives referring to the exchange of goods and services within a society as regulated by custom or law." The word *mean* also has the sense of "low or poor," the common people as seen by an elite looking down. Other senses include "medium" or "average" (to which is linked to *means*, "method of achieving something or property/wealth") and the verb from which *meaning* is derived, "to denote, signify, intend, bring about." Thus, the common people share meanings (cultural symbols) as a means of achieving their practical purposes together.

So money is a means, but it is also an end; and one of its ends may be to express all meanings and none. Money no longer persuades primarily as a concrete way of inducing people to sell what is theirs, if it ever did. It persuades through its potential control of meaning in general. Money can be held over time and lets us defer commitment to any particular meaning. It works something like a dictionary.[11] It is in this sense a memory bank; but it also allows us to erase memories, by temporarily emptying our mind of particular meanings. Money's value could be said to lie in its having no immediate value beyond its ability to valorize anything later. As Buchan suggests, this is one reason for money's centrality in the modern imagination. Advertising plays on our fantasies by offering an escape from the everyday and it is money that allows this. Money supports the retention of memories, but it also lends itself to their destruction, by allowing us to generate new meanings.

All of this feeds into the changing landscape of identity construction. If wealth was always a marker of identity, then the shift to wealth in the immaterial form of money, a process speeded up and expanded by the rise of the internet, contributes to the growing volatility of identity. Once, fixed or "real" property was dominant as a marker of identity, but this function has now been split between value realized in consumption (e.g., Bourdieu 1984) and hierarchies of value expressed as abstract quantities. Money is intrinsic to both of these and credit ratings are an increasingly powerful gauge of personal identity.

In this way, money defines each of us by articulating the relationship between individuals and their communities. One of the great unsettled questions of our day is whether the strong association of community with the nation-state is being eroded by current developments or the opposite is the case. The nation-state has enjoyed such tremendous success over the last century or two that we find it difficult to imagine society in any other form. I identify four ideal types of community, all of them exemplified by the synthetic notion of the nation-state (Munro and Hart 2000). The nation-state has been a *political community*, capable of offering its citizens a single vehicle for relating to the world outside, as well as the framework of law regulating their internal affairs. It has been a *community of place*, resting on territorial principles of association with definite boundaries of land and sea. It has also been an *imagined* or *virtual community*, a constructed cultural identity relying on symbolic abstraction of a high order. It has finally been a *community of interest*, in both the subjective and objective senses, uniting members in trade and war by a shared purpose.

Establishing control over money was always a principal means toward achieving this synthesis. The general principle of states monopolizing the supply of paper or *fiat* money is quite recent, although it was pioneered by Kublai Khan in the thirteenth century (Weatherford 1997: 125–27). But the nation-state, by centralizing society as a single agency and conflating that with the dominant idea of national community, has led us to lose sight of the potential of money to be plural, and its ability to link us to all of the forms of association we may wish to join (Hart 2006). The rise of the internet makes it less plausible than before to assume that community is singular and stops at national borders.

The recent introduction of a new currency, the euro, allows us a contemporary glimpse of money's symbolic role in defining and shaping collective identity, in this case the European Union (Hart 2005a). An editorial under the heading "Rubicon" in the French newspaper, *Libération*, celebrated the introduction of euro notes and coins on 1 January 2002 as a revival of the spirit of the Roman Empire:

> Caesar's march on Rome was the founding act of a *Pax Romana* that extended the empire for several centuries from one end of Europe to the other, guaranteeing prosperity and civilization to the continent. The Europeans have never completely forgotten that golden age… The euro, a genuine icon of the European Union, is the new reincarnation of an eternal project of unification for an old continent haunted by its long history of bloody conflicts…
> (*Libération* 1 January 2002: 3)

Moneta returns to claim her cultural legacy and a left-wing newspaper temporarily abandons its republicanism to invoke the idea of empire. If money is memory, then the euro provokes very long memories indeed, as well as a degree of amnesia. The promise of overcoming the fragmentation of sovereignty inherited from feudalism is the huge symbolic prize conferred by monetary union. The citizens of Berlin, Rome, and Paris notice that the banknotes are the same in all of these places and derive notions of community and identity from that, just as they may sometimes be seen in bars checking the national origin of coins and expressing wonder that the Irish harp should be freely circulating in Continental Europe. Nothing quite succeeds as well as money in expressing political community; but that does not mean that the nation-state's monopoly is eternal.

Money is intimately linked to democracy as a political principle. This is because its impersonality dissolves differences between people: anyone can use it for their own purposes in the same way. It is not false to claim that we vote with our money whenever we buy a cinema ticket or a loaf of bread. But, of course, this system of voting is wildly unequal, since some have so much more of it. Money thus not only binds individuals together; it also separates them from each other. As an engine of class inequality, it has often been held to disrupt community. Seen from the perspective of its embodiment in capitalism as a specific social form, money breeds and enhances social differentiation; and that is why utopian communities of all sorts have sought to ban it. The Cold War was fought over this issue. The Americanization of the planet is at one level the universal projection of their way of money,[12] with its extreme individualization, competitiveness, and inequality, to the point of undermining national forms of state and culture elsewhere. Many feel that money's social dominance is now guaranteed as a result; but another global economic crisis would soon undermine abstract money's invincibility.

Spengler Revisited

These attempts to explain money's persuasive power have led me to an author whose work is hardly respectable these days. In *The Decline of the West*, Oswald Spengler ([1918] 1962) emphasized the part played by money and number in the history of Western European civilization and its North American offshoot.[13] The first idea I draw from him is that money is just one of several abstract universals of which number, time, and space may be more relevant than language. The second is that, for all their apparent universality, these should be approached as cultural particulars with their own historical patterns of growth and decline. Third, world history in our period has been dominated by the

West owing to its adoption of a specific form of economic life, based on money and machines, that normally goes by the name of "capitalism." Fourth, rather than adopt a timeless form of words for what interests us today, we should embrace the dialectic of "becoming and become," in order to understand both the immanent direction of our present circumstances (history) and their finitude[14] as the residue of what has already happened, the past (nature). So, finally, the question of money's persuasive power is historically and geographically relative: we need to attend to the relationship between the measurement of money as something perceptible to the senses (magnitude) and money as a category of thought expressed intangibly as abstract relations (function).

According to Spengler, the West had exhausted the historical impulse given by its modern version of economic life (featuring money and machines) and a new phase, based on politics, national religion, and war, was about to take over. This was not a bad prediction, but Spengler's interest for us lies in how he conceived of the relationship between money and other universals. I refer here to the beginning and end of the abridged English translation, "The meaning of numbers" (Spengler [1918] 1962: 41–69) and "The form-world of economic life: money and the machine" ([1918] 1962 : 398–415).

Following Goethe, Spengler made a contrast between history (becoming) and nature (what has become). The counterpart of *longing,* of the desire to move forward that is becoming, is the *dread* of having become, of finality or death; and this pair together drive cultural creativity.

> Life, perpetually fulfilling itself as an element of becoming, is what we call "the present", and it possesses that mysterious property of "direction", which men have tried to rationalize by means of the enigmatic word "time". (Spengler [1918] 1962 : 41)

On the one hand, there is measurement of time as duration; but the idea of history as becoming, as irreversible direction, is particular to the West. Number belongs to nature as the chief sign of completed demarcation, of all things that have become themselves.

> Mathematical number contains in its very essence the notion of a *mechanical demarcation,* number being in that respect akin to *word,* which ... fences off world-impressions. (Spengler [1918] 1962: 43, original italics)

Spengler identifies a break between classical antiquity and the modern West. For the Greeks, number is *magnitude,* the essence of all things perceptible to the senses. Mathematics for them was thus concerned with measurement in the here and now, visible and tangible. "Numbers are symbols of the mortal" (Spengler [1918] 1962: 52). All of this changed with Descartes, whose new number idea was *function*—a world of relations between points in abstract space. Whereas the Greeks sought perfection within the concrete limits of nature and society as they experienced them, now a passionate Faustian tendency toward the infinite took hold, married to abstract mathematical forms that increasingly freed themselves from concrete reality in order better to control that reality. The new mathematics was thus immaterial, resting on abstract analysis, dissociated from magnitude, and transferred to a transcendental relational world, a process culminating in "victory over the popular and sensuous number-feeling in us all" (Spengler [1918] 1962: 56).

> The nexus of *magnitudes* is *proportion,* that of *relations* is *function* ... All proportion assumes the constancy, all transformation the variability of the constituents ... Every *construction* affirms, and every *operation* denies appearances, in that one works out what is optically given and the other dissolves it.... The classical mathematic of small things deals with the concrete *individual instance* and produces a once-for-all construction, while the mathematic of the infinite handles whole *classes* of formal possibilities, *groups* of functions, operations, equations, curves ... [T]here has been growing up *the idea of a general morphology of mathematical operations.* (Spengler [1918] 1962: 63-64, original italics)

Western mathematics is "the copy and the purest expression of the idea of the Faustian soul" (Spengler [1918] 1962: 68). This leap from a geometry of the concretely real to a world of pure relations was mediated by the algebra of the "Magian" Arabs (and, we may add, by the Indian discovery of the number zero).

Spengler returns to this theme when considering "the form-world of economic life." Economics is British, materialistic, and has no room in it for a notion of the national soul. There has been a shift, parallel to that in mathematics, from thinking in terms of goods to thinking in terms of money.

> [A] form of limit-defining is abstracted from the visible objects of economics just as mathematical thought abstracts something from the mechanistically conceived environment. Abstract money corresponds exactly to abstract number. Both are entirely inorganic. The economic picture is reduced exclusively to quantities, whereas the important point about "goods" has been their quality. (Spengler [1918] 1962: 404)

He points to the widespread confusion between pieces of money, the value-token, and money as a category of thought. In fact, tangible property has been replaced by fortune, a purely numerical quantum of money that is mobile and undefined. The middleman elevates mediation between producer and consumer to the level of monopoly and ultimately primacy. "He who commands this mode of thinking is the master of money." The result, citing G.B. Shaw, is that money and life "are inseparable: money is the counter that enables life to be distributed socially: it *is* life." "Every idea, to be actualized, has to be put into terms of money" (Spengler [1918] 1962: 406–7).

The Apollonian idea of money as magnitude (which is classical) and the Faustian conception of money as function are opposites.[15] "Classical man saw the world surrounding him as a sum of bodies; money is also a body" (talents, coins) (Spengler [1918] 1962: 407). With the rise of double-entry bookkeeping, economic function became not even the ledger entry, but the act of writing it. When a businessman signs a piece of paper to mobilize remote forces, this gesture stands in an abstract relationship to the power of labor, machinery, etc., which only takes the form of money numbers in a retrospective accountancy process. In this way, western economic life was progressively emancipated from the notion of magnitude. Modern money is the result of creative thinking, mentally devised as an instrument of Faustian life. Thinking in money generates money. It turns the world into subjects and objects, consisting of a few executives and the many who follow them. Each individual is either a part of the money force or just a mass."And so they created the idea of the machine as a small cosmos obeying the will of man alone" (Spengler [1918] 1962: 411). Spengler concludes with a prophecy that the world of money and machine-industry will be overthrown by "blood" as the dominant life principle; and at this point we leave him. But his framework contains much of value for an analysis of the conscious and unconscious influence of money on our actions today.

Spengler points to the important relationship of money to time, specifically as a *promise* to pay in future. This obligation, as is well known, is of uncertain value (Pritchard 1940). It therefore requires *belief* for the promise to work; and this may take the form of faith, trust or confidence (Hart 1988). The degree of our emotional attachment to a belief is inversely related to the empirical evidence for holding it, strong in the case of "blind faith," weak for "open-eyed confidence," with "trust" somewhere in between. Money therefore always exists in time as something apparently certain, yet deeply uncertain. It appears in society temporally both as "work," a tangible principle of scarcity (magnitude), and as a principle of virtual increase, "interest" (function). The payment of money, like words and numbers, fixes the transience of life and lends it a certain finality.[16] But, in the historical form of modern capitalism, money also makes a break with the object-world and becomes the aspiration to infinite growth. The power of money to mobilize resources at a distance is commanded by only a few—once the "captains of industry," now in the age of finance, "masters of the universe"—while the masses experience money mainly as the immediate consequences of an anonymous force organizing their lives. Spengler's argument that magnitude was replaced by function in Western history would serve our purposes better if conceived of as an ongoing dialectical relationship. In this context, we must also acknowledge the machine revolution of the last two centuries, the latest stage of which involves perhaps the most dramatic transformation of money to date, its digital separation from material existence (from atoms to bits) as a virtual artifact of the internet.[17]

While this development, linked to widespread acceptance of "neoliberal" economic policies by ruling elites, has generated unheard of disparities of wealth within and between communities, it may also contain the seeds of a democratization of money, in the sense that powers, hitherto exercised only by a wealthy few,[18] may become diffused by degrees into the population at large. For some time now, since Keynes (1936) in fact, it has been acknowledged that modern economies are driven by consumer demand or the "purchasing power" of ordinary people in the mass. As a result of the extension of instruments of personal credit in the digital age, this power may be realized by individuals to an ever-greater degree (Hart 2000). Perhaps this helps to explain why persuasion is now largely directed at separating consumers from their money rather than from the goods they produce.

Money and Persuasion

Money is the primary vehicle of social abstraction, lending objectivity to our ideas, actions, and status. Only idealists think that retreating to some higher realm of abstract value is the goal itself. Money is a means to many ends, but in capitalist societies it often seems that money is the end, and not just a means. It is easy to lose sight of the common human purposes it was designed to realize and of the myriad particular actions it makes possible. To paraphrase Marx on the method of political economy in the introduction to *Grundrisse* (1973), we start from the concrete circumstances we live in, develop some abstractions after it, and then insert them back into the concrete circumstances, which is the main point of it all. In this respect, we need to learn from and improve on structural linguistics.[19] Grammar is at the heart of language; it is both universal and highly variable, operating for the most part at an unconscious level. Can we talk even vaguely about the grammar of money and, if so, what would it look like? It may be profitable to explore money's rules and how they are understood, consciously or unconsciously. But the structuralist movement elevated the generation of universal grammars to a position of precedence over concrete communication; and, it should be the other way around. The grammar of structural codes must be complemented by a grammar of usage in which the potentiality of meanings is temporarily fixed in speech events, as in money transactions. The reflexivity of money and language as signifying practices is formalized by a grammar of usage.[20] The danger then is to lose sight of structure in a morass of detail. It is easy to get stuck at one pole or the other of the dialectic.[21]

The central role of persuasion or rhetoric in economy was understood by those who have most influenced our economic ideas and behavior. Thus, Adam Smith (1762) spent fifteen years lecturing on rhetoric and left instructions in his will for these lectures to be destroyed, presumably so that his *Wealth of Nations* (1776), the founding text of economic science, would not be seen as the self-conscious literary artifact that it is.[22] Gudeman (1986) argues that David Ricardo (1817) was able to establish the hegemony of his own approach to economics because his "derivational" model was more a self-conscious cultural construction than a realistic depiction of economic life in his time. This model depended for its effectiveness on reproducing established western logical forms and, at least initially, on collapsing the difference between the physical and social dimensions of an economy poised between agriculture and manufacturing. Maynard Keynes likewise devoted a dozen years to his *Essays in Persuasion* (1932), trying to get across one simple message—that economic recovery would only come when the Victorian recipe of saving for capital accumulation was abandoned. His mantra was "Spend, don't save. Spend, don't save." More than any sophisticated academic treatise, such as the *General Theory* (1936), this rhetorical project accounts for the eventually favorable reception of his ideas. Now that we have all absorbed his message, the time is probably ripe for another one.

Even so, it is Smith's project that should most engage us here. Endres (1991) provides a detailed account of how the compositional rules laid down in Smith's *Lectures on Rhetoric* were applied in the writing of *The Wealth of Nations*. But Bazerman (1991) goes further toward explaining how he was able to influence modern thinking so thoroughly; and Bazerman makes an explicit connection between Smith's general approach and the persuasive power of money.

> If philosophy is near the pinnacle of the division of labour, for Smith persuasion is at its basis, for persuasion is what makes barter possible. (Bazerman 1991: 188)

> Money becomes a symbolic repository of material value with the added suasive effect of interchangeability, fairness of measure and consistency of value…. (Bazerman 1991: 189)

> In Smith's system … words and other symbolic systems are subordinated to the primary symbolic system of finance, because as a least common denominator, money forms the surest grounds for shared social meanings … Words serve to help persuade people of deals … and provide ideology and instructions for the economic order. But money provides the grounding of value….

> [M]athematicizing of economics only takes this reduction one step further. Money—countable and therefore open to complex mathematical representations and manipulations—becomes the primary mediational tool of social relations. (Bazerman 1991: 194)

> People loved money before Smith, but now they had an ideology, rationale and calculus for it. (Bazerman 1991: 195)

The problem of persuasion lies at the core of any attempt to change the forms of money today. I have explored the potential of community currencies in today's world (Hart 2006).[23] Given the cultural longevity of conventional money and the powers of indoctrination held by ruling institutions, it is not surprising that most people are initially reluctant to embrace community currencies; but the situation is psychologically complex. On the one hand, conventional money flatters our sense of self-determination: with some money, we can exert power over the world at will, moving from infinite potentiality to finite determination, and back and forth. On the other hand, there is another kind of comfort in the notion that money, as presently constituted, is not in our control at all. The fact that it embodies an exogenous force of necessity serves, in a manner analogous to number, to generate clarity of judgment and action where otherwise things might be frighteningly wide open. Similarly, with community currencies, people would not only be freer, but would have greater responsibilities also.

There is a strong parallel with slavery. People feel that the monopoly claimed by national money must be inevitable, since no one would freely choose it. To be told there is an alternative that they could choose makes nonsense of a lifetime's enslavement to an unrewarding system. So they cling to what they know as the only possibility. We often talk about wanting to be free, but we choose the illusion of freedom without its real responsibility. This is perhaps why we prefer money not to be of our own making. We spend it, but we never have enough of it because "they" keep it scarce. This is perhaps the underlying reason why eminently sensible schemes for do-it-yourself money get such a poor reception. It is not enough to develop a superb design for exchange circuits employing community currencies. People have to be sold the idea; and this involves engaging with their most cherished beliefs.[24]

For all of the temporary success of nation-states in persuading their captive populations to ignore what goes on elsewhere, it is the case that people's experience of money today is as much global as it is local. In this respect, there is clearly an "elective affinity" (Goethe again) between capitalism and the English language. This could merely be a consequence of the recent domination of the world economy by Britain and the United States; or the cultural association could have been established earlier.[25] In succession and together, they have made English the world language, a role that is becoming more deeply entrenched as a result of the internet. If the word "economy" was invented by the Greeks, it is the English-speakers who made it central to our understanding of modern society (Hann and Hart forthcoming). Economics is an English discourse (as Spengler noted): the vast majority of Nobel prize-winners in economics are English-speakers, indeed, American. Certainly, English is the international language of business. All of this is historically relative: world production and capital accumulation now seem to be moving inexorably toward countries like China, India, Russia, and Brazil. Even so, despite the palpable evidence of economic decline there, the United States—and its west coast in particular—is still the place where exploitation of the moneymaking implications of the digital revolution in communications is advancing fastest and furthest.

It is too soon[26] to make out how money, markets, and digital information are interacting through the medium of the internet. The latter enhances the dematerialization and cheapening of monetary transactions. In the short run, this seems to have increased money's persuasive power in world society, but the long run effect may be to dilute money's significance. Thus, it is an observable consequence of experiments with community currencies that, once money loses its scarcity, the real purposes of exchange in communities take precedence over the idea of getting more for less (Hart 2006; North 2006). Moreover, the dissemination of massive amounts of information at little or no cost makes it easier to keep track of the transaction histories of specific individuals, a contradictory process that I have referred to as "repersonalization" (Hart 2000). Taken much further than at present, these trends might lead to the uncoupling of money from the numerical values assigned to it by the state. People would be free to make up their own world-algebra, employing constraints appropriate to themselves, whether as individuals or in communities of their own design. We might then be able to talk about the emergence of "people's money," a true democracy rather than the apology for inequality we are stuck with now.

Digital information is itself also both a means and an end, in the sense that people get in return the same thing that they give. The difference between conventional money and digital information is that the latter is reproducible by anyone at virtually no cost and without removing the original. This underlies the extraordinary effort now being made by the West's media corporations to promote the idea that copying digital products is theft, even "piracy" (Hart 2005b). The result is an ongoing war between rival systems of exchange—corporate private property (with its origins in the seventeenth century) and the "free and open source software" movement (FOSS) that has grown up only in the last two decades. It would be surprising if this contradiction did not lead to new combinations of money and exchange; and, indeed, experiments with alternative forms of money point in that direction. In the meantime, a massive propaganda campaign is aimed at persuading us that cloning or remixing a text, song or movie is like "stealing my cow."

Conclusions

In *Money and the Morality of Exchange* (Parry and Bloch 1989), an excellent collection of anthropological essays, a convincing case is made that, for many of the world's peoples, money lacks the apparent autonomy it enjoys in the West and is usually subordinated to the long-term social purposes of groups. I have drawn on Spengler here to highlight the cultural sources of such a contrast. In capitalist societies, money has come to define an infinite field of possibilities and, within that field, has acted to create groups of relationships between abstract entities, as well as to increase practical control over innumerable social activities. Modern money only connects with concrete magnitudes after it has created this relational network. The realistic image of money as concrete number is a somewhat illusory formulation of its social significance, an instance perhaps, in Whitehead's (1925) phrase, of "the fallacy of misplaced concreteness." Those anthropologists, who reject the higher-order abstraction that quantification makes possible in order to embrace particular cultural meanings as indicators of quality, are giving voice to a deep-seated mistrust of the idea that money is somehow isomorphic with its own concrete properties. Nevertheless, I have tried to show here why this one-sided rejection of money's dialectical unity is anachronistic.

It is relatively easy to debunk religion, but in order to understand its social force, one has to enter the minds of believers. Searching for the source of money's power to persuade is like asking how God gets us to believe in Him. Of course we made Him up, just as we made up and make up Money. Since all we can ever know is the past, why would anyone accept a claim to guarantee the unknowable future? But we do, because we have to—and faith is the glue sticking past and future together in the present. Simmel (1900) made a good case, I think, for why money is able to make this spurious claim. Because all of our ephemeral transactions are made in terms of it, it seems to be more stable than the rest, even though we know it really is not. The river bank seems to be solid and yet it is in reality just slower-moving deposits thrown up by the fast-moving water. But, if we are drowning, we settle for its presumptive stability. The physicist may have worked out what is going on at an abstract level, but for practical purposes, we do not need to know what he knows about the movement of particles.

In this chapter, I have for the most part taken at face value an idealist premise that money has a mind of its own, since it seems to me that most members of capitalist societies are caught in it. The very rich do not have to accept this premise, but they are happy for the rest of us to believe in the story of our own captivity. I want us all eventually to have what the rich have—the creative ability to manipulate money. Hence, I have tried to discover something here of what they know about money and what stops the masses from catching on. This has also meant excavating my own socialization as a dupe of the existing money system who has spent his life trying to escape from it. It is easier to embrace a rationalist or materialist alternative than to give credit to this murky stuff, learnt at my mother's knee in the age of austerity. Spengler helped me to begin to understand some of my own irrational attitudes towards money. Why do I find it so hard to fill in tax returns or travel claim forms? Because being fixated on money as magnitude is a way of killing off the drive to grasp its infinite potential.

Money is the ocean we swim in these days. Despite or because of this, its role in human affairs continues to be demonized and the attempt to return it to the marginal role it was confined to in agrarian civilizations always finds a ready audience (Polanyi 1957). The question of where money's persuasive power comes from is probably unanswerable as such. Perhaps one answer lies in its rhetorical ability to bring lexis and logos uneasily together, if only to veer from one to the other. Money surely generates value and significance in human interactions as much as it erodes it. It is a symbol of our relationship as an individual person to society (hitherto more often singular than plural). This relationship may be conceived of as a durable ground on which to stand, anchoring identity in a collective memory whose concrete symbol is money. Or it may be viewed as the outcome of a more creative process in which we each generate the personal credit linking us to society.[27] The potential for shifting meanings, identities, and memories lies in the reflexivity of money and language. This latter outlook, however, requires us to abandon the notion that society rests on abstract grounds that are more solid than the transient exchanges we participate in. Few people at present are prepared to take that step, preferring to receive the money they live by, rather than make it. When the meaning of money is seen to be what each of us makes of it, we may be less inclined to think of Money as the somewhat archaic God of capitalism that it has become. Maybe, in the long run of human evolution, it will turn out that money is just a tool, as Simmel said; but, for now, it often seems that the tool does the talking.

Notes

I am grateful to Steve Gudeman, Huon Wardle, Kal Applbaum, Ingrid Jordt, Bill Murphy, Sandy Robertson, John Tresch, William Mazzarella, Eduardo Gianetti, Jeff Morrow, Aram Yengoyan, Roger Sansi-Roca, Johan Fredriksson, Chris Hann, Alan Thorold and Ivo Strecker for their help.

1. "Selling Malcolm X," BBC Radio 4, 7 February 2005.
2. Bill Maurer (2006), reviewing recent work on money from a position within a US American cultural anthropology that saturates everything with meaning, emphasizes rather the pragmatics of money, or what money does, a strategy that I partially follow here.
3. It is so widely believed that, for many, it is not a myth at all, but part of the bedrock of economic knowledge. I have spelled out my reasons for designating it as myth in Hart (2000: 267–68) and (2005a).
4. This mediation is semiotic (Mertz and Parmentier 1985), whereby the potentiality of codes of meaning is realized in processes of finite money transactions.
5. This connection is explored at length in Shell (1986). His *The Economy of Literature* (1978), especially the discussion there of writing and money as "invisible" social forces placing strain on the "visible" human relations made by the contract (*symbolon*), has long been a source of inspiration for me (Hart 2000: 53–54).
6. Thomas Crump, a follower of Simmel, has been a pioneer both of the anthropology of money (1981) and of number (1990). In an article bringing money, number, and language together, Crump (1978) suggests that money achieved a cultural transformation in colonial Mexico that religion could not, partly because numbers are the most abstract of words.
7. The principle is nothing new, as Thorstein Veblen (1899, 1904) made clear a century ago.
8. Sources include *The American Heritage Dictionary* (3rd edition), Lewis & Short's *Latin Dictionary*, and Buck's *Dictionary of Selected Synonyms in the Principal Indo-European Languages*. Silver (1992) argues that the main sense embodied in Moneta is one of warning and relates to trust and the duty not to abuse trust. See Silver generally on the gods as economic inputs.
9. This is a variant of Spengler's more dramatic dialectic of longing and dread (becoming and become, life and death).
10. This is why I named my website "The memory bank" (http://www.thememorybank.co.uk).
11. Toward the end of the seventeenth century, England, not least thanks to Locke's efforts, pioneered central banking and dictionaries of the national language at the same time.
12. See Oliven (1998) for an insightful description of a Brazilian anthropologist's encounter with California's system of money.
13. Huon Wardle referred me to Spengler. Spengler has largely disappeared from view, but he was a major source both for Ludwig Wittgenstein and for the author of the twentieth century's best-selling anthropological text, Ruth Benedict's *Patterns of Culture* (1934).
14. I take this expression, meaning relative position in time and space, from Heidegger's (1930) late metaphysics, which I have used elsewhere to explore the anthropology of the internet (Hart 2004).
15. For an extended treatment of Goethe's critique of industrial capitalism and the idea of Faust as a modern alchemist, see Binswanger's *Money and Magic* (1994).

16. Hence perhaps, Benjamin Franklin's claim that, "There is nothing certain in life beyond death and taxes."
17. It is important not to confuse a very rapid change in technique, the use of an electronic medium rather than paper and ink, for a much more gradual change in the fundamentals of money. One of the first steps in the transformation of money from a thing into information was recognition in Roman law of the validity of the banker's book. See also De Roover (1999) for further developments in medieval European banking.
18. The global number of the very rich is growing exponentially, encouraging resort by the corporate apologists for plutocracy to the anodyne acronym, HNWI or 'henwee', High Net Worth Individual.
19. The story of how de Saussure's (1916) distinction between *langue* and *parole* inspired not only modern linguistics, but also Lévi-Strauss's (1958) structural anthropology lies beyond the scope of this essay.
20. The idea of grammar as a structure of usage in social practice (Lucy 1993), rather than as a structure of signs (syntax), comes from Pierce (1985) and Wittgenstein (1958).
21. The analogy is much more general than a simple comparison between money and language. Molecular biology has given us genomics, but so far has not given an effective way of treating Alzheimer's. Algorithms in modern computing, such as Google's famous secret formula, likewise reveal their potential in use. We may not be interested in how we get 6,500,000 hits when we type in a phrase, even less in seeing all of those millions of entries. But we do need to develop practical methods for sorting the results and the algorithm itself would be of no value unless it permitted effective searches.
22. The lectures were discovered in the form of apparently complete student notes in the twentieth century and eventually published as Volume IV of the Glasgow omnibus edition (Smith 1985). See Endres (1991), Bazerman (1991).
23. See North (2006) for a theoretically aware and empirically grounded account of alternative currency movements. I am indebted to Michael Linton, inventor of LETS, one of the most successful varieties of community currency systems, for much of my knowledge in this area.
24. A "belief" meant in origin "something held dear," which is to say that exchanges involving money entail at some level a vision of humanity bound by mutual love. This is how the young Marx ends his remarkable essay on "The power of money" in the 1844 manuscripts: "If you love without evoking love in return, i.e. if you are not able, by the manifestation of yourself as a loving person, to make yourself a beloved person, then your love is impotent and a misfortune" (Marx 1844).
25. To take just one example, English has an impersonal possessive pronoun ("its"), which supports the fiction that corporations are legal persons (Hart 2005b). This feature originated in the seventeenth century, during England's political, commercial, and scientific revolutions, when the East India Company and the Bank of England were invented and the Mayflower expedition took place.
26. It is still little more than a decade since the internet began the transition from being a closed club for scientists, government officials, and the military to the global marketplace it is today. The changes that have occurred only since the diffusion of broadband after the millennium are unrecognizable when seen from the perspective of the dot com boom of the late 1990s.
27. Simmel makes this dialectical proposition the cornerstone of his *Philosophy of Money* (1900). His outlook has been the guiding thread on this journey.

CHAPTER 10

The Money Rhetoric in the United States

Ruby George Oliven

■ ■ ■ ■ ■ ■

The United States is frequently depicted as a country where monetization—the increase in the proportion of all goods and services bought and sold by means of money—has taken place. Money has become a central value, and commoditization has fully extended to all spheres of life. In this sense, it vindicates Marx's idea of the *Vergeldlichung* (monetization) of society. In reality, this process is much more complex, as Zelizer (1994) has shown when she argues that there are different sort of monies such as gift certificates, Christmas savings accounts, and food stamps.

Foreigners coming to the United States are frequently surprised about how explicit and pervasive money is in that country. Whereas in other societies there is frequently a diffident attitude toward money, in the United States money is a central question and part of day-to-day rhetoric. People are constantly speaking about money and measuring things and persons in monetary terms. "How much?" is therefore a natural and central question.

When I decided to go to the United States, where I spent a year and a half as a visiting professor in the Department of Anthropology of the University of California, Berkeley, North American scholars who knew my previous work suggested I should study some minority group in the San Francisco Bay Area, such as the Brazilians who live there in growing numbers. Because I had published a book on cultural diversity in Brazil (Oliven 1996), this would be the "natural" continuation of what I had been doing at home. Somehow the idea did not appeal to me. I came to the conclusion that this was what one would expect from a Brazilian anthropologist in the United States, i.e., that he or she should study the periphery in the center. As I had already worked on money in the lyrics of Brazilian popular music (Oliven 1997), it occurred to me that money would be a more fascinating subject. When I told North American anthropologists about my plan, they were usually enthusiastic about it, but tended to say it was a very broad subject. I was of course also concerned about the feasibility of my project. Actually, I had no idea on how to start it and where to focus my attention.

But from the moment I arrived in the United States (this was the first time I was staying a longer period of time in that country), I realized that money was around me all of the time and that I was literally submerged in my research topic and would have no difficulty finding material. I noticed people were constantly speaking about money and that most things were expressed through a monetary rhetoric.

Rhetoric here refers to how money is discussed and communicated and to its appearances outside the market as opposed to its "contents." Part of money's value lies in its pervasive and persuasive capacity as a vehicle of communication to express a variety of values, especially through metaphor and synecdoche.

Money is effective not only as a means of exchange, but mainly as a means of communication. It helps to mold and organize thought and action. Its effectiveness can be gauged through its persuasiveness. Money is persuasive in use, in talk, in understanding others, and in thinking about the self, and probably just thinking alone.

Money is a phenomenon that has simultaneous implications and is expressed in different dimensions of social life. Abstractly, it is a measuring rod for comparing things, a means by which they are exchanged and stored for holding value (see Hart's preceding essay), but what is the value that money "stores"? If Gudeman (this volume) looks at the power of market rhetoric and the way it cascades in theory and on the ground into other economic modes, I shall consider how the money form cascades into everyday life in the United States and becomes a vehicle for communicating local values.

Money is an integral part of North American culture and as such it is constitutive of social reality in the United States. It expresses the history, the life cycle, market participation, food, cleanliness, different regions of the country, the future, individualism, religious differences, race relations, and fundamental values of citizenship.

I soon realized that money in the United States could be looked at as a *total social fact*, to use Mauss's concept. Believing that money is a key to understanding North American society, I decided to look at any instance that could bring me clues: scholarly and non-scholarly articles, financial magazines, books on personal finance, proverbs, expressions, banks, investment companies, health insurance, service clubs, compulsive spenders, restaurants, and shops. Looking at the multifarious aspect of money in the United States, I ended up making North Americans my "tribe."

I am, of course, aware of the difficulties of the anthropologist dealing with complex societies and I do not want to sound ethnocentric in reverse by giving the impression that I believe that a complex society is nothing more than a simple society that has turned complex. I know there are important differences of scale. I know how difficult it is to generalize for so large a nation as the United States, which can be seen as having not one, but several, cultures. I am aware that the relation to money varies according to class, race, and gender, and other categories. I know also that California, the place I was living in, cannot be taken as representative of the whole of the US and I am well aware that a year and a half of observation might not be enough. But in spite of the difficulties of this sort of study, I believe it is important to look at the mainstream rhetoric of money that is widespread in the United States and to compare it to other countries.

My ethnography is presented in a specific style. In order to make the familiar strange, I have opted for the standpoint of a newcomer to another culture. I am looking at things that are normally taken for granted by North Americans, but which look quite different from my previous experience (Oliven 1998).

Opening a Bank Account and Finding Out that Ralph Emerson was Right

Ralph Waldo Emerson (1803–1882), frequently considered "the last puritan" (Santayana 1936; Porte 1979), lived a century later than Benjamin Franklin (1706–1790), "the apostle of modern times." He can be seen as a champion of the virtues of capitalism stressing the idea of thriftiness and free enterprise. In his essay, "Wealth," published in *The Conduct of Life,* he makes an apology for money when he says "The world is his, who has money to go over it" (Emerson 1983: 994). It is interesting that he relates wealth to nature. He argues that "Wealth is in applications of mind to nature; and the art of getting rich consists not in industry, much less in saving, but in a better order, in timeliness, in being at the right spot" (Emerson 1983: 989). He also stressed that, "Men of sense esteem wealth to be the assimilation of nature to themselves, the converting of the sap and juices of the planet to their incarnation and nutriment of their design" (Emerson 1983: 993). Emerson goes on in his analogy and argues that

> It is a doctrine of philosophy, that man is a being of degrees; that there is nothing in the world, which is not repeated in his body; his body being a

sort of miniature or summary of the world: then that there is nothing in his body, which is not repeated as in a celestial sphere in his mind: then, there is nothing in his brain, which is not repeated in a higher sphere, in his moral system. Now these things are so in Nature. All things ascend, and the royal rule of economy is, that it should ascend also, or, whatever we do must always have a higher aim. Thus it is a maxim, that money is another **kind of blood.** *Pecunia alter sanguis:* or, the estate of man is only a larger kind of body, and admits of regimen analogous to his bodily circulations. (Emerson 1983: 1010, emphasis added)

When I arrived in the United States, I decided to open a bank account with Bank of America. The representative who helped me asked what kind of current account I wanted. When I said I just wanted a simple checking account, she explained they had six checking accounts: the *Versatel Checking,* the *Standard Checking,* the *Interest Checking,* the *Alpha Account,* the *Prima Account,* and the *Limited Checking.* I asked her to advise me as to what type of account I should open. She said she could not decide that for me and showed the charges, the minimum balance required to avoid monthly charges, the outstanding features, and to whom each plan was recommended. I finally decided on the Standard Checking thinking I would then be rid of more decisions. The representative asked me for general information including my social security number, which of course I did not have. Then another unexpected decision: what sort of checkbooks would I like to have? In Brazil, banks usually have only one sort of checkbook. It might have different colors if you are considered a special client, but that is all. Nevertheless, in Bank of America you must choose whether you want a checkbook with or without a stub, or wallet style and what pictures you want on the check. I decided for the eagle because it is the symbol of the United States and I thought, "when in Rome, do as the Romans."

I must have looked pretty exhausted and confused at the end of the operation. Noticing it the bank representative said: "Don't worry: nothing is written in blood, you can always change your account plan."

Here we come full circle, the Bank of America's representative mirroring Emerson organic metaphor in spite of the fact that she probably did not read him. This made me think about the relation between money and blood. It also reminded me about pacts. As a matter of fact, several pacts involve blood. God demands the blood of circumcision when he makes a pact with Abraham; in *The Merchant of Venice,* Shylock lends money to Antonio on the condition that if the latter does not repay him, he is entitled to a pound of his flesh, but when he wants to take it he finds out he cannot have it because the bond does not entitle him to a jot of blood; the devil asks Faust to sign his pact with him in blood. Is money the blood that runs through the veins of US American society? Are you expected to enter in an implicit pact that involves money when you live in the United States?

Life, Love, Death, and Money

In the US, money is a matter that should not be taken lightly. A lot of time (and hence money) is devoted to financial matters. A leaflet of the Bank of America, *For Our Customers,* has an article called "Teach Your Children Lessons in Saving the Easy Way." Children are of course aware of the financial cost of things. I was visiting a US couple that had a teenager son. The conversation turned to children and the husband mentioned casually that maybe they should adopt a child. The teenager immediately reacted: "Dad, did you know that it costs 100,000 dollars to raise a child until he or she is eighteen?" It is interesting that the boy, feeling threatened by having to share his parents' love and attention, couched his fears in monetary terms.

There are several books that teach you how to administer your personal money. Bookstores frequently have several shelves under the section of *Personal Finance.* There are even books that teach you how to administer love and money. Actually, *Love and Money* is the title of a book (Porter 1985). It teaches you everything about this equation and has sections such as: "The Cost of Getting Married," "The Actual and Hidden Costs of Divorce," "Wills and Funeral Arrangements," "Taking your Spouse on a Business Trip," and "Maintaining a Mistress or a Male Lover." This particular section will teach you facts such as: "If you'd like to keep a mistress or a male lover, the most important thing to bear in mind is that it can be very expensive;" or "If you'd like to be a mistress or a male lover, the fundamental thing to remember is the extent of your rights in this capacity" (Porter 1985: 22).

The February 1994 issue of *Money* has an article written by the magazine's managing editor entitled, "The Cost of One Bullet: $2 Million." It starts by saying: "Looking at a bullet smaller than the tip of your pinkie, you wouldn't imagine that it could sever a man's spine, shatter a family, devastate a company and ultimately cost society more than $2 million. But that's what this 40 cents hollow-point bullet—and the .38 revolver it was fired from—did to David Johnstone, his family, his company and in fact to all of us" (Lalli 1994: 7). As one can imagine, the article tells a tragedy and the ordeal the victim (who died after some weeks of treatment) and his family went through because of a teenage mugger. It is well written and discusses, among other questions, gun control. But it is not only focused on suffering, loss, and grief. It is concerned about costs. And it decides to add up all of the expenses and damages involved, including hospital bills, air ambulance, social security, and worker's compensation, police investigation, juvenile sentencing hearing, prison costs, and productive years the victim had ahead of him.

An article that mixes money and a deceased person would be inconceivable in Brazil. Brazil has nevertheless extremely high rates of death related to work and traffic accidents, which reveal little concern about life. But there is a difficulty in Brazil of speaking about the social and economic costs of the injuries and deaths caused by the neglect that causes so many accidents.

Whenever there is natural disaster (earthquakes, hurricanes) in the United States, the news provide the number of casualties and, immediately after, the material loss in millions of dollars. There is a direct continuity from lives to dollars. Calculations are made as to how much the damage is and from where the money to repair it is going to come.

INVESTING

If you call Fidelity Investments, the US's largest stock fund manager, they send you a whole literature about how to invest. The *Fidelity Catalog* opens with a welcome from its chairman, who tells you that his father, who founded the enterprise in 1946, "was a strong individualist, and admired independence in others. But when it came to investing, he observed that everyone needs some help. Today, these ideas are still the foundation of our business. We believe that given the right tools, individuals make their own best investment decisions. After all, no one understands your situation better than you do" (Fidelity Investments n/d: 2). In sum: we can provide you with the information, but the decision is yours. In order to arrive at a decision, you should read the information, consider your time horizon, and analyze your needs. One of the main factors involved concerns the relation between risk and reward. As you are told, a rule of thumb is that "Risk and reward usually go together" (Fidelity Investments n/d: 15). You must also know for what you are investing: retirement, college expenses, building your savings, diversification, lower taxes, or alternatives to Certificates of Deposit.

One of the items in the literature is the *Fidelity Fund Match Workbook,* which comes with a worksheet that asks you twelve questions to which you attribute points. Depending on your final score, you fall in one of the following categories: 100 percent short-term portfolio, capital preservation portfolio, moderate portfolio, wealth-building portfolio, or 100 percent stock portfolio. Fidelity products and services are divided into Money Market Funds, Income Funds, and Growth Funds.

I made an appointment with a Fidelity financial representative at their San Francisco Investor Center and, for that purpose, filled in the worksheet. I was received by one of their brokers. He looked at my results, asked questions, gave me some information, and then asked me what sort of investments I had in mind. I mentioned a figure and he said I could divide it between conservative, moderate, and aggressive funds. The use of the word aggressive is interesting. Fidelity has *spartan* versions of many funds. They "offer the potential for higher returns through lower expenses." The military metaphor is present. Money is a war in which in order to win you have to be aggressive and spartan. But at the same time this war is highly unpredictable. You are always told that investing is like gambling. In a sense, the war takes place in a casino.

Money and Food

I was invited to give a talk on Brazil at a service club in a city of the San Francisco Bay Area. The person who invited me said that the club members knew very little about Brazil and would be interested in hearing what it is to live there—its social life, its economics, and its politics. Approximately twenty people attended the luncheon that took place at a hotel. It was held simultaneously as a formal meeting and a leisurely event. The president, after introducing the guests, started asking everybody to sing the national anthem and then to pledge allegiance to the flag. Then, the members started slowly to eat, but to my surprise, people got up and started to donate "happy dollars." It went like this: someone would stand up and say: "I finally got a telephone call through to Los Angeles [where an earthquake had taken place two days before] and learned that my relatives are all safe" and he would put a dollar in a small bowl. Another member of the club said a person who had stolen money from his business was finally convicted and put in jail and that he would donate a dollar for that. Another person donated a "happy dollar" for something pleasant that happened to him and a "sad dollar" because a relative of his was shot. While this was happening, people were eating and I could not stop thinking that in Brazil to mix money and eating in such a way would be considered strange. In Brazil, there are of course business lunches and political campaign dinners, but they avoid dealing directly with money, and money bills are not touched in these occasions.

During lunch, my host started asking me questions about Brazil and taking notes on them: when was Brazil discovered, what was the name of the discoverer, which were the two largest cities. I could not quite understand why he wanted to know all of that and I joked with him that if he gave all this information out to the public before I spoke, nothing would be left for me to talk about. When lunch finished, before introducing me, he started to ask the public the very questions he had asked me and he fined them a dollar for each wrong answer. I finally gave my talk and answered the questions that had been posed. At the end, I received a Certificate of Appreciation and an extra-large T-shirt that says: "I spoke at the X Club of X city and they loved me."

When you eat out with friends in Brazil, you usually split the bill according to the number of people who were present regardless of how much you eat or drink (in other words, there is no point in having less because you still will pay for what others had). In the United States, however, at the end of the meal frequently someone plays the role of the banker and goes into a great accountancy effort to figure out exactly who ate and drank what in order to have everybody pay exactly what he or she had. It is also interesting to see that in the US the *maître d'* will come to the table and announce what special dishes are being served that particular day. After he explains the dish, he immediately states the price, thus translating the pleasure principle into the reality principle. In Brazil, a waiter will not bring the bill until you ask for it. And then it probably will still take him a long time to do it. In the United States, waiters frequently bring you the bill, without being asked to, after you finish the main course, and sometimes without bothering to ask whether you want desert. To a Brazilian this reads more or less like a message saying, "You are on your way now, aren't you?" But my US friends to whom I commented about this said they tend to see it as positive attitude of the waiter, who is assuming that customers are frequently in a hurry and do not like waiting too long to pay their bill. Time is money!

The Cleanliness of Money

There are several expressions in the United States directly related to money. "To add my two cents to the discussion" means you want to voice your opinion regarding a subject that is being debated. "They don't buy it" means they do not agree or accept the idea. "I would put my money on this" means that this is what is going to happen in the future regarding a certain trend. "For one's money" means "according to one's preference or opinion" (Webster 1988: 1458). Thus, one could say: "For my money, the film is very good." A friend of mine, reading a research proposal I wrote for the United States, advised me that proposals are shorter in the US than in Brazil and that every sentence of a proposal must "sell" an idea. You must be assertive (or aggressive) in the statements you write in your proposal. And "a penny for your thoughts" implies that theoretically everything is for sale, including your most intimate feelings. In Brazil, you buy a discussion (*comprar uma discussão*) and you buy a fight (*comprar uma briga*), both having a conflictive meaning.

Whereas in the US money is explicit, in Brazil there is a diffident attitude toward it. In Brazil, to talk about money is frequently considered shameful. The polite way to ask for money there is "Can you lend some?" (*"Você pode me emprestar algum?"*). In the US, money is more easily seen as an integral part of the person—thus the saying, "Not a penny to my name." In the US, when referring to the amount of wealth a person owns, newspapers frequently use the expression "Mr. X is worth so many million dollars." In Brazil, one would not want to believe that a person could be defined by the money attached to him or her in spite of or because of the fact that social inequality is greater there.

In English you pay attention, you pay a visit, you pay a compliment, you pay your respect, you pay your way, and you pay lip service. In Brazil, you pay for your sins (*pagar seus pecados*) and you pay promises you made to a saint from whom you have asked for help (*pagar promessas*). Whereas in the United States you will ask a person if you can buy him or her a drink, in Brazil you would ask if you can get or offer someone a drink. In Brazil, asking if you can buy someone a drink would implicitly mean that you are trying to buy the person.

In Brazil, money is regarded as more polluting than in the US. Actually, in Brazil when a person is totally out of money, he or she is "clean" (*limpo*), or when a gang robs a bank, they "clean" it. But when a person is very wealthy, he or she is "rotten rich" (*podre de rico*), the equivalent of the US version, "stinking rich." In Brazilian slang the word *poupança* (savings) is used to refer to the buttocks. And when you are totally out of money, you can say: "I haven't got a whorish penny" (*"Estou sem um puto tostão"*).

In the US, however, poverty is filthier. In this respect, one can be "dirt poor." There are other expressions relating poverty to dirt in English: something can be "dirt cheap" (again, the dirt is in the lack, not in the abundance of money). On the other hand, "pay dirt" according to the dictionary is "earth containing enough ore to be profitably worked by a miner" or "something which turns out to be a valuable source of information" (Webster 1988: 738). Notice how money (gold) breeds from dirt. Referring to US society, Knight argues that, "Today poverty is recognized as an evil and money as the potential means of much good—of enjoying the arts, the education, travel, medical care, philanthropy, as well as the material necessities and comforts of life" (Knight 1968: 11).

Some US proverbs attest to the idea that money in America is seen as less dirty than, for example, in Brazil: "All money is clean, even if it's dirty," "Money doesn't get dirty" (Mieder 1991: 415), and "Money doesn't smell." Some proverbs compare money to feces, but the classical Freudian equation between these terms (Freud 1953; Ferenczi 1956) is weak. Thus, the parody "Money talks, bullshit walks" makes money the strong element and feces the weak one. The payment day is "when the eagle shits." Although here there is an association between money and feces, the animal providing people with money is not the filthy pig, but the eagle, the symbol of the United States. And there is an instance of a direct equation of money to feces: "Money is like manure: it's only good when spread around" (Mieder 1991: 416). But the element that is stressed is the fertilizing aspect of feces. Because in earth feces are not "matter out of place," to quote Douglas' (1966) expression, in this particular circumstance, money and manure cannot be considered dirty.

Actually, there is a strong incidence of US proverbs that lend a positive connotation to money. To give some examples: "Money talks," "Money makes the mare to go," "Make money honestly if you can, but make money," "Money is power," "Money is the sinews of trade," "Money must be made, or we should soon have the wolf at the door," "Nothing but money is sweeter than honey," and "Nothing makes money faster than money." There seem to be fewer negative proverbs about money. Among them are: "Money can't buy happiness" and "Money isn't everything." But even the biblical proverb "Money is the root of all evil," is frequently transformed into a parody negating its statement: "Money is the root of all wealth," "Money is the root of the Bank of America," "Money is the root of all evil and man needs roots," "Money is the root of all evil, but it does seem to grow some mighty fine plants," "Money is the root of all evil, but it's still number one as the root of all idylls," "Money is the root of all evil, but has anyone ever discovered a better route?," or "Money is the root of all evil and also of a good many family trees." In the same way "Money can't buy happiness" is transformed into "Happiness can't buy money." And "Money isn't everything" becomes "Money isn't everything, only half." "Virtue is its own reward" becomes "Money is its own reward" (Mieder 1989: passim).

Things are Different in the South of the United States

Ralph Emerson and Benjamin Franklin were born in Boston. Their attitudes toward money represent a more capitalist and northern view of a society based on free labor and the idea of the self-made man, giving equal possibilities to everybody. Analyzing southern folkways prior to the Civil War regarding money, Ogburn (1964), in an article originally published in 1943, shows that things were different in the Old South, which did not have a very developed money economy because farmers were mainly self-sufficient. According to him, although the South changed since the Civil War and money became much more widely used, "some ideas, characteristic of the days of self-sufficing plantation economy, have persisted into the industrial civilization of the twentieth century" (Ogburn 1964: 199). Examples of the survival of attitudes of a moneyless economy are the resistance to the use of money in settling personal differences, the fact that it would be rude to come quickly to business matters without any preliminaries, the fact that tipping would be less common a custom than it is in northern cities, or expressions such as "this is something money cannot buy." Ogburn argues that these attitudes have a lot to do with an aristocratic society whose wealth is based on land and not on money, and who look down at merchants and businessmen. He draws a comparison with seventeenth and eighteenth century Europe, which was not yet a fully monetary economy: "The attitudes of the aristocrats were like the attitudes of a moneyless economy. They high-hatted tradesmen and people who worked for money" (Ogburn 1964: 203).

Of course, "money is making an inroad into such personal transactions, but slowly and with resentment" (Ogburn 1964: 203). Ogburn sees these attitudes as survivals which sooner or later will disappear:

> Several of the manners and customs of the South become clearly understood when they are seen as survivals of attitudes of a moneyless society. Money appears first in a limited sphere of transactions in a society. But gradually it penetrates into wider and wider circles of exchanges and relationships. But in doing so, it is opposed. Many of these attitudes of the South after the Civil War are best understood as oppositions to this wider use of money. In the course of time, these survivals will disappear, and the adoption of money will be as complete in the South as elsewhere. (Ogburn 1964: 206)

Why Should We Save?

Some of the attitudes about money mentioned by Ogburn as applying to the Old South can also be noticed in Brazil. Being one of the last countries to abolish slavery (in 1888), Brazil has no tradition of valuing work, especially manual labor. To toil in Portuguese is called *mourejar,* something that according to the Portuguese should be left to the moors. A racist expression referring to hard work is *trabalho para negro* (work for a Negro), a direct reference to slavery. But even after the abolition of slavery and introduction of wage labor in factories, work has never been very valued, because the social order continued to be highly exclusive. Until the beginning of the twentieth century, Brazil was an essentially rural society. When industrialization and urbanization started to become more important in the 1930s, there was a strong reaction against working and the growing monetization of life. At that time, one could find the same "resentment against expressing values in money" about which Ogburn (1964: 205) speaks in relation to the Old South. The *horror ao batente* (hatred of manual work) developed into *malandragem* (idleness), which can be seen simultaneously as a survival strategy and a conception of the world through which some segments of the lower classes refused to accept the discipline and monotony associated with the wage-earning world.

The negative side of labor is reflected in Brazilian popular music. As I have shown elsewhere (Oliven 1984) during the 1930s and 1940s when an urban-industrial society was in the making in Brazil, *samba* composers used to eulogize idleness. *Malandragem* developed into a way of life and a way of regarding life. Instead of developing a work ethic (in the Weberian sense), Brazilians were developing a *malandro* ethic. This was so widespread that during the 1937–45 dictatorship, the State decided to intervene through its censorship department by prohibiting songs which praised *malandragem* and at the same time giving prizes to those which praised work.

The same composers who praised *malandragem* also depicted money as something ignoble generally demanded by women who did not understand that the men they were asking it from had something much more precious to offer them: their love. Of course, one can see here a "sour grapes complex": knowing they would never make much money no matter how hard they tried, those men looked down at the *vil metal* (filthy lucre). But on the other hand, in several of the lyrics of these songs, one can notice that money is a reality from which one cannot escape in a monetized society. But all of this is seen in a melancholic fashion. Nobody is happy to work. And money after all is very destructive: it ends love and friendship, and it invites falsehood and treason. As Noel Rosa, perhaps the greatest of all the composers of the 1930s, put it in the song *Fita Amarela* (Yellow Ribbon) in 1933: "I haven't got any heirs/ and I don't own a single penny/ I lived owing to everybody/ But I didn't pay anybody back" (*Não tenho herdeiros/ Nem possuo um só vintém/ Eu vivi devendo a todos/ Mas não paguei a ninguém*).

Work in and of itself has never been something to be proud of in Brazil, even if most of the population works more hours than does the North American population. If you ask a Brazilian what he is doing, there is a strong likelihood he will reply: "nothing." Actually, "to do nothing" is a native category that perhaps makes little sense in English, but which is full of meaning in Portuguese.

Of course, people in Brazil work very hard and are interested in money. Rebhun, who carried out anthropological field work in Brazil, argues that:

> impoverished and working class Northeast Brazilians claim to believe in a sharp moral divide between *amor* (love) and what they call *interesses* or economic interests. However, in practice, the two are inextricably intertwined. Especially today, in this impoverished region characterized by a fractured, unstable, hyper inflated economy, the depth of love is increasingly measured

in terms of the worth of generosity. In addition, the weakness of cash makes the emotionally-loaded relations of family and social network increasingly important as avenues of access to goods and services. (Rebhun 1993: 1)

INDIVIDUALISM AND GROUP HELP

When I arrived at the University of California, Berkeley, I was invited to attend an *Information Meeting for New International Scholars*. Part of the meeting was a lecture given by the director of Services for International Students and Scholars. Among other interesting things, he emphasized that US Americans like to be independent. According to him, "if you are independent, you don't want to depend on friends." This is why you see twelve-year old middle class children doing some sort of work to earn some money. He also stressed that US Americans also are supposed to value hard work, which is why they value goods.

But if in the US people are usually doing things by themselves, in Brazil you are always asking or offering help, which is a way of making friends and building networks. In a more personal society like Brazil, it is difficult to survive without friends and social networks. In contrast, in a more individualistic society like the US, people are more reluctant to ask or give advice. Of course, there are friends and networks in the US, but their role is weaker than in Brazil. This can be seen even in day-to-day life and the "do it yourself" attitude that prevails in US culture. To give just one example, for a Brazilian it is quite impressive to see handicapped people in their wheelchairs going from one place to another without any personal help.

Even organizations based on the idea of solving problems through group help have a very individualistic character in the US. I went to meetings of *Debtors Anonymous,* an organization based on a similar model of the "Twelve Steps" of the *Alcoholics Anonymous* and which is widespread in the US. Their objective is to help people who are compulsive debtors through help provided by the group. But although the group is essential as a support provider, there is a strong emphasis on the individual and the moral aspect of his or her problem. Listening and talking to the people who go to the meetings, I found out that owing money, like alcohol abuse, is seen as a physical, emotional, and spiritual problem. Although the word was never pronounced, it is treated like a symptom of a disease. The causes of the disease are family maladjustment (parents who are too authoritarian, lack of dialogue) and a society that pressures you to constantly spend. The whole thing is very related to a spiritual awakening and revival. The meeting actually started and ended with a prayer. During the ending prayer, everybody was in circle holding hands. The word *recovery* is used frequently. It is, however, a different type of disease. Whereas Alcoholic

Anonymous tries to stop people from drinking alcohol, and presumably Gambler Anonymous does the same with gambling, Debtors Anonymous has a different task: to teach people how to deal with money in a non-compulsive way in a society constantly compelling you to spend.

One of the meetings I went to was almost entirely devoted to business matters. It dealt with moving future meetings to a more accessible place, changing its time, electing a new treasurer, collecting voluntary donations, and raising money to send a delegate to a national meeting in New York. I was impressed with the degree of organization of the meeting. Thirteen people who had serious financial problems were conducting a meeting in an extremely formal way, following *Robert's Rules of Order* as if this were an assembly general. Everything was very orderly. Also, money was dealt with in a very proper way, the treasurer saying exactly what they had collected, and how much they needed. Nobody would guess that those persons are compulsive spenders who cannot organize their budget. The sharing part of this and other meetings I went to gave every member up to four minutes to speak about him or herself. For me, it was impressive to see people speak, sometimes almost in tears, about their problems and stop when told that their time was up. Order and self-help were very present in the atmosphere.

Catholics Versus Protestants

Saving and investing leads us to the question of a "Catholic" versus a "Protestant" view of money. In his letter to Timothy, the apostle Paul says that, "The love of money is the root of all evil" (I Timothy, 6:10). We know that usury was condemned by Thomas Aquinas and could only be practiced in the Middle Ages by non-Christians, that is, Jews (Le Goff 1988). But with Protestantism, more specifically with Calvinism, came the conception that success (measured by profit) was the indication that the chosen vocation pleased God. Dislike of work was seen as a sign of failure that is displeasing to God. As Weber (1958) has shown in *The Protestant Ethic and the Spirit of Capitalism,* Calvinism allowed and to a sense consecrated the drive to become rich, thus reconciling wealth with a good conscience.

It is of course difficult to make generalizations about Catholic versus Protestant views of money. Schama shows that in Holland in the Golden Age "riches seemed to provoke their own discomfort, and affluence cohabited with anxiety." For him:

> The official creeds of both Calvinism and humanism, then, were agreed that lucre was indeed filthy, and that devotion to its cult constituted a kind of pol-

luting idolatry. In its extreme forms of avarice and cupidity it could unhinge the conscience and reason and turn the free souls into fawning slaves. This strong sense of the reprehensible nature of money-making persisted, even, while the Dutch amassed their individual and collective fortunes. The odd consequence of this disparity between principles and practice was to foster expenditure rather than capital accumulation, as a way to exonerate oneself from the suspicion of avarice. Admittedly, the forms of such expenditure had to be collectively sanctioned and regarded as morally unblemished by clergy and laity alike. (Schama 1987: 326 and 334)

Catholicism is frequently seen as an important influence on Brazilian culture. Moog has even tried to discuss the Weberian thesis (Weber 1958) in a comparison between Brazil and the United States. He argues that Brazilian culture is characterized by the "dislike of useful work and all that is connected to it: initiative, organization, cooperation, and the technical and scientific spirit." But in North American culture, "the sanctity of debt and the dignity of labor are notions that neither the Puritan, nor the Yankee or the crypto-Yankee are disposed to let perish" (Moog 1964: 210 and 154).

As a matter of fact, Brazilian authors who wrote in the 1930s frequently argued that Brazil was not a capitalist society. Thus, Holanda who coined the term "cordiality" to explain Brazilian society, maintained that it was characterized by social relations, which were personalized, affective, particularistic, and clientelistic (Holanda 1969). In a similar perspective, although from a different political standpoint, Vianna maintained that in Brazil there prevailed what he called a pre-capitalist mentality or spirit, in spite of the fact that materially the country was capitalist (Vianna 1987; Gomes 1989, 1990).

Dumont (1980) establishes a contrast between what he calls hierarchical societies and egalitarian societies. The first are based on the concept of person, whereas the second are based on the concept of a free individual. India would be the classical example of a hierarchical society, whereas the US would be the most developed example of an egalitarian one. Drawing on Dumont's model, DaMatta (1991) argues that today Brazil is somehow in-between hierarchical and egalitarian societies. Whereas the United States tends to be a society very much based on the egalitarian individualistic model, Brazil is closer to the hierarchical and personal model. There would exist a dilemma between the adherence to an impersonal individualistic model existing formally in Brazilian laws, and the day-to-day tendency to constantly revert to personal relations. Hence, the greater aversion in dealing directly with money and the more face-to-face relations involved in transactions.

DaMatta also goes into the Catholicism versus Protestantism question. Commenting on the expression *"dinheiro não trás felicidade"* (money does not bring happiness), he argues that it "adds to the underlying cultural equation that tells how work corresponds to punishment and how the accumulation of wealth equals something dirty or illicit" (DaMatta, 1991: 181). Analyzing the cultural matrix of the Brazilian inflation he argues that,

> of course we want to have money, but we can compensate its absence through the presence filled with value of friends, of health, of "education" and, above all, of "happiness." This incapacity to regard money—and above all the possession of money—as a positive activity, as a hegemonic measure of competence and success, as the aim of all things, creates areas of tolerance and of social compensation that seem important in the Brazilian case. (DaMatta 1993: 172)

WHY WAS MARTIN LUTHER KING'S SPEECH *I HAVE A DREAM* SO PERSUASIVE?

On 28 August 1963, Martin Luther King delivered his famous speech "I Have a Dream" on the steps at the Lincoln Memorial in Washington, D.C. as the keynote address of a civil rights march on Washington. This speech had an impressive impact and marks a turning point in racial relations in the United States. The part of the speech that is most mentioned is the sentence "I have a dream that one day this nation will rise up and live out the true meaning of its creed: 'We hold these truths to be self-evident, that all men are created equal'" (King Jr. 2003: 330). But before this sentence, which gave name to King's speech, there is a series of sentences that are couched in financial terms. Thus, King asserts that,

> In a sense we have come to our nation's capitol **to cash a check**. When the architects of out great republic wrote the magnificent words of the Constitution and the Declaration of Independence, **they were signing a promissory note** to which every American was to fall heir. This note was a promise that all men, yes, black men as well as white men, would be guaranteed the "inalienable Rights of Life, Liberty, and the pursuit of Happiness." It is obvious that **America has defaulted on this promissory note** insofar as her citizens of color are concerned. Instead of honoring this sacred obligation, America has given the Negro people **a bad check, a check that has come back marked "insufficient funds."** But we refuse to believe that there are **insufficient funds in the great vaults of opportunity** of this nation. And so we've come **to cash this check, a check that will give us upon demand the riches of freedom and the security of justice.** (King Jr. 2003: 328–29, emphasis added)

There are two reasons Martin Luther King's speech was so persuasive. The first is that he was arguing quite simply that, if the North American creed is based on the idea that all men are created equal, there should not be discrimination against Black people; hence apartheid countered the tenets of the founding fathers.

The second reason, which is central to the argument of this chapter, is that his speech is couched in a rhetoric that is common sense in the US, that is, the monetary rhetoric; hence the idea that the Constitution and the Declaration of Independence were promissory notes and that African Americans had come to Lincoln's statue to cash a check, which until then had been marked "insufficient funds." This is a speech pattern that makes sense in the United States.

CHAPTER 11

THE THIRD WAY
A CULTURAL ECONOMIC PERSPECTIVE

Arjo Klamer

■ ■ ■ ■ ■ ■

EXORDIUM

"TINA—There Is No Alternative," the neoliberal politician responds to questions about the market rhetoric that dominates political discourse. "And what's wrong with making a profit?" "Why should education not be a commodity bought and sold in a market?" "And why should people not be able to buy the health care they desire?" "We need to further the market process in order to keep up with the global economy!"

Presumably, there is no alternative when the state is passed over, when collective provisions of welfare programs, subsidies, regulations, and public governance are the subject of doubt and incredulity. In the early twenty-first-century public—or is it socialist?—rhetoric has grown dull and impotent in a world dominated by market rhetoric. Even civil servants have taken to market talk—heralding efficiency, promoting their products, aspiring for measurable results, and speaking of citizens as their customers.

Yet, there is another alternative. Of course, there is. The alternative of which I am thinking pictures society large—the entity that according to Margaret Thatcher, the former conservative British prime minister, does not exist. Call it a third way, if you wish—as long you do not associate the third way with Tony Blair, the labor prime minister, and his advisor, Anthony Giddens, which is about collaborations between the market and the state sectors. No, this third way is really a third way as it points at a most undervalued domain of value creation.

It's Not the Economy, Stupid; It's Society!

The inability to see the third way and the incomprehension I meet when I try to show it, may betray a rhetoric that dominates to the point of becoming an ideology. In order to change the conversation to one that makes the third way a regular option, I chose the strategy of exposing the TINA claim as belonging to a particular conversation with its own logic and rhetoric. If market talk is a conversation, surely other conversations must be feasible, and maybe even preferable.[1]

By talking about rhetoric, I allude to the theme of difference. The introduction of culture in the conversation furthers the theme, allows us to see market behavior as cultural, and behavior in the sphere of the state as cultural as well, but in a different way. The notion of culture calls for an analysis of values. When we have reached the question as to the different ways in which values can be generated, changed, and realized, we are ready to perceive the third way. (When the anthropologically trained reader is now thinking that the option of the third way is obvious, I would like to ask him or her why it does not play a role in public discussions, and extend the invitation to explore together how to get it on the agenda of economists as well as politicians. I do so by making a link with the themes of this volume: culture and rhetoric.)

Narratio

The notions of rhetoric and culture stimulate the imagination to see the economy and the thinking about it in another way. These notions enable us to consider the rhetoric of markets, for example, or the cultural context of consumption behavior and trade. However, before an economist might speak about culture and rhetoric in a meaningful and interested way, a lot needs to change. Like the hardnosed attitude toward science, for instance, and the almost religious commitment to thinking in terms of rational decision making in highly formalized settings—that much an encounter with the conversations of anthropologists makes clear.

In the following sections, I will explore a few of the possible consequences of making the shift to include culture and rhetoric within the conversation of economics. In doing so, I will outline a *cultural-economic perspective*. This will not only help us to see a third way but also stimulate us to face the gap that currently separates the conversations of economists and anthropologists.

In this enterprise, fellow travelers are economists like Deirdre McCloskey and Metin Cosgel, and anthropologists like Stephen Gudeman. We hark back to a longstanding, but somewhat forgotten tradition of interpretive, pragmatic, and historical reasoning as can be found in Aristotle, Thomas Aquino, Adam Smith, Karl Polanyi (here, McCloskey will bark because of what she calls his gross misconceptions of markets in history), Ronald Coase, and others. In doing so, we veer away from the modernist tradition in economics, exemplified by the work of Paul Samuelson, Kenneth Arrow, and Gerard Debreu. We prefer words above equations and diagrams, and look for concepts and forms that help us to make sense of a world that continues to amaze and puzzle us. I am not sure if I speak for all of my fellow travelers when I state that the objective is not just to formulate striking and revealing characteristics of the economic world but also to seek direction for how to do good in that world. Deirdre McCloskey concurs as she points in the direction of bourgeois virtues: celebrate and admire men and women who display the virtue of prudence, especially if they combine such a virtue with the virtue of courage as shown in entrepreneurial activity, and the virtues of faith, hope, and love. She, an ardent advocate of the free market, continues on the path that Adam Smith set out, and revives economics as a moral science (McCloskey 2006). The point is not just to interpret the world but also to find a direction for right action (without claiming that our scientific findings will be resolute and definite about what to do—we have learned to respect the difference between "teoria" and "phronesis.") The exploration starts with the rhetorical turn in the thinking about economics.

The Rhetorical Turn

Thanks to Deirdre McCloskey, the notion of rhetoric is circulating in the conversation among economists (McCloskey 1984). Her claim, that economists practice rhetoric as much and as pervasively as poets do, caused somewhat of a stir. It evoked the Rortyan idea that all economics is mere rhetoric, and a scientific claim is nothing more than an opinion (Rorty 1979), which does not go over well when practitioners take a hardnosed attitude toward their science, with a firm belief in its methods as the only scientific methods imaginable and acceptable (see Milberg in this volume). To say that economics is rhetorical is then understood as to deny that there are grounds for such a belief and to assert that the science of economics lacks solid foundations.

McCloskey's attack on the modernist dogma of that time aimed to have just that effect. She wanted to attack the dogmatic adherence to a highly formalized methodology (see Carrier in this volume). Economics is not physics, she keeps saying to her colleagues; it is more like poetry. The latter analogy is important to her; in the end, she likes to see economists join what she calls the human conversation. Instead of talking among each other, she would like to see economists converse as easily with mathematicians as literary scholars and sociologists. The first step is to get them to see what they have in common with other scholarly pursuits. Accordingly, her move has a moral connotation; it is perlocutionary in the sense that it is a call to economists to change their tune, to expand their bookcase and to start reading poetry, for example, or get interested not only in mathematics and physics as related disciplines, but in philosophy, sociology, and anthropology as well.

My disagreement with her is due to a different reading of the consequences as well as the purpose of the rhetorical perspective. The purpose as I see it is to be able to recognize and understand differences among economists, and between economists and everyone else. Although anthropologists and economists have a great deal in common—it is all right to stress the common elements, especially when we try to communicate with each other—the differences are substantive. If we would ignore the differences, we would fail to grasp the miscommunications and to read the frustrations that arise when we are really trying to talk with each other about subjects that matter to us. The differences show in the way we speak and write, that is, in our rhetoric. We use different metaphors and concepts, and I would not be surprised if a closer scrutiny would show that our (implicit) narratives are different, too. Whereas economists tend to see themselves as Policy Advisors or Academic Professionals in a more or less well defined context, anthropologists appear to project themselves as Traveling Scholars interested in The Other (Klamer and Colander 1989; Klamer 2007). Would it be an exaggeration to say that they present themselves as more socially minded than the economist, more sensitive to difference, too? Not all economists will recognize themselves in this projection. Even so, ask them what they really think of anthropologists and you will most likely discern a distinct characterization to which many anthropologists will object. It is a difference that anthropologists should easily grasp, because they are sensitized to it.

A different rhetoric is an expression of a different culture. Economists share stories, ways of speaking, a history, including a history of disputes and controversies, institutions, and particular values that make their culture distinct from, for example, that of anthropologists. You do not become a game theorist simply by studying game theory. Before you are in that conversation, as an accepted and recognized game theorist, you need to adopt a frame of mind, assimilate a set of values and practices, and moreover socialize in the world of game theorists. The other game theorists need to recognize and accept you as one of them. That is why you have to complete graduate school, do a dissertation, go to conferences, and demonstrate with contributions to the conversation that you are worthy of their attention. Having tried to become a cultural economist in the midst of my career, I had to earn my status by mingling and contributing. A chair in the subject may have helped, but it certainly did not suffice. Getting the right attention requires the right type of work.[2]

Differences in rhetoric and culture show in particular feelings, often ill feelings. McCloskey may surprise socially minded people with her talk about rhetoric and virtues, but when she displays her enthusiasm for the market and entrepreneurship, you see them shrink back. The code in academic meetings is to remain civil, but the feelings of annoyance and indignation usually show in the discussion that inevitably follows. You see them thinking: "how in the hell can she think that?" "She is so nice and then this…, it does not make sense." McCloskey herself has coined this the stupidity problem. It is the inclination to call those who do not think and talk like you do, stupid, or something else to that effect. So economists are used to calling politicians and business people stupid for their lack of economic sense and for not being able to heed the advice of economists. But the accused return the compliment by charging that economists are stupid, or something equivalent, for not being able to predict well, and speaking obscurely, and basing their advice on wildly unrealistic models. The asserted stupidities, I suggest, are signs of rhetorical differences. Politicians are in a different conversation, and although that conversation overlaps the conversation that economists are having, rhetorical differences stand in the way of mutual comprehension (see also Klamer 2007).

Conversation as a Key Metaphor

In order to make sense of the differences in rhetoric and culture, I would like to advance the metaphor of the conversation. Accordingly, economists are in a conversation, or better even, in a bunch of conversations, and so are anthropologists. Each conversation has its characteristic rhetorical practice and generates and sustains a distinct culture. By adopting the metaphor, I follow others who have done so, including the philosophers Gadamer and Rorty, and most significantly, Randall Collins in his *Sociology of Philosophies* (1998). Cosgel also uses the metaphor in his contribution to this volume.

Like rhetoric, conversation evokes meanings I do not intend to foreground. Just like the first associations with rhetoric should not be "mere rhetoric," or "deceitful," or "stylish talk," conversation as I use it here, does not, first of all, mean "chit chat" or "small talk," as it often means in everyday parlance. I think rather of conversation in the sense of "keeping company with" or "being conversant with." In a scientific context, conversations are about arguments and come in the form of books and articles; they consist of the texts that scientists produce in conference meetings, in the corridors of their departments, on email, and in living rooms and cafes. Small talk can be a part of this—as when economists discuss who is where and who is doing what and with whom—but the economic conversation comprises a great deal more. The metaphor also evokes the meaning of getting together and having something in common. Conversation is not just about what is going on, but contains the potential for further conversation. A conversation gains in potential with every contribution to its library of books, articles, and other works. Our writings are part of the conversation we are in, awaiting further discussion and scrutiny. Those who follow us may find something of value or some phrase worth citing, and thus keep it alive in the ongoing conversation. (Unfortunately, most of the writing will wait for readership in vain and will virtually die.) Accordingly, conversation is a common source for anyone making an effort to be part of it. (If a conversation were to develop involving both economists and anthropologists, those of us who are interested in such a conversation would benefit—and may be expected to contribute.)

In Klamer (2007), I argue that differences among conversations show in differences in rhetorical practices as in the use of (constitutive) metaphors, (constitutive) narratives, and argumentative strategies and styles, as well as in values. Seeing such differences helps us understand why the way everyday people talk about the economy is so dramatically different from the way academic economists want to talk about the same phenomena, with the effect that the phenomena themselves appear to become different. Whereas an academic economist would like us to talk about markets in terms of general equilibrium systems or game theoretic situations, in everyday talk, people think about markets in anthropomorphic and moral terms. For the latter, the market can go up and down, is good or bad, is about competition between firms, or is about satisfying consumers. It is all in the conversation.

This metaphor has been an eye opener for my perception of the economy. If economics is a conversation, or better yet, a bunch of conversations, so too could be the market. Whereas the standard economic metaphor portrays a market as a general equilibrium mechanism with the forces of supply and demand, the conversation metaphor focuses on the communication that constitutes markets, which is more or less obvious in an actual market place where we are struck by yelling and shouting, by the signs all over calling attention to the wares displayed and the asking price, by the haggling about the price, and by the discussions among the suppliers and between the suppliers and buyers. Artists discuss among each other and with their gallery owner what price they should ask for their painting, they chat with potential buyers at their studio, read what others write about art and the art market to develop a reference, visit openings, and chat some more, while potential buyers talk with their partners about what to buy or consult experts. Sure, the art market is a conversation as well, an ongoing conversation at that, or better even, a bunch of conversations (as the conversation among artists is quite distinct from the conversation that gallery owners conduct or the one that potential buyers are involved in [see Velthuis 2005]).

McCloskey and I have calculated that talk makes up a great deal of the economy as it is accounted for in economic measurements. The efforts of salesmen, advertising agencies, managers, stockbrokers, newspapers, the media, the travel industry, much of it, make up the talking in economic processes. We estimated that one third of the GDP stands for the costs of persuading others to buy, sell, work, and consume (Klamer and McCloskey 1995). Whereas traditional economic analysis presumes that agents calculate in isolation and in silence their optimal options, in reality you and I are continuously in one conversation or another to make up our minds. Before I buy a car, I have talked a great deal with friends, salespeople, and especially my wife, just to make up my mind. In a way, the car I buy is also an input for other conversations. A car is a statement after all, about the identity of the owner, for example, about social status, and for some, about inspiration.

The persuasion in conversation points to processes that all too easily are overlooked in a standard economic analysis. For instance, the conventional assumption is that preferences of "agents" are given. Yet, considering all of the talk in which they engage while considering the purchase of a complex good, such as a car or a painting, their preferences are not all that clear to begin with. Persuasion implies that people may change their mind, buying something that at first they were not considering. We university professors should be all too aware of the process. Quite a few of our students do not particularly care for what we want to teach them. Yet, exposed to our passionate teaching and inspired with the insights they gain, they may change their minds and decide to go on to graduate school. If the process of applying ones preferences to the available options is one of *valuation,* this process of being persuaded to change one's processes could be called *valorization.* It is what happens when you go to the gallery in search of a peaceful landscape for the wall behind the couch and proudly return home with a wildly colored abstract painting. Apparently, while at the gallery, you learned to value abstract painting. As others would put it, you acquired a taste for it. *Valorization* captures this very process. It occurs especially in the acquisition of cultural goods (Klamer 2004), but it occurs also when my little daughter discovers that her new shoes are not considered cool by her peers.

This line of argument accords with, for example, Bourdieu's argument that in their consumption, people reproduce their identity and social status (Bourdieu 1984). Buying and driving a Lamborghini is a statement. (In a

Dutch law firm where I did a research project, I noticed one of those machines in its garage, amidst a series of Volvo's and other family cars. The next time I came, the car had disappeared, as it turned out at the request of the management of the firm; the machine did not fit the solid and reliable image that the firm wants to radiate.)

Accordingly, the metaphor of conversation takes us to the literature on material culture and the world of consumption. Price figures in the analysis, of course, but the formation of preferences as well as their change has to become an explicit concern, in contradistinction to conventional economic analysis.

Organizations are conversations, too. After all, by setting up an organization, like a firm or a club, people agree on a framework within which they will work together toward a particular goal, like making a profit or playing soccer together. They do so discursively, agreeing on some rules, a division of labor, a strategy, the presentation to the outside world, and other things. The conversations that constitute an organization will have their own rhetoric and generate a particular culture. In an accounting firm, the talk is about professionalism, ambition, hard work, and dedication to the needs of the client. It is a way of talking, of course, and in practice not all partners may be as ambitious and hardworking. Yet, it is a story that they produce for each other, for their clients, and for anyone else who is interested. In the law firm to which I referred earlier, ambition is not a prominent subject in the conversation. Rather, the partners talk about the challenges they meet, their legal expertise, and the solidness of their work. "No, we are not very competitive among each other with each other/or among ourselves. When I am away on a trip, I do not have to fear that my colleagues will take over dossiers of mine." (At the accounting firm, internal competition is encouraged and it was a custom to lock one's dossiers away if on a trip with the key entrusted only to those who could be trusted.)

Organizations differ widely and the organization literature provides a plethora of classifications. Morgan articulates six metaphors to characterize firms (Morgan 2006). A highly organized and disciplined firm with predictable routines operates like a machine whereas a creative knowledge oriented firm is more like a brain. The metaphor is an indication of the rhetoric and culture of an organization. A brain talks differently than a machine.

Another consequence of the metaphor of the conversation is to view the entrepreneur as a rhetor, as someone who can be persuasive in distinctly different conversations. In that sense, the entrepreneur is more than one who is creative, willing to break with routines, and alert to opportunities, which are the characteristics usually attributed to the entrepreneur (Klamer 2006). As an academic entrepreneur, I had the vision of a new type of university. The idea came about during a meeting and it was not difficult to see the opportunity for such a university given the frustrations with existing universities in Europe.

This inspiration has not been even one percent of all of the entrepreneurial work I have been doing on the idea. Most of the time, I find myself talking. I talk with people in businesses for their participation and financial support, with state officials, and with all kinds of individuals to get them involved as participants, teachers, and co-workers. I had to persuade people with a certain social status to join the board of my foundation, the city government of Deventer (in the middle of Holland) to make buildings and some finances available, a developer to take a substantial risk in developing a campus, colleagues regarding the academic content, a few young scholars to join our research center rather than attending a regular university, and so on. Often, people are persuaded and so now and then they will act upon it (but certainly not always, as I found out). And let me not forget the people close to me who had to be persuaded that the time spent away from home is worth it.

The Cultural Turn

One important consequence of the rhetorical turn is, as I have already intimated, the recognition of the role that culture plays in human life, including the economical dimension. To recognize the relevance of this insight, consider dominant practice in the conversation of economists. Culture is not part of the standard vocabulary of economists. You will look for it in vain in the index of any economic textbook. It is one of the reasons why the rhetoric of economics is so different from that of anthropologists. The idea is presumably that in dealing with the profane and the mundane of everyday trading, supplying, and buying, social and cultural conditions can be presumed as given. Certainly, a Weberian analysis shows the influence of religion on the economic system of interest, as Swedberg observes in this volume, but it serves a historical interest rather than that of an economic analysis.

Recently, some economists are developing an interest in the relationship between culture and the economy. The *Journal of Economic Perspectives* of Summer 2006 even contained a series of articles on cultural economics. The basic question motivating these economists concerns the impact of cultural factors on economic behavior and economic outcomes. Cultural factors can be a constraint on economic behavior, as when religious convictions discourage entrepreneurial activities, and they could influence preferences of economics agents. In this approach, culture remains an exogenous factor.

A similar approach is followed by Harrison and Huntington in their volume, *Culture Matters* (2000). The issue motivating the studies in this volume is the relationship between culture and development. The difficulties of implementing development programs continue to baffle researchers. They have advanced a wide variety of explanations, such as the lack of natural resources (not critical), a lack of capital (idem), a lack of education (possibly), trade restraints (most likely), and failing governments (idem). The question remains why governments are failing in some countries and not in others, why education gets a great deal of attention in some developing countries and not in others. And so culture enters the analysis. Economists remain wary though, as the factor—culture—is difficult to capture in the formalized models that they prefer to use through which to think about things.

My wariness concerns the treatment of culture as a factor. It is as if economies are not embedded in cultures, and as if there is no effect of economic arrangements on culture. If markets are conversations, they are cultural in a sense. Here, I refer to culture to mean the values, histories, and current news that a group of people has in common, which makes them distinct from other groups of people. If I look for processes of persuasion and valorization, I am accepting the cultural contexts from which discursive strategies derive their meanings and effectiveness.

I also take issue with the cultural turn as Ray and Sayer perceive it in their introduction to *Culture and Economics of the Cultural Turn* (1999). They distinguish culture and the economy as distinctive realms and see the cultural turn as a shift of interest away from the economic realm to the cultural realm. As if the cultural realm, which in their book includes the making and enjoying of art, watching movies and giving whatever meaning to one's life, does not involve economic activities. How do people pay for the arts? When enjoying their leisure time, they do not work (and that signifies the existence of opportunity costs, which economists will never get tired of pointing out—then again, they are notably absent from this volume). Even if we were to restrict the subject of economics to the allocation of scarce resources, cultural activities have inevitably an economic dimension.

Admittedly, the emergence of post-materialistic values, as recorded by Inglehart (1997), points to a cultural change, as does the recent preoccupation with creativity by city officials and business leaders. Richard Florida has galvanized the world of local politics with his claim that the creative class is a critical factor in the future of local economies (Florida 2004). Cities need their fair share of artists, designers, architects, and researchers to keep up with the new economy. Business leaders are now talking a great deal about the importance of creativity for their organization, with one major outcome being a booming market for books that preach exactly that. But although these developments are significant, they do not signify an increasing importance of culture. Culture has been important all of the time. When an organization squashes any form of creativity and bans all forms of artistic activity, it still represents a culture, that is, a culture that does not value creativity and art.

Any economy is cultural. For someone like the semiotician, Barend van Heusden, this is obvious: "Listen, economists study human behavior and human behavior is in large part cultural, that is, semiotic behavior. So if economists decide to leave out culture from their theories of economic behavior, they have at least the duty to explain how this human being, cultural from head to toes, suddenly leaps out of culture when s/he is being 'economic'" (van Heusden 1996: 47). Humans are cultural in the sense that they participate in a culture and attribute meanings that make sense of the culture in which they are a part. A conversation is cultural because it represents a way of talking that is distinct from other conversations.

The Issue of Values and Goods

Culture, to repeat, refers to the values, histories, and current news that a group of people has in common, which makes them distinct from other groups of people. Accordingly, culture makes one think of values that a group has in common. My questions are how values are being generated, how they are sustained, and how they are realized. A distinctive feature of Dutch life is the high value attached to a private life. Start talking about how important your private life is and about your wish to work less to have more time for your private life, and you will find a responsive audience in the Netherlands, even if you are working for a prestigious law firm. Suggest something of the kind in US law firm, and you find your colleagues questioning your ambition and commitment to the law. So how do US Americans realize their valuation of ambition and commitment, and how do the Dutch succeed in sustaining the value of a private life that is independent of working life?

A distinctive feature of the cultural economic perspective that I am exploring and developing, here, is the attention to values. I propose to redefine economics as the study of values; more particularly, economics is a study of which values are realized and how they are realized. The conventional economic analysis focuses on economic values, such as the income people earn, or the profit that a company makes, or the economic growth a country achieves. These economic values, however, are nothing more and nothing less than instruments to generate other values. My income serves to buy goods, first of all, in support of my family and then to support me as a citizen in my society, as a participant in cultural activities, and as a professor at my university. My expenditures serve, therefore, first of all social values, like the values that I attach to having a private life, a family, friends, a social position, a profession, to being a member of a club and a society, and to being part of a conversation. Insofar as I dedicate some of my resources to cultural and religious activities, I could be said to have put my economic values to use for my cultural and spiritual values, like having an appreciation for aesthetics or having an identity and a faith (see also Klamer 2003; for the virtue of faith see McCloskey 2006).

In order to make the discussion of social and cultural values substantive, it helps to speak of social and cultural goods as distinct from economic goods. An economic good is good for the economic values it generates. A painting is an economic good in so far as it fetches a price in the market place, as is someone's education when it is good for additional income. A painting can also be a social good considering the social values it generates. Art can bring friends together—as in Yasmina Reza's play, Art—or can contribute to a national identity (as reflected in the question: "did you not know that we have an internationally renowned dance company?"). A family is social good because one has to make a serious effort to have and sustain one, and because it generates social goods such as companionship, a sense of belonging, care, and possibly even love. (Unfortunately, families can also turn into social "bads" when they become repressive and abusive.) Collegiality is a social good, too, and so is a vital society. We are just much better off when we "have" a well functioning society then when we are part of a conflict-ridden and divided society.

Cultural goods represent, or serve to realize, cultural values. Art is a cultural good insofar as it is a contribution to the conversation called art, or it inspires people and conveys a sense of beauty, or shock, for that matter. Temples, mosques, and cathedrals function as cultural goods when they evoke a sense of awe, or impress their visitors in special ways, but so too does the Erasmus bridge in Rotterdam, which functions as an inspiring icon for the Rotterdam people and has become the major symbol of the city. Not all cultural goods are tangible or material. A ritual is a case in point, as is music, a shared history, and a tradition. They all share the property that they can inspire awe, wonderment or convey a sense of the sublime. Their value is that they mean something over and beyond whatever economic and social values they have, like cows in the experience of Indians, an aboriginal painting in an aboriginal context, or an icon for a Rumanian Roman-Catholic.

"Cultural" here has the connotations of spiritual, sacred, symbolic, aesthetic, and artistic. The inclination is to bring in the social dimension and consider the value of cultural goods in terms of what they mean for a certain group of people. Flags stand for a nation and a ritual is what reminds participants of their common culture. Cultural goods often appear to have social functions. The Greeks view the Elgin Marbles to be Greek and want them back from the Brits to bolster Greek culture. The French are adamant on an exception for cultural goods in the GATT, arguing that countries should be able to protect their cultural heritage. In such an argument the social values are accentuated; the cultural values are implicit.

Some cultural goods are viewed as such the world over, like a Rembrandt, a Venetian palazzo, or an ancient Buddha statue. A number of them show up on the world heritage list of UNESCO. Most cultural goods operate as such within a culture, defining, bolstering, and representing that culture. Often, it is the appreciation of the outsider that gives the impetus to such an evaluation. The Dutch valued "their" Rembrandts, but became seriously interested only after the US and Russians had bought many of his paintings during the nineteenth century.

To see the relevance of distinguishing social and cultural goods, consider a religious service. An economic approach would focus on the economic values involved. Economic statisticians will record the expenses of the building, the compensation paid to the minister and the organist, as well as the donations of the participants. But such tabulation of economic values does not do justice to the goods that a service realizes. A service first of all affirms and sustains a sense of community. Those who attend presumably derive satisfaction from sharing their faith with others. The main intent of the service, however, is to contribute to the faith of the community, to stir religious sensations, and to inspire by means of the liturgy, the music, and the sermon—not necessarily in that order. But the same distinction applies to more mundane events like a visit to a café with a friend. The statisticians will record the expense of the drinks the two friends have. But that is not the value realized. Most important of all is the value of companionship, of the friendship, and possibly the atmosphere in the café. At times, it is even more than that. So now and then the two friends may get into a flow that makes them forget about the time and leaves them with a very special feeling. You could call that the cultural value of their visit. Having such moments is immensely valuable; just as having a good conversation is valuable. Accordingly, the regular accounting does not do justice to the values that the two friends are actually realizing with the visit to the café.

The use of "good" may be confusing, as the usual association is with something tangible. I use the notion of good to refer to anything of value that we own. By ownership, I do not mean just legal ownership, but also symbolic ownership in the sense that you "own" a family, a friendship or a society. In the latter sense, ownership means that you can call the good yours. Accordingly, Dutch society is mine for the simple reason that I was born into that society and participated in it. One question that presents itself is how can we account for all of these goods, or, how to measure them? Clearly we cannot in all cases. But we can watch what people do to acquire a certain good or sustain ownership of one. I could not tell you what the value of my being Dutch is for me, but when you watch me give up my US American life to return to the Netherlands, you can observe that I significantly value having a Dutch background. And when I notice that you are willing to sacrifice your family life in pursuit of an academic career, it is my best guess that you highly value your academic good.

The Realization of Values

In the standard economic treatment goods become commodities and as a consequence, their economic value stands out. Such a selective perspective begins already with Karl Marx, who starts *Capital* as follows: "The wealth of societies in which the capitalist mode of production prevails appears as an 'immense collection of commodities'; the individual commodity appears as its elementary form" (1977 [1867]: 126, the quotation marks are his). He continues with a few remarks on the use value of a commodity ("use values are only realized in consumption") and then focuses on the exchange value by means of which a commodity becomes a quantity. The latter value subsequently gets his undivided attention as he tries to figure out its relationship with the value of embodied labor power.[3] Not long after, Marx's standard economic analysis would dispense with the labor theory of value, but would keep the focus on goods as commodities, that is, goods to be exchanged. Goods are to be produced for exchange and to be consumed. Their value equals their price in exchange. When actual exchange is impossible, as in the case of public goods (think of national defense), a price is lacking and economists are compelled to derive a price by means of contingent valuation studies and the like. Either way, the analysis begins and ends with the moment of exchange—as the critical moment of valuation.[4]

When goods become candidates for exchange, they become commodities (Appadurai 1986). It is a phase in their life, possibly an important one, but a phase nonetheless. In that phase their economic value is being realized. You might not say so when you give the floor to economists, but goods have a life beyond that phase. Their being a commodity is just one moment in their biography (Appadurai 1986; Kopytoff, 1986). Things have a life and pass various stages in which their values are being realized, sustained, affirmed, questioned, and so on, in characteristic ways. During their gestation, goods are the subject of conversations dealing with their production. A painting comes about in conversations about techniques, art in general, and the world of artists. In those conversations, the producer and others involved value its qualities and evaluate the values that are being applied ("I want to paint again as an antidote to all the technique." "But why in this way? This is really cliché." "No it is not, I just take off on the work I have done earlier." Etc.).

When the good enters the phase of exchange, in a store or wherever, it becomes the subject of totally different conversations, like those of the marketers, salespeople, and consumers. Now its price will be just as major a subject as its use. (An example of such a conversation is: "It is a pretty large painting and given the track record of the artist, I'll price it at 10000 euro." "But don't you run the risk to miss the buyer who looks for interesting art above the couch?" "Yeah, but why would my work be priced less than that of my friend? Maybe I should take it to another gallery that can appreciate it better." "Listen, it has nothing to do with that. We just assess where the market is. We can do no better than this. In the end the buyer determines whether the price is right."[5])

Some goods, however, will never be in such a phase as they are "blocked from exchange" (cf. Walzer 1983: 100). A good, such as friendship, is one example, freedom of speech another, divine grace, and, in the western world, marriage and political office. The valuations of such goods take place in conversations that are distinct from others ("You are not going to risk imprisonment/ your life to defend your freedom of speech! I don't want to loose you." "Yes, I will." "So that freedom is worth more to you than our relationship?" Etc.).

The consuming of the good constitutes again another stage of the good. In the conventional economic account the economic process ceases with consumption; as soon as the good ends up in the hands of the consumer the story ends, and so does the analysis. For quite a few goods the consuming is a timely process that involves various people and comprises all kinds of experiences, valuations, evaluations, and so on. When people pay a visit to a museum, they are said to consume the services of the museum, i.e., the exhibition. Yet, what actually happens? They may visit the museum with their family, and so the outing may actually be important for the life of the family. They may have used the visit to have a nice lunch in the museum or to enjoy being in the building itself. They may have gone to the museum in the hope of meeting certain people. They may experience something in the museum that has a lasting impact. They may have conversations about their experiences afterward so that the museum visit may have a longer life than the mere visit. People may have learned something; and they may have to account for what they did. So, it is not immediately obvious what the consumption is all about. It is obvious, however, that the valuation of the museum visit, that is, its consumption, is an entirely different matter, and subject of again different conversations, than its economic valuation.

The notion of "the life of things" alerts us to the valuations and valorizations outside of the commodity phase. Indians realize the cultural value of a cow when they refuse to remove it from the road or slaughter it when they are in need of food. The cow has significant value, yet no market has a role in determining that value. Daily religious practices bring out the cultural value of a temple or church; critical discursive practices as well as institutions like museums account for the cultural value of Van Gogh. And the value of a flag may prove itself in the heat of the battle or at a funeral. Accordingly, we would not do justice to the life of any good, and its values, if we were to focus on its commodity phase only. Valuations and evaluations take place in different settings and in distinct spheres.

Spheres of Valuation: The Market and the State Sphere

One problem blocking the view of a third way of realizing values is the current fixation in economic and political discourse on only two spheres of valuation. The fixation is on the market sphere, on the one side, and the state sphere, on the other. Whether the concern is cars, education or healthcare, we are led to think of the opposition of markets versus governments. As an economist myself, I will be the last one to deny the relevance of the quid pro quo of market exchanges and the rule-based actions in the state sphere. I only want to show that there is a third alternative. I will do this by way of a few pictures.

The two squares represent the spheres of the market and of the state. Let me stress that they stand for ideal types as imagined in common economic and political discourse. Accordingly, the square for the market stands for the square logic of the market, based on the measurement in monetary terms, well-defined conditions of exchange, and an explicit quid pro quo. Adam Smith described the logic of the market deal in the following, famous, words:

> Give me that which I want, and you shall have this which you want, is the meaning of every such offer; and it is in this manner that we obtain from one another the far greater part of those good offices which we stand in need of. It is not from the benevolence of the butcher, the brewer, or the baker, that we expect our dinner, but from their regard to their own interest. We address ourselves, not to their humanity but to their self-love, and never talk to them of our own necessities but of their advantages. (Smith 1776: book I, chap. 2: 19)

Figure 11.1. The Spheres that Dominate the Political and Economic Discussions

THE SPHERE OF THE MARKET	THE SPHERE OF THE STATE

In contemporary talk, the logic of the market inspires talk about products (like the products of healthcare), demand driven production, explicit pricing, monetary incentives, the importance of profit, efficiency, and results. We are now able to recognize in this talk a particular rhetorical genre. To speak of a course in cultural economics as a product of the university is to speak metaphorically. A story about a company becoming innovative due to the profit motive is just that—a story.

One hears the rhetoric of the market most lucidly and pristinely in the company of economists. It is also clearly present in the discourse of administrators and, remarkably, many a policymaker. And one encounters it in market settings, when the deal is made and the terms of the transaction become explicit.

The logic of the state is the logic of collective action, the law, and bureaucracy. In its pure form it involves talk about public goods, corrections of market imperfections, protection of property rights, guaranteeing due process, and redistribution. When artists want to realize the value of their work by means of the state sphere, they will have to conform to the stipulations of the subsidy program, fill in the right forms, and meet the standards of a committee of experts. They will do none of this when they try to realize the value of their work in the market sphere, for then they have to appeal to the commercial sense of a gallery owner and to the taste of potential buyers.

Both the logic of the market and that of the state are purely formal and devoid of social and moral content, as several essays in this volume suggest. There is no need for relationships in either sphere. In the market, agents seek a transaction with whatever party offers the best deal; allocation occurs by means of the objective price mechanism; and valuation equals pricing according to this logic. In the sphere of the state, agents are dependent upon the outcomes of political processes. The bureaucracy is presumed to be neutral in allocating goods and services in accordance with the preferences of the public administration. There is no need for a relationship with the civil servant. The process of allocation is mechanical and follows distinct rules. Valuation, here, is political; the outcome of a democratic process: elections and parliamentary debates determine the value of healthcare, for example, or education, that is, they determine which part of the budget is being allocated to either cause.

Dominant economic and political discourse follows basically the logic of both squares. The leading question is whether markets do better than states in valuing and allocating goods and services. It is a question of ownership, or of who decides. In the market sphere, ownership is private and accordingly individuals or private entities choose and decide. Because ownership is collective in the state sphere, collective entities such as parliaments and governments have to choose and decide who gets what.

Two Additional Spheres of Valuation: First, the Oikos

The difficulty that audiences—students as well as the general public—have in imagining alternative spheres attests to the persuasiveness of the combined logic of the market and state spheres. The presumption is that they are responsible for the realization of all important values and goods that provide values. Either a good receives its value in the sphere of the market or, as in the case of public goods such as national defense and social welfare, in the sphere of the government. Yet, there are other spheres, each with a distinct logic of valuation and valorization. We need to consider them in order to see how values come about outside the spheres of the state and the market. I focus below on two such spheres.

The first is the *oikos,* or home. The oikos is the sphere in which people realize values by means of the logic of connectedness and immediate solidarity. It comprises all of our actions and interactions based on, or implying, kinship or another deeply felt connectedness. Driven by this logic, I share my income with my wife and children without even considering the quid pro quo, at least not explicitly.

Oikos usually refers to the sphere of kinship, of family. It is the place to which people go when they go home. People tend to grow up in an oikos themselves and bring up children in an oikos. But the oikos stands for more. Oikos does not have to be a house or a nuclear family. For a Chinese student of mine, it is the extended family and includes aunts, uncles, nieces, and nephews. For Indians, it might be their tribe, and for others, the local community. A friend claims that his circle of friends has developed into his oikos—with his mother and sister at great distance. The oikos might be a country, like it is for people who have been away from their home country for a long time; astronauts may experience the earth as their oikos after circling around it for some time. People may become part of an oikos by means of a traumatic or deeply felt shared experience. The Stockholm syndrome shows how this happens in the case of hostage dramas. It happens with people who fought together in a war; it also happens with rapist and murderers who strangely become a member of the oikos of their victims. The oikos is about connectedness. People may experience the connectedness as a valuable common good, but connectedness can also have a negative value, like in the case of a rapist, or of a bad relationship with a parent.

The logic of connectedness is about conversations that bring about shared values, or common goods, such as a family, a common history, a special relationship. It is the logic of kinship, of the mother-child and father-child relationship. Most humans do not know much more than this logic in the first years of their lives. They are dependent upon the care of others, they learn how to get their food and their share of the prey by participating in the oikos somehow, by jostling for position, or by competing with their siblings for attention of their parents.

The logic of connectedness does not go well with the logic of the market. The cash nexus plays a subsidiary role, if any, in the oikos. Surely, valuation takes place in the oikos, but it has rather a moral and social connotation. When I fail to deliver as a father, my moral standing suffers. ("How could he forget picking up his child at school! "What a lousy father he is!") Life in the oikos consists of constant haggling and deliberating about who contributes what and how much, about recognition for what one has put in to the oikos. The logic is not only of connectedness, but also of reciprocity ("I do this for the family, we agree not to measure my contribution, but I expect some form of recognition in return," or "if I do the dishes, you can put the children to bed." Disputes within the oikos are often the manifestation of an imbalance in the endless gives and takes. "Listen, I bought all this just for you, so why don't you shut up!" "Yes, but I do not care for all this luxury. All I want from you is a little bit of loving attention." "Don't you see what I am doing for the kids? Isn't that loving attention?"). Would money ever be able to restore the imbalance in the oikos, as it usually does in the market sphere? Parents may try to transfer large sums of money to their children to compensate for a lack of attention, but they may find out that this gesture only increases the anger of their children toward them.

Dealing with people to whom we are connected is dramatically different from dealing with people with whom we only have a relationship for the sake of the deal. When I buy my shoes at a store, I may have a friendly chat with the salesperson, but we both know that the interaction is merely instrumental for the deal. I usually will not feel any social obligation after I have paid for the shoes and walked away. If that person had been an uncle, or the rapist of my sister, it would have been a different matter altogether. In either case, the buying of the shoes would mean a contribution to the shared good that is our relationship.

The logic of the government also does not work well in the sphere of the oikos. Only in exceptional cases does the state step in by means of the court and the law, forcing the quarreling members in an oikos into some kind of settlement, or a divorce. Usually, social deliberation does the trick ("Listen, I am having a hard time. Sorry to have let you down. I do love you, you know." "It's okay. I see how busy you are. Just leave the dishes. I will take care of them later. You take a rest.").

The oikos is social through and through. In contrast to the spheres of the market and the government, it revolves around relationships. Positions do matter. It matters in the valuation of interactions and relationships whether you are the (grand)parent, the father, the mother, the child, the oldest, the youngest, an in-law, a stepchild, or whatever. It matters whether I relate as a father to my own children or to my stepchildren.

The logic of connectedness implies the sharing of goods. The oikos is an oikos because members have things in common. They share common goods as in the form of a family history, memories, a sense of family, or community, and a culture in the form of shared values and practices. One oikos may have as a custom that the head of the household receives the best cut of the meat; in another, the youngest children are the lucky ones. In one oikos they share a faith; in another, they do not. The oikos itself is a common good (see Klamer 2005). No individual can claim its ownership, so it is not a private good. It is not a collective or public good either. It cannot be bought or sold, and is not controlled by a state agency.

The oikos is good for all kinds of things, and it requires effort, time, attention, and often money to sustain it. You lose your oikos when your partner leaves with your children. Children lose at least one dimension of their oikos when they leave home. For some, having an oikos is their most important possession ("my family comes first!"); for others, it is a burden. The oikos may generate a great deal of value to its members. A few members organize the shelter and bring in the food, clothes, and other goods to allot them to the other members in some way or another (see for a good discussion of the process of allotment Gudeman 2001). But that is not all. Daily interactions among the members generate all kinds of goods and bads. They realize, for example, values such as love, care, and responsibility, but also bring about paternalism, dependency, suppression, and abuse.

Recalling Hirschman's three options—exit, voice and loyalty—we perceive the oikos as the realm of loyalty and possibly of voice (cf. Hirschman 1970). Exit is problematic in the oikos. You do not choose an oikos and leave it when the membership ceases to satisfy you. You cannot choose another mother just like that or another father, for that matter. Sure, you can abandon your oikos, but just like the prodigal son found out, your oikos may not leave you. Although divorce appears to be the exit option, you may find out that you continue to be linked to the former partner by means of the children that you have in common. Connections in the oikos can run deep.

Clearly, the sphere of the oikos is complex. An oikos is dynamic because its composition is continuously subject to change. The variety of oikoi is endless. I hope to learn more from anthropologists about the various forms in which they appear and about their functioning. The point for now is that the oikos stands for a distinctive sphere of valuation, one that most people know best as they have grown up with it and live in it everyday. It is distinctive because of their common goods, that is, the goods that their members have in common

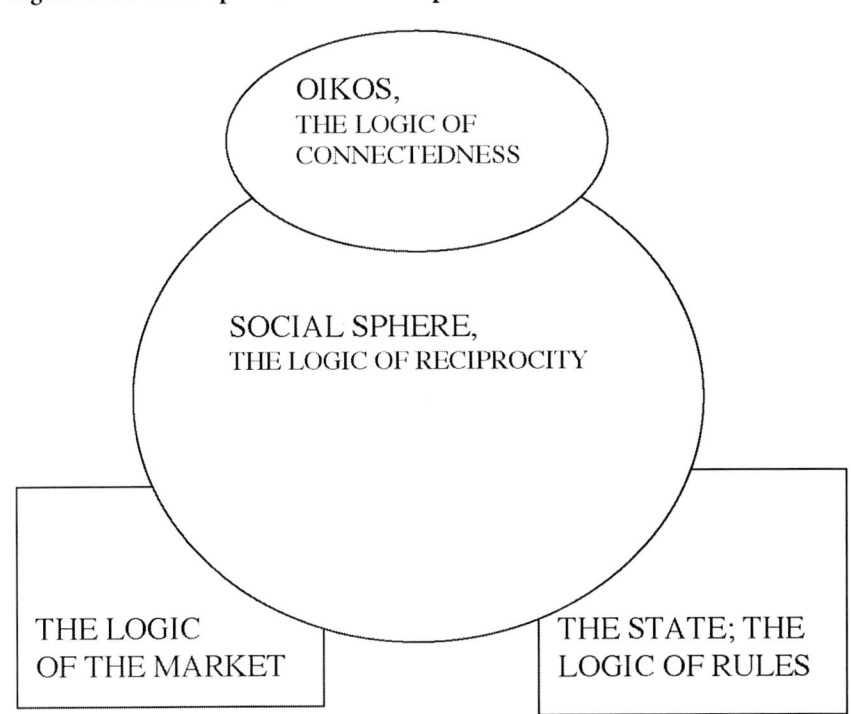

Figure 11.2. Four Spheres Make a Complete Picture

OIKOS, THE LOGIC OF CONNECTEDNESS

SOCIAL SPHERE, THE LOGIC OF RECIPROCITY

THE LOGIC OF THE MARKET

THE STATE; THE LOGIC OF RULES

and their social way of allotting and apportioning goods (Gudeman 2004). The oikos is a common good for its members. You cannot live without one.

The oikos does not quite suffice for everyone all of the time. Especially in "developed" societies, people develop an urge to engage with people outside of their oikos. They experience it as a liberation from the bonds in their oikos. When the economists Hayek and Friedman celebrate the freedom of the market, they mean the negation of the logics of the oikos and the state. They see the market as the escape. To them, the sphere of the market is where people should realize the most relevant values. Yet, there is another sphere to which we turn in order to realize important values.

The Most Important Sphere of all: Society

Usually, we turn to the social sphere instead of turning to the other spheres. Or call it society. This sphere comprises social interactions outside the oikos and away from the spheres of the market and the state. So whenever you and I interact in a way that does not follow the logic of the market, the state or the oikos, we most likely are interacting in the social sphere. Just observe people forming groups. Social animals that they are, they are drawn to each other, and before you know it, they speak of "us," and "our group." They can do so without being connected in any serious way. They do not need to engage in a transaction, exchanging one thing for another, and no formal rules or laws form a constraint. They do not draw up contracts, yet they are a group, a commons you could call it as they share the group. Being part of a group has value for all of them. In a positive sense, it may convey a sense of belonging, an identity even, or possibly a sense of security. (Groups can also work in a negative sense—restraining and even suffocating its members; in that case, people may want to get out.)

Groups come in all forms, sizes, and manifest a wide array of characteristics. Take friendship. Two friends form a group; the friendship has value for them. They can claim the friendship as something of value to them, as a good, as a common good, I would add. In general, you cannot purchase a friendship and you cannot sell it either. (Even though you think of your therapist as your friend, the difference here is that you pay the therapist, and the payment allows you to step out of the relationship without serious consequences.) With your neighbors you form a neighborhood, with your colleagues an organization or a community, and with all kinds of people and other groups a society.

The logic that sustains groups and defines the processes of valuation and valorization in the social sphere is that of reciprocity. The understanding is like this: I do something for someone or for a group—I help in some way, I give attention or recognition, I tell you I really liked your paper, I offer important advice, I dedicate myself to science for the betterment of this world, etc.—and I expect something in return—thanks, recognition, status, additional earning in the future—but the terms of the exchange remain unspecified and are usually unclear. I cannot know for certain when, how, and even by whom a favor is returned. Economists, and possibly thanks to Mauss [1990]) also anthropologists, easily confuse this logic with that of the market. They differ in a fundamental respect. In the logic of the market, the terms of trade have to be made explicit. The quid pro quo has a contractual basis. This is not so according to the logic of the social sphere. Here, interactions involve relationships and the give and take that characterizes relationships ("I helped you move so how about going out with me?"). In the case of reciprocity, the terms of the give and take are left unambiguous and are the subject of endless deliberations, often conducted internally. Playing the game of give and take, of reciprocity, requires a great deal of social knowledge, which is usually unique for a certain group, society or professional group.

Note that the social sphere also manifests itself in commercial organizations. The inclination is to place all commercial activity in the square of the market. Even if their goal is profit maximization and the focus is on the market, employees chat in the morning, give or follow orders during the working day, have holiday parties, discuss personal affairs, help each other out, pay attention, and receive recognition, and they maybe even develop relationships. Commercial organizations, therefore, are part social. The logic of the market only applies to a subset of interactions, like when a deal is struck, when managers value their employees on the basis of the contribution to the bottom line, or when shareholders dictate the decisions. Most of the time, however, the people in commercial organizations are as social in their interactions as they would be outside of it, applying the logic of reciprocity more so than the logic of the market. Similar social processes show up in governmental offices. Thus, organizations are embedded in society.

Markets can also be social. As Lane (1991), Anderson (1993), and McCloskey (2006) have shown, interactions in the setting of markets generate all kinds of social values. Markets bring about bourgeois virtues such as prudence, entrepreneurship, independence, creativity, and responsibility. For those who want to escape from the suffocating effects that the oikos and social settings can have, the market represents the freedom to choose. These values are not economic values per se; they are not prices that can be attached to things. You might say that they are spillovers of the engagement in exchange relations (cf. van Staveren 2000); economists would call them externalities. Interacting in market relations implies the valorization of the values that are common to all such relations, that is, to the culture of the market. The culture of the market stands for a series of typical values—typical as they do not readily pop up in situations in the sphere of the oikos or that of social groups.

The social sphere is good for all kinds of values and goods. Commonly, the most important values of cultural goods are generated in the social sphere. As we have seen, the life of cultural goods may include moments of exchange, but an important part of their values come about, or is sustained, in a series of conversations among curators and other experts, with governmental officials who need to be persuaded to provide subsidies, family members (the oikos), and other people. This social process is one of valorization. Trying to change people's mind (by means of public relations, advertising, and the like) and trying to impact their valuation is a social process requiring social interactions and some kind of social relationship. That is the reason that the market rhetoric—"products," "customers," "efficiency," "demand driven supply," "profit," and similar expressions—is inappropriate when schools try to draw students into the conversation about science, and when artistic groups try to seduce people to join their conversation. Social organizations would like people to participate, to share in their social or cultural values somehow, and, therefore, they do not want people to position themselves as customers as if they are only interested in a quid pro quo interaction.

The Third Sector

Part of the social sphere is the so-called third sector (Klamer and Zuidhof 1998). This is the sphere of gifts, as in donations, volunteering, and the like. Characteristically, institutions in this sphere tend to be nonprofit or nongovernmental. The better term would be social. Social organizations do not have a profit motive, are nongovernmental, and usually have the mission to generate one common good or another. The people who form an artistic organization, for example, try to contribute to the commons, that is, the arts. Researchers at universities try to contribute to the commons of science. Social organizations are not exempt from the logic of the market altogether or, for that matter, from that of the state. They, too, engage in market transactions, draw up contracts with employees, and can set up a fund drive as if it is a commercial operation. Yet, to qualify as a social organization, an organization needs to stress the social logic, like the logic of reciprocity and of commonness, rather than the logic of the market or that of the state.

Conclusion

By picturing (in Figure 11.2) the social sphere below the oikos and on top of the squares of the market and the state, we can appreciate its pivotal place in daily life. It also becomes clear that the logic of the market—so dominant nowadays in political parlors—has a subordinate role. The same applies for the logic of the state. In our daily interactions, the logic of connectedness dominates insofar as we dwell in our oikos and the logic of reciprocity and commonness dominates in our social life. By focusing on the latter logic, we can distinguish the third way in a political sense. We can appreciate the social processes that bring about critical social values; we will understand that cultural goods owe their social and cultural values to the valorization in the social sphere away from the logic of the market and the state. And we may reevaluate the contribution of the third sector and look for ways in which we allow the logic of the market and that of the state, when they are appropriate, and make space for the logics of connectedness, reciprocity, and commonness.

And if we come to reassess the potential of interactions between economists and anthropologists, we might conclude that the latter stand to benefit from the former in terms of their insight into the logic of the market, and that anthropologists can guide economists to a common understanding of how social logic works. This exercise is intended to clear away a few of the rhetorical barriers that stand in the way of such a collaboration. Whether it is successful depends on how the mutual conversation develops.

Notes

1. This contribution is political in the sense that it does not only aim at furthering the conversation among economists and anthropologists, but it also aims at furthering the political conversation. I myself am involved in political discussions in the Netherlands to call attention to the neglect of society.
2. I elaborate on the notions of the conversation, rhetoric, and culture extensively in Klamer (2007).
3. With his notion of commodity fetishism, he criticizes the focus on the commodity phase; in no way does he call to attention that the values of a good can be realized outside the situation of exchange.
4. "Economic goods are goods that are properly valued as commodities and properly produced and exchanged in accordance with market norms…. I call the mode of valuation appropriate to pure commodities 'use'. Use is a lower, impersonal, and exclusive mode of valuation" (Anderson 1993: 143–44).
5. See Velthuis (2005).

Contributors

∎ ∎ ∎ ∎ ∎ ∎

Nurit Bird-David studied Economics and Mathematics at the Hebrew University of Jerusalem and Social Anthropology at Cambridge University. She is currently a senior lecturer of Social Anthropology at the University of Haifa, and a visiting scholar at the department of Anthropology, Harvard University. She is the author of many articles, including on cultural-economics and its contribution to the study of small-scale indigenous economies.

Asaf Darr studied Organizational Behavior at the School of Industrial and Labor Relations, Cornell University. He is currently a senior lecturer of Organization Studies at the University of Haifa. He is the author of *Selling Technology: The Changing Shape of Sales in an Information Economy,* published in 2006 by Cornell University Press. His current research is on the social fabric of mass markets.

James G. Carrier has taught anthropology and sociology and has carried out research on economy in Papua New Guinea, the United States, and Great Britain. His publications include *Wage, Trade and Exchange in Melanesia* (U. Cal. P. 1989, J. Carrier and A. Carrier), *Gifts and Commodities: Exchange and Western Capitalism since 1700* (Routledge 1995), *Meanings of the Market* (Berg 1997, J. Carrier, ed.), and *A Handbook of Economic Anthropology* (Edward Elgar 2005, J. Carrier, ed.). He is currently Adjunct Professor of Anthropology at the University of Indiana and Honorable Research Associate at Oxford Brookes University.

Metin M. Cosgel is Professor of Economics at the University of Connecticut, Storrs, CT, USA. His research interests include rhetorical analysis of the economy, particularly consumption. He has also written on the political economy of religion and the economic history of the Ottoman Empire. Recent publications of his have appeared in *Explorations in Economic History* (2006), *Journal of Economic History* (2005), *Review of Social Economy* (2004), *Historical Method* (2004), and *Journal of Socio-Economics* (2004). He is also maintaining a website on the "Economic History of the Ottoman Empire" (ottoman.uconn.edu). Personal Website: cosgel.uconn.edu.

LaRay Denzer is a historian of twentieth-century Africa, specializing in West African social history, with an emphasis on women's participation in public life and governance in Sierra Leone and Nigeria. Author of the biography of Folayegbe M. Akintunde-Igbodalo, first female permanent secretary in Nigeria, and collaborator in the mediated autobiography of Constance A. Cummings-John, mayor of Freetown, she has also published many articles. She collaborated in all of the newspaper collections for the project analyzed in this paper.

Stephen Gudeman is Professor of Anthropology at the University of Minnesota, and currently Associate Member of the Max Planck Institute for Social Anthropology. The author of six books, his most recent publication is *Economy's Tension* (Berghahn 2008). He has undertaken fieldwork in Panama, Colombia, Guatemala, and Cuba, where he has focused on social life and especially economy. He works to develop an anthropological economics by focusing on culture, figurative language, local voices, formal models, and the interaction of markets and material life.

Jane I. Guyer is Professor of Anthropology at Johns Hopkins University, having served on the faculty at Harvard and Boston University, and as Director of the Program of African Studies at Northwestern. She was elected to the National Academy of Sciences in 2008. The present essay is one of a series of publications on money and modern economies in Africa, which includes most recently *Marginal Gains. Monetary Transactions in Atlantic Africa* (Chicago University Press 2004) and a Forum article in the *American Ethnologist* 34, 3: 409–21, "Prophecy and the near future: Thoughts on macroeconomic, evangelical, and punctuated time".

Keith Hart is Professor of Anthropology Emeritus at Goldsmiths, University of London and Honorary Research Professor in the School of Development Studies, University of Kwazulu-Natal. His work in economic anthropology has focused recently on money, the internet, and informal economy. He is the author of *The Memory Bank: Money in an Unequal World* (2000), *The Hit Man's Dilemma: or Business, Personal and Impersonal* (2005), and *The African Revolution: Africa in the Twenty-first Century World* (forthcoming); and is editor with Chris Hann of *Market and Society: The Great Transformation Revisited* (2009).

Arjo Klamer is Professor of the Economics of Art and Culture at Erasmus University in Rotterdam, The Netherlands, and holds the world's only chair in the field of cultural economics. Prior to that and after acquiring his PhD at Duke University, he taught for many years at several universities in the US, including Wellesley College and George Washington University.

In 1984, he attracted a great deal of attention with his *Conversations with Economists*. In his latest book, *Speaking of Economics* (Routledge, 2007), he pursues themes that emerged from that book. He has collaborated with Deirdre McCloskey to promote the rhetorical perspective on economics. *The Economic Conversation,* a textbook forthcoming in early 2008 (Palgrave) and co-authored with McCloskey and Stephen Ziliak, employs a groundbreaking "open-method" approach to teaching first-year micro- and macroeconomics.

His current research focuses on the cultural dimension of economic life and the values of art. He is a member of the board of various cultural organizations and chairman of the board of trustees of "Het grafisch lyceum" te Rotterdam. He is actively involved in public debates in the Netherlands and is founding director of a new university, Academia Vitae in Deventer.

William Milberg is Associate Professor of Economics at the New School for Social Research in New York. He is the author of *The Economic and Social Consequences of Global Supply Chains* (forthcoming) and co-author (with Robert Heilbroner) of *The Crisis of Vision in Modern Economic Thought.*

Ruben George Oliven is Professor of Anthropology at the Federal University of Rio Grande do Sul in Porto Alegre, Brazil and fellow of the Brazilian Academy of Sciences. He received his PhD from the University of London (London School of Economics and Political Science) and was a visiting professor at several universities, among them the University of California, Berkeley, the University of Paris, and the University of Leiden. He was the President of the Brazilian Anthropological Association and the President of the Brazilian Association for Postgraduate Studies and Research in Social Sciences.

Richard Swedberg is Professor of Sociology at Cornell University, Department of Sociology since 2002. He is a Swedish citizen and his specialties are economic sociology and sociological theory. He has a law degree from Stockholm University and a PhD in Sociology from Boston College. Before coming to Cornell, he worked at the Department of Sociology at Stockholm University, where he in 1996 was appointed "Professor of Sociology, especially Economic Sociology." His works include *Max Weber and the Idea of Economic Sociology* (1998), *Principles of Economic Sociology* (2003), and *Tocqueville's Political Economy* (forthcoming in 2009). He is also the co-editor together with Neil Smelser of *The Handbook of Economic Sociology* (1994; 2005).

References

Abacha, Sani. 1996. "Budget of Consolidation: Full Text of the 1996 Budget Address." *The Guardian,* 16 February: 18, 24.
Acemoglou, D. and J. Robinson. 2004. *Economic Origins of Dictatorship and Democracy.* New York: Cambridge University Press.
Adedoyin, Ademola and Isodi Dike. 1991. "The Oil Subsidy Debate Again." *The Sunday Magazine,* 3 November.
Adeleye, Deji with Femi Olatunde. 1991. "Combating the Deficit Scourge." *Times Week,* 23 December: 51–53.
Adewale, Terry, Lanre Alabi, Aisu Owens, and Olusola Bello. 1996. "Thrills and Spills of the '96 Budget." *Vanguard,* 19 February: 12–13.
Agbese, Pita. 2005. "The 'Stolen' Okigbo Panel Report: Of Malfeasance and Public Accountability in Nigeria." In *Vision and Policy in Nigerian Economics: The Legacy of Pius Okigbo,* edited by L. Denzer and J.I. Guyer, 55–75. Ibadan: Ibadan University Press.
Agrawal, V. and D. Farrel. 2003. "Offshoring: Is It a Win-Win Game?" McKinsey Global Institute, August 2003.
Ake, Claude. 1988. In "Fiery Welcome to Hikes." Sola Akinrinade, *Newswatch,* 19.
Akerlof, George. 1970. "The Market for Lemons: Quality Uncertainty and the Market Mechanism." *Quarterly Journal of Economics* 84, no. 3: 488–500.
Akinrinade, Sola. 1988. "Fiery Welcome to Hikes." *Newswatch,* 2 May: 14–19.
Albrow, Martin. 1990. *Max Weber's Construction of Social Theory.* London: Macmillan.
Alchian, Armen A. and Harold Demsetz. 1973. "The Property Rights Paradigm." *Journal of Economic History* 33, no. 1: 16–27.
Amiti, M. and S-J Wei. 2005. "Fear of Service Outsourcing: is it Justified?" *Economic Policy,* 307–47. April.
Anderson, David G. 1998. "Property as a Way of Knowing on Evenki Lands in Arctic Siberia." In *Property Relations,* edited by C.M. Hann, 64–84. Cambridge: Cambridge University Press.
Anderson, Elizabeth. 1993. *Value in Ethics and Economics.* Cambridge: Harvard University Press.
Andrews, Edmund L. 2005. "Low Rates Could be Around for Long Term." *New York Times,* 27 June: C1 and C9. <http://www.nytimes.com/2005/06/27/business/27fed.html>.
Appadurai, Arjun, ed. 1986. *The Social Life of Things: Commodities in Cultural Perspective.* Cambridge: Cambridge University Press.
Apter, Andrew. 2005. *The Pan African Nation. Oil and the Spectacle of Culture in Nigeria.* Chicago: University of Chicago Press.

Armstrong, W.E. 1924. "Rossel Island Money: A Unique Monetary System." *The Economic Journal* 34, no. 135: 423–29.
Armstrong, W.E. 1928. *Rossel Island.* Cambridge: Cambridge University Press.
Arrow, K. and G. Debreu. 1954. "Existence of an Equilibrium for a Competitive Economy." *Econometrica* 22: 265–90.
Arrow, K. and F. Hahn. 1971. *General Competitive Analysis.* San Francisco: Holden-Day.
Ashwe, Chichi. 1987. "The Petroleum Subsidy Bogey: No Deal." *The Nigerian Economist:* 24–27 October: 51.
Associated Press. 2005. "Upbeat talk by Greenspan Gives Share Prices a Lift." *New York Times,* 10 June. <http://nytimes.com/2005/06/10/business/10stox.html?_r=1&oref=slogin>.
Babbage, Charles. 1835. *On the Economy of Machinery and Manufactures.* London: C. Knight.
Bank of America. 1994. *For Our Customers.* June.
Bardhan, Pranab. 1989. *Conversations between Economists and Anthropologists.* Delhi: Oxford University Press.
Bateson, Gregory. [1936] 1958. *Naven.* Stanford: Stanford University Press.
Baxstrom, Richard, Naveeda Khan, Bhrigupati Singh, and Deborah Poole. 2005. "Networks Actual and Potential: Think-Tanks, War Games and the Creation of Contemporary American Politics." *Theory and Event* 8, no. 4.
Bazerman, Charles. 1991. "Money talks: the rhetorical project of *The Wealth of Nations.*" In *Economics and Language,* edited by W. Henderson, T. Dudley-Evans, and R. Backhouse, 173–99. London and New York: Routledge.
Becker, Gary S. 1968. "Crime and Punishment: An Economic Approach." *Journal of Political Economy* 76: 169–217.
———. 1976. *The Economic Approach to Human Behavior.* Chicago: University of Chicago Press.
———. 1981. *A Treatise on the Family.* Cambridge: Harvard University Press.
———. [1981] 1991. *A Treatise on the Family.* Enlarged edition. Cambridge: Harvard University Press.
———. 1993. "Nobel Lecture: The Economic Way of Looking at Behavior." *The Journal of Political Economy.* 101, no. 3: 385–409.
———. 1996. "Religions Thrive in a Free Market, Too." *Business Week:* 15 January: 7.
Belshaw, Cyril. 1989. "Anthropology in the Spectrum of Knowledge." Unpublished manuscript, International Social Science Council.
Bendix, Reinhard. 1960. *Max Weber: An Intellectual Portrait.* New York: Doubleday & Company.
Benedict, Ruth. 1934. *Patterns of Culture: an analysis of our social structure as related to primitive civilizations.* New York: Penguin Books.
Benhabib, J. and A. Przeworski. 2004. "Economic Growth under Political Accountability." Working Paper, Department of Economics and Department of Politics, New York University.
Bentley, Arthur. [1908] 1967. *The Process of Government.* Cambridge: Harvard University Press.
Bernstein, Basil. 1971. "A Sociolinguistic Approach to Socialization." In *Class, Codes and Control,* edited by B. Bernstein. Volume 1. London: Routledge & Kegan Paul.
Berri, D. et al. 2006. *The Wages of Wins: Taking Measure of the Many Myths in Modern Sports.* Stanford: Stanford Business Books.
Bhagwati, J. et al. 2004. "The Muddles Over Outsourcing." *Journal of Economic Perspectives,* vol. 18, no. 4, Fall: 93–114.

Billig, Michael S. 2000. "Institutions and Culture: Neo-Weberian Economic Anthropology." *Journal of Economic Issues* 34, no. 4: 771–88.

Binswanger, Hans. 1994. *Money and Magic: a Critique of the Modern Economy in the Light of Goethe's 'Faust'*. Chicago: University of Chicago Press.

Bird-David, N. 1990. "The Giving Environment: Another Perspective on the Economic System of Gatherer-hunters." *Current Anthropology* 31(2): 183–96.

———. 1992. "Beyond 'The Original Affluent Society': a Culturalist Reformulation." *Current Anthropology* 33(1): 25–47.

———. 1997. "Economies: a Cultural-economic Perspective." *International Social Science Journal* 154(II): 463–77.

Bizzell, Patricia and Bruce Hertzberg. 1990. *The Rhetorical Tradition: Readings from Classical Times to the Present*. Boston: St. Martin's Press.

Blaug, M. 1980. *The Methodology of Economics, or How Economists Explain*. New York: Cambridge University Press.

———. 2001. "No History of Ideas, Please, We're Economists." *Journal of Economic Perspectives*, vol. 15, no. 1, Winter: 145–64.

Bohannan, Paul and George Dalton, eds. 1965. *Markets in Africa*. New York: Doubleday Anchor.

Booyens, J. 1998. "Economics and Anthropology: In Search of Partnerships." *South African Journal of Economics* 66, no 4: 584–95.

Bourdieu, Pierre. [1979] 1984. *Distinction: A Social Critique of the Judgment of taste*. Cambridge: Harvard University Press.

———. 1986. "The Forms of Capital." In *Handbook of Theory and Research for the Sociology of Education*, edited by J.G. Richardson, 241–58. New York: Greenwood Press.

———. 1998. *Practical Reason: On the Theory of Action*. Stanford: Stanford University Press.

Brown, Vivienne. 1994. "The Economy as Text." In *New Directions in Economic Methodology*, edited by R. Backhouse. London and New York: Routledge.

Buchan, James. 1997. *Frozen Desire: An Enquiry into the Meaning of Money*. London: Picador.

Buckley, Peter J. and Malcolm Chapman. 1996. "Economics and Social Anthropology—Reconciling Differences." *Human Relations* 49, no 9: 1123–50.

"Budget '95: Three Months After." 1995. *Daily Times*, 22 April: 7 and 15.

Business Times. 1994. 6 February: 21.

Caffentzis, George. 1989. *Clipped Coins, Abused Words and Civil Government in John Locke's Philosophy of Money*. New York: Autonomedia.

Cagan, Phillip. 1989. Monetarism. In *The New Palgrave. Money*, edited by John Eatwell, Murray Milgate, and Peter Newman, 195–205. New York: W.W. Norton.

Campbell, J.K. 1964. *Honour, Family, and Patronage: A Study of Institutions and Moral Values in a Greek Mountain Community*. Oxford: Clarendon Press.

Cancian, Frank. 1966. "Maximization as Norm, Strategy, and Theory: A Comment on Programmatic Statements in Economic Anthropology." *American Anthropologist* 68: 465–70.

Carbaugh, Donal. 1988. *Talking American: Cultural Discourses on Donahue*. Ablex Publishing.

Card, D. and A. Krueger. 1995. *Myth and Measurement: The New Economics of the Minimum Wage*. Princeton: Princeton University Press.

Carrier, J. 1990. "Gifts in the World of Commodities: The Ideology of the Perfect Gift in American Society." *Social Analysis* 29: 19–37.

———. 1991. "Gifts, Commodities and Social Relations: A Maussian View of Exchange." *Sociological Forum* 6: 119–36.

———. 1992. "Occidentalism: the world turned upside-down." *American Ethnologist* (2)19: 195–212.

———. 1995. *Gifts and Commodities*. London and New York: Routledge.

———, ed. 1995. *Occidentalism: Images of the West*. Oxford: Oxford University Press.

———. 2001. "Social Aspects of Abstraction." *Social Anthropology* 9: 239–52.

——— and Daniel Miller, eds. 1998. *Virtualism: A New Political Economy*. Oxford: Berg.

———. 1998. "Abstraction in Western Economic Practice." In *Virtualism: A New Political Economy*, edited by J. Carrier and D. Miller, 25–47. Oxford: Berg.

Casson, Mark. 1996. "Economics and Anthropology—Reluctant Partners." *Human Relations* 49, no. 9: 1151–80.

Cheal, D. 1988. *The Gift Economy*. New York: Routledge.

Chun, Allen. 2000. "From Text to Context: How Anthropology Makes its Subject." *Cultural Anthropology* 15, no. 4: 570–95.

Chwe, Michael Suk Young. 2001. *Rational Ritual: Culture, Coordination, and Common Knowledge*. Princeton and Oxford: Princeton University Press.

Coase, R.H. 1988. *The Firm, the Market, and the Law*. Chicago: University of Chicago Press.

Cockett, Richard. 1994. *Thinking the Unthinkable: Think-tanks and the Economic Counter-revolution, 1931–83*. London: Harper Collins.

Coddington, A. 1975. "The Rationale of General Equilibrium Theory." *Economic Inquiry*, vol. 13: 539–58.

Colander, D. 1999. "New Millenium Economics: How Did It Get This Way and What Way is It?" *Journal of Economic Perspectives*, vol. 14, no. 1.

———. 2000. "The Death of Neoclassical Economics." *Journal of the History of Economic Thought*, April.

———. 2005. "The Future of Economics: The Appropriately Educated in Pursuit of the Knowable." *Cambridge Journal of Economics*, vol. 29, no. 6: 927–41.

——— et al. 2004. "The Changing Face of Economics." *Review of Political Economy*, vol. 16, no. 4: 485–99.

Collier, P. and A. Hoeffler. 2004. "Greed and Grievance in Civil War." *Oxford Economic Papers*, vol. 56, no. 4: 563–95.

Collins, Randall. 1998. *The Sociology of Philosophies: A Global Theory of Intellectual Change*. Cambridge: Harvard University Press.

Cook, Scott. 1966a. "Maximization, Economic Theory, and Anthropology: A Reply to Cancian." *American Anthropologist* 68: 1494–98.

———. 1966b. "The Obsolete 'Anti-market' Mentality: A Critique of the Substantive Approach to Economic Anthropology." *American Anthropologist* 68: 323–45.

Cooter, Robert. 2000. "The Law and Economics of Anthropology." In *Encyclopedia of Law and Economics*, Volume 1. *The History and Methodology of Law and Economics*, edited by Boudewijn Bouckaert and Gerrit De Geest. Northampton, MA: Elgar.

Corrigan, P. 1989. "Gender and the Gift: The Case of the Family Clothing Economy." *Sociology* 23: 513–34.

Cosgel, Metin M. 1992. "Rhetoric in the Economy: Consumption and Audience." *Journal of Socio-Economics* 21, no. 4: 363–77.

———. 1994. "Audience Effects in Consumption." *Economics and Philosophy* 10, no. 1: 19–30.

———. 1997. "Consumption Institutions." *Review of Social Economy* 55, no. 2: 153–71.

———, and Arjo Klamer. 1990. "Entrepreneurship as Discourse." Unpublished Manuscript.

———, and Lanse Minkler. 2004. "Rationality, Integrity, and Religious Behavior." *Journal of Socio-Economics* 33, no. 4: 329–41.

Cribb, Joe. 2005. "Money as Metaphor (President's address of the Royal Numismatic Society)." *The Numismatic Chronicle*, vol. 165: 417–38.

Crump, Thomas. 1978. "Money and number: the Trojan horse of language." *Man* (n.s.) 13.4: 503–18.

———. 1981. *The Phenomenon of Money*. London: Routledge.

———. 1990. *The Anthropology of Numbers*. Cambridge: Cambridge University Press.

DaMatta, Roberto. 1991. *Carnivals, Rogues, and Heroes: An Interpretation of the Brazilian Dilemma*. Notre Dame: University of Notre Dame Press.

———. 1993. *Conta de Mentiroso. Sete Ensaios de Antropologia Brasileira*. Rio de Janeiro: Rocco.

Darr, A. 2003. "Gifting Practices and Interorganizational Relations: Constructing Obligation Networks in the Electronics Sector." *Sociological Forum*, 18(1): 47–67.

———. *Selling Technology: The Changing Shape of Sales in an Information Economy*. Ithaca and London: Cornell University Press.

Davidson, Basil. 1992. *The Black Man's Burden: The Myth of African Tribalism and the Curse of the Nation State*. New York Times Books.

Davis, J. 1972. "Gifts and the U.K. Economy." *Man* (n.s.) 7: 408–23.

———. 1992. *Exchange*. Minneapolis: University of Minnesota Press.

———. 2008. "The Turn in Recent Economics and Return of Orthodoxy." *Cambridge Journal of Economics*, forthcoming.

De Roover, Raymond. 1999. *Money, Banking and Credit in Medieval Bruges: Italian merchant-bankers, Lombards and money-changers: a study in the origins of banking*. London: Routledge.

De Saussure, Ferdinand. [1916] 1959. *Course in General Linguistics*. New York: McGraw Hill.

Debreu, G. 1959. *The Theory of Value: An Axiomatic Approach to Economic Equilibrium*. New Haven: Cowles Foundation Monograph Feenstra.

Demsetz, Harold. 1967. "Toward a Theory of Property Rights." *American Economic Review* 57, no. 2: 347–59.

Dewey, John. 1929. *The Quest for Certainty*. New York: G.P. Putnam's Sons.

Dixit, A. and J. Stiglitz. 1977. "Monopolistic Competition and Optimum Product Diversity." *American Economic Review* V. 67, No. 3, June: 297–308.

Djebah, Oma. 1996. "Storm over Budget Surplus." *The Guardian*, 17 September.

Dobbs, L. 2004. *Exporting America: Why Corporate Greed is Shipping American Jobs Overseas*. New York: Warner Business Books.

Dogan, Mattei and Robert Pahre. 1990. *Creative Marginality: Innovation at the Intersections of Social Sciences*. Boulder: Westview Press.

Douglas, Mary. 1966. *Purity and Danger An analysis of concepts of pollution and taboo*. New York: Praeger.

Dow, L. 1977. "High Weeds in Detroit: The Irregular Economy among a Group of Appalachian Migrants." *Urban Anthropology* 6: 111–28.

Dowling, John H. 1982. "The Relationship between Anthropology and Economics." *Journal of Economic Issues* 16, no. 2: 481–84.

Dumont, Louis. 1970. *Homo Hierarchicus: The Caste System and its Implications*. London: Weidenfeld and Nicolson.

———. 1977. *From Mandeville to Marx: The Genesis and Triumph of Economic Ideology.* Chicago: University of Chicago Press.
———. 1980. *Homo Hierarchicus. The Caste System and Its Implications.* Chicago: Chicago University Press.
Durham, D. 1995. "Soliciting Gifts and Negotiating Agency: The Spirit of Asking in Botswana." *Journal of the Royal Anthropological Institute* 1: 111–28.
Durkheim, Emile. [1897] 1951. *Suicide: A Study in Sociology.* New York: The Free Press.
———. [1893] 1984. *The Division of Labour in Society.* London: Routledge & Kegan Paul.
Eagleton, Terry. 2000. *The Idea of Culture.* Oxford: Basil Blackwell.
Easterly, W. 2006. *The White Man's Burden: Why the West's Efforts to Aid the Rest have Done so Much Ill and So Little Good.* New York: The Penguin Press.
Edemodu, Austin. 1996. *Guardian,* 5 January: 18.
Edmonds, E. and N. Pavcnik. 2005. "The Effects of Trade Liberalization on Child Labor." *Journal of International Economics,* March.
Eichengreen, Barry. 1996. *Globalizing Capital: A History of the International Monetary System.* Princeton: Princeton University Press.
Elleh, Nnamdi. 2002. *Architecture and Power in Africa.* Westport: Praeger.
Emerson, Ralph Waldo. 1983. *Essays and Lectures.* New York: Literary Classics of the United States.
Endres, A.M. 1991. "Adam Smith's Rhetoric of Economics: An Illustration Using Smithian Compositional Rules." *Scottish Journal of Political Economy,* vol. 38.1: 76–95.
Ensminger, Jean, ed. 2002. *Theory in Economic Anthropology.* New York: Altamira Press.
Epstein, T. Scarlett. 1975. "The Ideal Marriage between the Economist's Macroapproach and the Social Anthropologist's Microapproach to Development Studies." *Economic Development and Cultural Change* 24, no. 1: 29–45.
Fanon, Frantz. 1963. *The Wretched of the Earth.* New York: Grove Weidenfeld.
Farrell, Joseph. 1995. "Talk is Cheap." *American Economic Review* 85, no. 2: 186–90.
Feenstra, R. and G. Hamilton. 2006. *Emergent Economies, Divergent Paths: Economic Organization and International Trade in South Korea and Taiwan,* New York: Cambridge University Press.
Ferber, Marianne A. and Julie A. Nelson, eds. 1993. *Beyond Economic Man: Feminist Theory and Economics.* Chicago: University of Chicago Press.
Ferenczi, Sandor. 1956. "The Ontogenesis of the Interest in Money." In *Sex in Psychoanalysis.* New York: Dover.
Ferguson, James. 1990. *The Anti-politics Machine: "Development," Depoliticization, and Bureaucratic Power in Lesotho.* New York: Cambridge University Press.
Fidelity Investments. n.d. *The Fidelity Catalog (Your Complete Guide to Fidelity's Products and Services).*
Fine, Ben. 1998. "The Triumph of Economics; Or, 'Rationality' Can Be Dangerous to Your Reasoning." *Virtualism: A New Political Economy,* edited by James G. Carrier and Daniel Miller, 49–73. Oxford: Berg.
Firth, Raymond. 1936. *We, The Tikopia.* London: George Allen & Unwin.
Fishelow, David. 1993. *Metaphors of Genre.* University Park, PA: Pennsylvania State University Press.
Florida, Richard. 2004. *The Rise of the Creative Class.* New York: Basic Books.
Foley, R. 1985. "Optimality Theory in Anthropology." *Man* (n.s.) 20: 222–42.
Forrest, Tom. 1995. *Politics and Economic Development in Nigeria.* Boulder: Westview Press.

Freud, Sigmund. 1953. "Character and Anal Erotism." In *Collected Papers*. London: Hogarth.
Frey, Bruno S. 1997. *Not Just For the Money: an Economic Theory of Personal Motivation*. Brookfield, VT: Edward Elgar.
Friedman, Milton and Rose Friedman. 1980. *Free to Choose: A Personal Statement*. New York: Harcourt Brace.
Friedman, T. 2005. *The World is Flat: A Brief History of the 21st Century*. New York: Farrar, Straus and Giroux.
Frisby, David and Derek Sayer. 1986. *Society*. London: Tavistock.
Gahia, Chukwuemeka. 1996. "Antinomies of a Fiscal Policy." *The Post Express*, 15 August: 17.
Geertz, Clifford. 2002. "An Inconstant Profession: The Anthropological Life in Interesting Times." *Annual Review Of Anthropology* 31:1–19.
Gerth, Hans and C. Wright Mills, eds. 1946. *From Max Weber*. New York: Oxford University Press.
Gigerenzer, Georg. 2002. *Calculated Risks: How to Know When Numbers Deceive You*. New York: Simon and Schuster.
Goldschmidt, Walter. 2000. "A Perspective on Anthropology." *American Anthropologist* 102, no. 4: 789–807.
Gomes, Ângela de Castro. 1989. "A Ética Católica e o Espírito do Pré-Capitalismo." *Ciência Hoje* 9 (52): 23–8.
———. 1990. "A Dialética da Tradição." *Revista Brasileira de Ciências Sociais* 5 (12): 15–27.
Goodenough, Ward H. 2002. "Anthropology in the 20th Century and Beyond." *American Anthropologist* 104, no. 2: 423–40.
Graeber, David. 2001. *Toward an Anthropological Theory of Value: the false coin of our own dreams*. New York: Palgrave.
Granovetter, Mark. 1985. "Economic Action and Social Structure: the Problem of Embeddedness." *American Journal of Sociology* 91: 481–510.
Greenfield, Sidney M. 1982. "Anthropology and Institutional Economics." *Journal of Economic Issues* 16, no. 2: 485–87.
Gregory, C.A. 1980. "Gifts to Men and Gifts to God: Gift Exchange and Capital Accumulation in Contemporary Papua." *Man* 15: 626–52.
———. 1982. *Gifts and Commodities*. London: Academic Press.
Grossbard, Amyra. 1978. "Towards a Marriage between Economics and Anthropology and a General Theory of Marriage." *American Economic Review* 68, no. 2: 33–37.
Grossman, G. 1986. "Strategic Export Promotion: A Critique." In *Strategic Trade Policy and the New International Economics*, edited by P. Krugman. Cambridge: MIT Press.
Grusky, David, ed. 2001. *Social Stratification*. 2nd ed. Boulder: Westview Press.
Gudeman, Stephen. 1978. *The Demise of a Rural Economy*. London: Routledge.
———. 1986. *Economics as Culture: Models and Metaphors of Livelihood*. London: Rouledge Kegan Paul.
———. 1986. "Ricardo's representations." In *Economics as Culture: Models and Metaphors of Livelihood*, 48–70. London: Routledge.
———. 2001. *The Anthropology of Economy: Community, Market, Culture*. Malden: Blackwell.
———. 2006. "Trade's Reason." *Max Planck Institute for Social Anthropology*. Working Papers, Haale/Saale. ISSN 1615–4568.
———. 2008. *Economy's Tension*. New York: Berghahn Books.
——— and Alberto Rivera. 1990. *Conversations in Colombia*. Cambridge: Cambridge University Press.

Guiso, L. et al. 2006. "Does Culture Affect Economic Outcomes." *Journal of Economic Perspectives,* Spring, vol. 20, no. 2: 23–48.
Guyer, Jane I. 1997. *An African Niche Economy: Farming to Feed Ibadan 1968–88.* Edinburgh: Edinburgh University Press.
———. 2004. *Marginal Gains: Monetary Transactions in Atlantic Africa.* Chicago: University of Chicago Press.
———. 2005. Confusion and Empiricism: Several Connected Thoughts. In *Christianity in Africa: Essays in Honor of J.D.Y. Peel,* edited by Toyin Falola, 83–97. Rochester: University of Rochester Press.
———, LaRay Denzer, and Adigun Agbaje. 2002. *Money Struggles and City Life: Devaluation in Ibadan and Other Urban Centers in Southern Nigeria, 1986–1996.* Portsmouth: Heinemann.
Habermas, Jürgen. 1987. *The Theory of Communicative Action.* Volume 2. Cambridge: Polity Press.
Hampshire, Stuart. 1983. *Morality and Conflict.* Cambridge: Harvard University Press.
Hands, D.W. 2001. *Reflection Without Rules: Economic Methodology and Contemporary Science Theory.* New York: Cambridge University Press
Hann, Chris, ed. 1995. *Property Relations.* Cambridge: Cambridge University Press.
Hann, Chris and Keith Hart. Forthcoming. "A Short History of Economic Anthropology." In *Market and Society: The Great Transformation Today,* edited by Chris Hann and Keith Hart. Cambridge: Cambridge University Press.
Harcourt, G. 1978. *The Social Science Imperialists and Other Essays.* London: Routledge and Kegan Paul.
Hardin, G. 1968. "The Tragedy of the Commons." *Science,* no. 162: 1243–48.
Harrison, Lawrence E. and Samuel P. Huntington, eds. 2000. *Culture Matters: How Values Shape Human Progress.* New York: Basic Books.
Hart, Keith. 1982. "On Commoditization." In *From Craft to Industry: the Ethnography of Proto-industrial Cloth Production,* edited by E. Goody, 38–49. Cambridge: Cambridge University Press.
———. 1988. "Kinship, contract and trust: the economic organization of migrants in an African city slum." In *Trust: Making and Breaking Co-operative Relations,* edited by D. Gambetta, 176–93. Oxford: Blackwell.
———. 2000. *The Memory Bank.* London: Profile. (Republished in 2001 as *Money in an Unequal World.* New York and London: Texere).
———. 2004. "Notes Towards an Anthropology of the Internet." *Horizontes Antropologicos* 10. 2: 15–40.
———. 2005a. " Money: One Anthropologist's View." In *Handbook of Economic Anthropology,* edited by James Carrier, 160–75. Cheltenham: Edward Elgar.
———. 2005b. *The Hit Man's Dilemma: or business, personal and impersonal.* Chicago: Prickly Paradigm.
———. 2006. "Richesse Commune: Construire une Démocratie Économique à l'aide de Monnaies Communautaires." In *Exclusion et liens financiers—Monnaies Sociales: Rapport 2005-6,* edited by J. Blanc. Paris: Economica: 135–52.
Hayek, Frederick von. 1937. "Economics and Knowledge." *Economica* 4: 33–54.
———. 1944. *The Road to Serfdom.* Chicago: University of Chicago Press.
Heidegger, Martin. [1930] 1983. *The Fundamental Concepts of Metaphysics: World, Finitude, Solitude.* Bloomington: Indiana University Press.

Heilbroner, Robert. 1961. *The Worldly Philosophers: The Lives, Times and Ideas of the Great Economists.* New York: Simon and Schuster.
Heilbroner, Robert, ed. 1986. *The Essential Adam Smith.* New York: W.W. Norton.
Heilbroner, Robert and W. Milberg. 1995. *The Crisis of Vision in Modern Economics.* New York: Cambridge University Press.
Helgason, Agnar and Gísli Pálsson. 1997. "Contested Commodities: The Moral Landscape of Modernist Regimes." *Journal of the Royal Anthropological Institute* 3: 451–71.
Henderson, Willie. 1995. *Economics as Literature.* New York: Routledge.
Herrmann, G. 1997. "Gift or Commodity: What Changes Hand in the U.S. Garage Sale?" *American Ethnologist* 24: 910–30.
Herskovits, Melville J. 1965. *Economic Anthropology.* New York: W.W. Norton.
Herzfeld, M. 2001. *Anthropology, Theoretical Practice in Culture and Society.* Oxford: Blackwell.
Heusden, Barend van. 1996. "The Value of Culture: a Dialogue with Arjo Klamer." In *Value of Culture,* edited by Arjo Klamer, 44–55. Amsterdam: Amsterdam University Press.
Hill, Kim, Kristen Hawkes, Magdalena Hurtado, and Hillard Kaplan. 1984. "Seasonal Variance in the Diet of Ache Hunter–Gatherers in Eastern Paraguay." *Human Ecology* 12: 101–35.
Hirschman, Albert O. 1970. *Exit, Voice and Loyalty.* Cambridge: Harvard University Press.
———. 1977. *The Passions and the Interests: Political Arguments for Capitalism before Its Triumph.* Princeton: Princeton University Press.
———. 1986. "The Concept of Interest: from Euphemism to Tautology." In *Rival Views of Market Society and Other Recent Essays.* New York: Viking.
Hirshleifer, J. 1985. "The Expanding Domain of Economics." *American Economic Review,* vol. 75, no. 6: 53–68.
Hodgson, G. 2007. "Evolutionary and Institutional Economics as the New Mainstream." *Evolutionary Institutional Economics Review,* vol. 4, no. 1: 7–25.
Holanda, Sérgio Buarque de. 1969. *Raízes do Brasil.* Rio de Janeiro: José Olympio.
Holmes, D. 1989. *Cultural Disenchantments: Worker Peasantries in Northeast Italy.* Princeton: Princeton University Press.
Holmes, Stephen. 1990. "The Secret History of Self-Interest." In *Beyond Self-Interest,* edited by Jane Mansbridge. Chicago: University of Chicago Press.
Humphrey, Caroline and Verdery, Katherine. 2004. "Introduction: Raising Questions about Property." In *Property in Question,* edited by Katherine Verdery and Caroline Humphrey, 1–25. Oxford: Berg.
Hyde, L. 1983. *The Gift: Imagination and the Erotic Life of Property.* New York: Random House.
Imirhe, Toma. 1991. "Short of the Magic Wand." *The African Guardian,* 14 January: 29–30.
Inglehart, Ronald. 1997. *Modernization and Post-Modernization: Cultural, Economic and Political Change in 43 Societies.* Princeton: Princeton University Press.
Innis, Harold. 1951. *The Bias of Communication.* Toronto: University of Toronto Press.
Isaac, Barry L. 2005. "Karl Polanyi." In *Handbook of Economic Anthropology,* edited by James G. Carrier. Cheltenham: Edward Arnold.
Iyeke, Peter. 1996. *The Vanguard,* 19 February: 1 and 2.
Johnson, Craig. 2004. "Uncommon Ground: The 'Poverty of History' in Common Property Discourse." *Development and Change* 35: 407–33.
Kahn, Joel S. 1990. "Towards a History of the Critique of Economism: The Nineteenth Century German Origins of the Ethnographer's Dilemma." *Man* 25: 230–49.

———. 1997. "Demons, Commodities and the History of Anthropology." In *Meanings of the Market*, edited by James G. Carrier. Oxford: Berg.

Kalberg, Stephen. 1985. "The Role of Ideal Interests in Max Weber's Comparative Historical Sociology." In *A Weber-Marx Dialogue*, edited by Roberto Antonio and Ronald Glassman. Kansas: University of Kansas Press.

———. 1994. *Max Weber's Comparative Historical Sociology*. Chicago: University of Chicago Press.

Kaplan, Michael. 2003. "Iconomics: The Rhetoric of Speculation." *Public Culture* 15, no. 3: 477–93.

Keane, Webb. 2003. "Self-Interpretation, Agency, and the Objects of Anthropology: Reflections on a Genealogy." *Comparative Studies in Society and History* 45, no. 2: 222–48.

Keen, Suzanne. 2003. *Narrative Form*. NY: Palgrave Macmillan.

Keynes, J.M. 1936. *The General Theory of Employment, Interest and Money*. London: Macmillan.

Keynes, John Maynard. 1932. *Essays in Persuasion*. New York: Harcourt, Brace and Company.

King Jr, Martin Luther. 2003. "I Have a Dream." In *Racism. A Global Reader*, edited by Kevin Reilly, Stephen Kaufman, and Angela Bodino. M.E. Sharpe: Armonk & London.

Kirzner, Israel. 1976. *The Economic Point of View: An Essay in the History of economic Thought*. Kansas City: Sheed and Ward.

Klamer, Arjo. 1983. *Conversations with Economists*. Totowa: Rowman and Allanheld.

———. 1991. "Towards the Native Point of View." In *Economics and Hermeneutics*, edited by Don Lavoie. London: Routledge.

———. 2003. "A Pragmatic View on Values in Economics." *Journal of Economic Methododology*, vol. 10 (2): 191–212.

———. 2004. "Cultural Goods are Good for More Than Their Economic Value." In *Culture and Public Action*, edited by V. Rao and M. Walton. Stanford: Stanford University Press.

———. 2007. *Speaking of Economics: How to be in the Conversation*. London: Routledge.

——— and David Colander. 1989. *The Making of an Economist*. Boulder: Westview Press.

——— and David Throsby. 2000. "Paying for the Past: the Economics of Cultural Heritage." In *World Culture Report, 2000*, 130–45. Paris: Unesco Publishing.

——— and P.W. Zuidhof. 1998. "The Role of the Third Sphere in the World of the Arts." Paper presented at the ACEI conference.

Kletzer, L. 2001. "Job Loss from Imports: Measuring the Costs." Washington, D.C., Institute for International Economics.

———. 2005. "Globalization and Job Loss, From Manufacturing to Services." *Economic Perspectives*, 2Q, 2005: 38–46.

Knight, Frank. [1921] 1971. *Risk, Uncertainty, and Profit*. Chicago: University of Chicago Press.

Knight, Frank. 1941. "Anthropology and Economics." *The Journal of Political Economy* 49, no. 2: 247–68.

Knight, James A. 1968. *For the Love of Money. Human Behavior and Money*. Philadelphia: J.B. Lippincott.

Knudsen, Christian. 2004. "Alfred Schutz, Austrian Economists and the Knowledge Problem." *Rationality and Society* 16, no. 1: 45–89.

Kocourek, Albert. 1917. "The Nature of Interests and Their Classification." *American Journal of Sociology* 23: 359–68.

Kopytoff, I. 1986. "The Cultural Biography of Things: Commodification as a Process." In *The Social Life as Things*, edited by Arjun Appadurai, 64–91. New York: Cambridge University Press.

Krueger, A. 1999. "Experimental Estimates of Educational Production Functions." *Quarterly Journal of Economics*, vol. 114, no. 2: 497–532.

―――― and D. Whitmore. 2000. "The Effects of Attending a Small Class in the Early Grades on College-test taking and Middle School Test Results: Evidence from Project Star." Working Paper 7656, National Bureau of Economic Research, April. <http://www.nber.org/papers/w7656>.

Krugman, P. 1983. "New Theories of International Trade." *American Econonomic Review*, vol. 73: 343–48.

Krugman, Paul. 2005. "Un-Spin The Budget." *New York Times*, 11 July. <http://www.nytimes.com/2005/07/11/opinion/11krugman.html>.

Kuhn, Thomas. 1970. *The Structure of Scientific Revolutions*. Chicago: University of Chicago Press.

Lalli, Frank. 1994. "The Cost of One Bullet: $2 Million". *Money* 23 (2): 7–8.

Lane, Robert E. 1991. *The Market Experience*. Cambridge: Cambridge University Press.

Langlois, Richard. 1992. "Orders and Organizations: Toward an Austrian Theory of Social Institutions." In *Austrian Economics: Tensions and New Direction*, edited by Bruce Caldwell and Stephan Boehm. Dordrecht: Kluwer Academic Publishers.

―――― . 2003. "The Vanishing Hand: the Changing Dynamics of Industrial Capitalism." *Industrial and Corporate Change*, vol. 12, no. 2: 351–85.

―――― and Nicolai J. Foss. 1999. "Capabilities and Governance: the Rebirth of Production in the Theory of Economic Organization." *Kyklos* 52, no. 2: 201–18.

Lavoie, Don. 1990. "Hermeneutics, Subjectivity, and the Lester/Machlup Debate: Toward a More Anthropological Approach to Empirical Economics." In *Economics as Discourse: An Analysis of the language of Economics*, edited by Warren J. Samuels. Boston: Kluwer Academic Publishers.

Le Goff, Jacques. 1988. *Your Money or Your Life. Economy and Religion in the Middle Ages*. New York: Zone Books.

Leach, Edmund. 1982. *Social Anthropology*. NY: Oxford University Press.

Leacock, Eleanor. 1954. "The Montagnais 'Hunting Territory' and the Fur Trade." *American Anthropological Association*, memoir no. 78, vol. 56: 5.

Leamer. 1983. "Let's Take the Con out of Econometrics." *American Economic Review*, vol. 73: 31–43.

LeClair, Edward E., Jr and Harold K. Schneider, ed. 1968. *Economic Anthropology: Readings in Theory and Analysis*. New York: Holt, Rinehart and Winston.

Leonhardt, David. 2003. "'Egalitarian Recession' Keeps Anger At Bay." *New York Times*, 15 June, Week in Review. <http://query.nytimes.com/gst/fullpage.html?res=9B0CEFD81738F936A25755C0A9659C8B63>.

Lepsius, M. Rainer. 1986. "Interessen und Ideen. Die Zurechnungsprobematik bei Max Weber." In *Kultur und Gesellschaft*, edited by Friedhelm Neidhardt et al. Opladen: Westdeutscher Verlag.

Lévi-Strauss, Claude. [1958] 1967. *Structural Anthropology*. New York: Anchor.

Levitt, S. and S. Dubner. 2005. *Freakonomics: A Rogue Economist Explores the Hidden Side of Everything*. New York: William Morrow.

Levy, D. 2005. "Offshoring in the New Global Political Economy." *Journal of Management Studies*, vol. 42, no. 3 (May): 685–91.

Lévy-Bruhl, Lucien. 1923. *Primitive Mentality.* London: George Allen & Unwin.
Lindbeck, Assar. 1992. Presentation speech. Bank of Sweden Prize in Economic Sciences in Memory of Alfred Nobel. <http://nobelprize.org/economics/laureates/1992/presentation-speech.html> 13 January 2005.
Lipton, Michael. 1992. "Economics and Anthropology: Grounding Models in Relationships." *World Development* 20, no. 10: 1541–46.
Locke, John. [1690] 1960. *Two Treatises of Government.* Cambridge: Cambridge University Press.
Lodewijks, John. 1994. "Anthropologists and Economists: Conflict or Cooperation?" *Journal of Economic Methodology* 1: 81–104.
Lowenthal, M. 1975. "The Social Economy in Urban Working Class Communities." In *The Social Economy of Cities,* edited by Gary Gappert and Harold M. Ross, 447–69. Beverly Hills: Sage.
Lucy, John, ed. 1993. *Reflexive Language: reported speech and metapragmatics.* Cambridge: Cambridge University Press.
MacLennan, Carol A. 1997. "Democracy under the Influence: Cost-Benefit Analysis in the United States." In *Meanings of the Market,* edited by James G. Carrier. Oxford: Berg.
Macpherson, C.B. 1962.*The Political Theory of Possessive Individualism.* Oxford: Clarendon Press.
———. 1979. "Property as Means or End." In *Theories of Property: Aristotle to the Present,* edited by Anthony Parel and Thomas Flanagan, 3–9. Waterloo, Canada: Wilfrid Laurier University Press.
Malinowski, Bronislaw. 1922. *Argonauts of the Western Pacific.* London: Routledge & Kegan Paul.
———. 1926. *Crime and Custom in Savage Society.* London: Routledge and Kegan Paul.
———. [1935] 1978. *Coral Gardens and Their Magic.* New York: Dover Publications.
Mandeville, Bernard. [1714] 1981. *The Fable of the Bees: or, Private Vices, Publick Benefits.* New York: G. Olms.
Markus, Hazel and Shinobu Kitayama. 1998. "The Cultural Psychology of Personality." *Journal of Cross-cultural Psychology* 29, no. 1: 63–87.
——— and Shinobu Kitayama. 2003. "Models of Agency: Sociocultural Diversity in the Construction of Action." In *Cross-Cultural Differences in Perspectives on the Self,* edited by Virginia Murphy-Berman and John Berman. Nebraska Symposium on Motivation 49: 18–74.
Marshall, Alfred. 1890. *Principles of Economics.* London: Macmillan.
Martin, Wallace. 1986. *Recent Theories of Narrative.* Ithaca: Cornell University Press.
Martindale, Don. 1960. *The Nature and Types of Sociological Theory.* Boston: Houghton Mifflin Company.
Marx, Karl. 1844. "The Power of Money." In *The Economic and Philosophical Manuscripts of 1844.* <http://www.marxists.org/works/1844/manuscripts/power.htm>.
———. [1867] 1967. *Capital.* Volume 1. New York: International Publishers.
———. [1867] 1970. *Capital: the Critique of Political Economy,* Volume 1. London: Lawrence and Wishart.
———. [1857–58] 1973. *Grundrisse.* New York: Vintage Books.
———. 1988. *Economic and Philosophic Manuscripts of 1844.* New York: Prometheus Books.
———. [1865] 1995. *The Poverty of Philosophy.* New York: Prometheus Books.
Maurer, Bill. 2006. "The Anthropology of Money." *Annual Review of Anthropology,* 35.2 (March).

Mauss, Marcel. 1954. *The Gift.* Translated by Ian Cunnison. London: Cohen and West.
———. [1938] 1985. "A Category of the Human Mind: The Notion of Person; the Notion of Self." In *The Category of the Person,* edited by Michael Carrithers, Steven Collins, and Steven Lukes. Cambridge: Cambridge University Press.
———. [1925] 1990. *The Gift: The Form and Reason for Exchange in Archaic Societies.* London: Routledge.
Mayer, T. 1995. *Doing Economic Research: Essays on the Applied Methodology of Economics.* Brookfield, VT: Edward Elgar.
Mayhew, Anne. 1994. "Transactors and Their Markets in Two Disciplines." *History of Political Economy* 26, Supplement: 295–312.
———. 1999. "The Troubled Courtship of Economics and Anthropology." In *Research in the History of Economic Thought and Methodology,* Volume 17, edited by Warren Samuels and Jeff Biddle. Stamford, CT: JAI Press.
Mbembe, Achille. 2001. *On the Postcolony.* Berkeley: University of California Press.
McCloskey, D. 1983. *The Rhetoric of Economics.* Madison: University of Wisconsin Press.
———. 1985. "A Conversation with Donald McCloskey about Rhetoric." *Eastern Economic Journal,* vol. 11, no. 4, Oct.–Dec: 293–96.
———. 1994. *Knowledge and Persuasion in Economics.* Cambridge: Cambridge University Press.
———. 1996. *The Vices of Economists, the Virtues of the Bourgeoisie.* Amsterdam: Amsterdam University Press.
———. 2006. *Bourgeois Virtues.* Chicago: University of Chicago Press.
——— and Arjo Klamer. 1995. "One Quarter of GDP is Persuasion." *American Economic Review* (May): 191–96.
——— and S. Ziliak. 1996. "The Standard Error of Regressions." *Journal of Economic Literature,* vol. 34, no. 1, March: 97–114.
McLeary, R. and R. Barro. 2006. "Religion and Economy." *Journal of Economic Perspectives,* Spring, vol. 20, no. 2: 49–72.
McMichael, Philip. 1998. "Development and Structural Adjustment." In *Virtualism: A New Political Economy,* edited by James G. Carrier and Daniel Miller. Oxford: Berg.
Merton, Robert K. 1946. *Mass Persuasion: The Social Psychology of a War Bond Drive.* New York: London, Harper & Brothers.
Metz, Elizabeth and Richard Parmentier, eds. 1985. *Semiotic Mediation: Sociocultural and Psychological Perspectives.* Orlando FA: Academic Press.
Mieder, Wofgang. 1989. *American Proverbs. A Study of Texts and Contexts.* New York: Lang.
———. 1991. *A Dictionary of American Proverbs.* New York: Oxford University Press.
Milberg, W. 1996. "The Rhetoric of Policy Relevance in International Economics." *Journal of Economic Methodology,* vol. 3, no. 2.
———. 2001. "Decentering the Market Metaphor in International Economics." In *Postmodernism, Knowledge and Economics,* edited by S. Cullenberg, D. Ruccio, and J. Amariglio. London: Routledge.
———. 2004. "After the 'Economics'—Pragmatist Turn?" In *Dewey, Pragmatism and Economic Methodology,* edited by E. Khalil. London: Routledge.
———. 2007. "The Shifting and Allegorical Rhetoric of 'Neoclassical' Economics." *Review of Social Economics,* vol. LXV, no. 2: 209–22.
Milgrom, Paul and John Roberts. 1992. *Economics, Organization and Management.* Englewood Cliffs, NJ: Prentice Hall.
Mill, John Stuart. 1874. "On the Definition of Political Economy; and on the Method of

Investigation Proper to it." In *Essays on Some Unsettled Questions of Political Economy*, 2nd ed. London: Longmans, Green, Reader & Dyer. Reprinted by Augustus M. Kelley.

———. [1836] 1992. "On the Definition of Political Economy; and on the Method of Investigation Proper to It." In *Essays on Some Unsettled Questions of Political Economy*. Bristol: Thoemmes Press.

Miller, Daniel. 1998. "Conclusion: A Theory of Virtualism." In *Virtualism: A New Political Economy*, edited by James G. Carrier and D. Miller. Oxford: Berg.

Miller, Rich. 2005. "Too Much Money. The Surprising Consequences of a Global Savings Glut." *Business Week*, 11 July: 48–56.

Mirowski, Philip. 1988. *Against Mechanism: Protecting Economics from Science*. Totowa, NJ: Rowman and Littlefield.

———. 1989. "The Probabilistic Counter Revolution." *Oxford Economic Papers*, vol. 41: 217–35.

———. 1989. *More Heat Than Light*. Cambridge: Cambridge University Press.

———. 1994. "Tit for Tat: Concepts of Exchange, Higgling, and Barter in Two Episodes in the History of Economic Anthropology." *History of Political Economy* 26, Supplement: 313–42.

———. 2000. "Exploring the Fault Lines: Introduction to the Minisymposium on the History of Economic Anthropology." *History of Political Economy* 32, no. 4: 919–32.

———. 2002. *Machine Dreams: How Economics Became a Cyborg Science*. New York: Cambridge University Press.

———. 2004. *The Effortless Economy of Science?* Durham: Duke University Press.

——— and S. Sklivas. 1992. "Why Econometricians Don't Replicate (Although They Do Reproduce)." *Review of Political Economy*, vol. 3: 146–63.

Mitchell, Timothy. 2002. *Rule of Experts: Egypt, Techno-politics, Modernity*. Berkeley: University of California Press.

Mokyr, J. 2000. *The Gifts of Athena: Historical Origins of the Knowledge Economy*. Princeton: Princeton University Press.

Mommsen, Wolfgang. 2000. "Max Weber's 'Grand Sociology': The Origins and Composition of Wirtschaft und Gesellschaft. Soziologie." *History and Theory* 39: 364–83.

Moog, Clodomiro Vianna. 1964. *Bandeirantes and Pionners*. New York: George Braziller.

Morgan, Gareth. 2006. *Images of Organization*. London: Sage Publications.

Mosse, David. 2004. *Cultivating Development: An Ethnography of Aid Policy and Practice*. London: Pluto Press.

Munro, Gillian and K. Hart. 2000. '*The Highland Problem*': *state and community in local development*. Aberdeen: Arkleton Research Papers, no. 1.

Neusner, Jacob. 1990. *The Economics of the Mishnah*. Chicago: University of Chicago Press.

Newbreed. 1993. "Budget of Deceit: Old Wine In New Bottles." 8 March: 4–15.

Newswatch. 1987. 30 November, Cover.

Newswatch. 1988. 25 July: 36.

Newswatch. 1989. "Sap Not Evil Speech." 19 June 1989: 20.

Nigerian Hand Book Review. 1992: 119–20.

North, Douglass. 1990. *Institutions, Institutional Change and Economic Performance*. Cambridge: Cambridge University Press.

North, Pete. 2006. *Alternative Currency Movements as a Challenge to Globalisation? A case study of Manchester's local currency networks*. Aldershot: Ashgate.

O'Driscoll, Gerald P., Jr. 1977. *Economics as a Coordination Problem: The Contribution of Friedrich A. Hayek*. Kansas City: Sheed Andrews & McMeel.

Ogburn, William F. 1964. "Southern Folkways Regarding Money." In *On Culture and Social Change*. Chicago: Chicago University Press.
Olaniyan, Tejumola. 2004. *Arrest the Music! Fela and his Rebel Art and Politics*. Bloomington: Indiana University Press.
Oliven, Ruben George. 1984. "A Malandragem na Música Popular Brasileira." *Latin American Music Review* 5 (1): 66–96.
———. 1996. *Tradition Matters: modern gaúcho identity in Brazil*. New York: Columbia University Press.
———. 1998. "Looking at Money in America." *Critique of Anthropology* 18 (1): 35–59.
———. 1999. "Money in Brazilian Popular Music." *Studies in Latin American Popular Culture* 18: 115–37.
Olson, Mancur. 1965. *The Logic of Collective Action: Public Goods and the Theory of Goods*. Cambridge: Harvard University Press.
Omokhodion, Lawson and Victor Iduwe. 1987. "A String of Deficit Budgets." *THISWEEK*, 2 February: 24–25.
Park, Robert and Ernest Burgess. 1924. *Introduction to the Science of Sociology*. Chicago: University of Chicago Press.
Parry, Jonathan and Maurice Bloch, ed. *Money and the Morality of Exchange*. Cambridge: Cambridge University Press.
Parry, Jonathan. 1986. "The Gift, the Indian Gift and the 'Indian Gift.'" *Man* 21: 453–73.
Pearson, Heath. 2002. "Primitive Economics: A Reply." *History of Political Economy* 34, no. 1: 273–81.
Peillon, Michel. 1990. *The Concept of Interest in Social Theory*. Lewiston: Edwin Mellen Press.
Persky, Victor. 1995. "The Ethology of *Homo Economicus*." *Journal of Economic Perspectives* 9, 2: 22–31.
Pierce, Charles. 1985. "Logic as Semiotic: the Theory of Signs." In *Semiotics: an Introductory Anthology*, edited by Robert Innis, 4–23. Bloomington: Indiana University Press.
Pieters, Rik and Hans Baumgartner. 2002. "Who Talks to Whom? Intra and Interdisciplinary Communication of Economics Journals." *Journal of Economic Literature* 40, no. 2: 483–509.
Pirolli, Peter and Stuart K. Card. 1998. "Information Foraging Models of Browsers for Very Large Document Spaces." *Proceedings of the Working Conference on Advanced Visual Interfaces*, 83–93. New York: ACM Press.
Polanyi, Karl. [1944] 1957. *The Great Transformation: The Political and Economic Origins of Our Time*. Boston: Beacon Press.
———. 1957. "The Economy as Instituted Process." In *Trade and Market in the Early Empires: Economies in History and Theory*, edited by K. Polanyi, Conrad M. Arensberg, and Harry W. Pearson. Glencoe, IL: The Free Press.
———, Conrad M. Arensberg, and Harry W. Pearson, eds. 1957. *Trade and Market in the Early Empires: Economies in History and Theory*. Glencoe, IL: The Free Press.
——— and Harry W. Pearson. 1977. *The Livelihood of Man*. New York: Academic Press.
Polanyi, Michael. 1949. "Review of F.A. Hayek, *Individualism and Economic Order*." *Economica*, August: 267.
Porte, Joel. 1979. *Representative Man. Ralph Waldo Emerson in His Time*. New York: Oxford University Press.
Porter, Sylvia. 1985. *Love and Money*. New York: William Morrow.
Porter, Theodore. 1996. *Trust in Numbers: the Pursuit of Objectivity in Science and Public Life*. Princeton: Princeton University Press.

Posner, Richard A. 1980. "Anthropology and Economics: Review Article." *Journal of Political Economy* 88, no. 3: 608–16.
Post Express. 1996a. "Antimonies of a Fiscal Policy." 15 August.
Post Express. 1996b. "1996 Budget Still Off-Target." 27 November.
Pritchard, Harold. [1940] 1968. *Moral Obligation, and Duty and Interest: Essays and Lectures*. London: Oxford University Press.
Pryor, Frederic L. 2005. *Economic Systems of Foraging, Agricultural, and Industrial Societies*. Cambridge: Cambridge University Press.
Putnam, Robert, Robert Leonardi, and Rafaella Y. Nanetti. 1994. *Making Democracy Work*. Princeton: Princeton University Press.
Radcliffe-Brown, A.R. 1952. *Structure and Function in Primitive Society*. London: Routledge & Kegan Paul.
Ratzenhofer, Gustav. 1907. *Sociologie: Positive Lehre von den menschlichen Wechselbesiehungen*. Leipzig: F.A. Brockhaus.
Ray, Larry and Andrew Sayer, eds. 1999. *Culture and Economy: After the Cultural Turn*. London: Sage Publications.
Rebhun, L.A. 1993. *Love and Interests. Negotiating the Value of Cash and Sentiment Under Economic Disruption in Northeast Brazil*. Paper presented at the 92nd Annual Meeting of the American Anthropological Association, Washington.
Reddy, William M. 1984. *The Rise of Market Culture: the Textile Trade and French Society, 1750–1900*. Cambridge: Cambridge University Press.
Ricardo, David. [1817] 1951. *On the Principles of Political Economy and Taxation*. Edited by Piero Sraffa. Cambridge: Cambridge University Press.
———. [1817] 1971. *Principles of Political Economy and Taxation*. Harmondsworth: Penguin.
Richards, Audrey. 1939. *Land, Labour and Diet in Northern Rhodesia*. London: Oxford University Press.
Richardson H. and N.A.M. Verbeek. 1986. "Diet Selection and Optimization by Northwestern Crows Feeding on Japanese Littleneck Clams." *Ecology* 67: 1219–26.
Rigney, Daniel and Donna Barnes. 1980. "Patterns of Interdisciplinary Citation in the Social Sciences." *Social Science Quarterly* 61: 114–27.
Robbins, L. 1932. *An Essay on the Nature & Significance of Economic Science*. London: Macmillan.
Rodrik, D. 1999. "Democracy Pays Higher Wages." *Quarterly Journal of Economics*, vol. 114, no. 3, August.
——— et al. 2002. "Institutions Rule: The Primacy of Institutions Over Geography and Integration in Economic Development." Mimeo.
Rorty, Richard. 1979. *Philosophy and the Mirror of Nature*. Princeton: Princeton University Press.
Rosaldo, Renato. 1987. "Where Objectivity Lies: The Rhetoric of Anthropology." In *The Rhetoric of the Human Sciences*, edited by J.S. Nelson, A. Megill, and D. McCloskey. Madison: University of Wisconsin Press.
Rose, Carol M. 1994. *Property and Persuasion: Essays on the History, Theory, and Rhetoric of Ownership*. Boulder: Westview Press.
Roth, Guenther and Wolfgang Schluchter. 1979. *Max Weber's Vision of History*. Berkeley: University of California Press.
Rousseau, Jean Jacques. [1762] 1913. *The Social Contract*. Translated by G.D.H. Cole. London: J. M. Dent and Sons Ltd.

Russell, Bertrand. 1945. *A History of Western Philosophy and Its Connection with Political and Social Circumstances from the Earliest Times to the Present Day*. New York: Simon and Schuster.
Sahlins, Marshall. 1963. "Poor Man, Rich Man, Big-man, Chief: Political Types in Melanesia and Polynesia." *Comparative Studies in Society and History* 5: 285–303.
———. 1972. *Stone Age Economics*. New York: Aldine Books.
———. 1976. *Culture and Practical Reason*. Chicago: University of Chicago.
———. 1996. "The Sadness of Sweetness: The Native Anthropology of Western Cosmology." *Current Anthropology* 37: 395–415, 425–28.
Said, Edward. 1978. *Orientalism*. Harmondsworth: Penguin.
Samuelson, Paul. 1938. "A Note on the Pure Theory of Consumer Behavior." *Economica* 5: 61–71.
Santayana, George. 1936. *The Last Puritan: A Memoir in the Form of a Novel*. New York: Scribner.
Scaff, Lawrence. 1989. "Weber before Weberian Sociology." In *Reading Weber*, edited by Keith Tribe. London: Routledge.
Schama, Simon. 1987. *The Embarrassment of Riches. An Interpretation of Dutch Culture in the Golden Age*. New York: Alfred A. Knopf.
Schotter, Andrew. 1981. *The Economic Theory of Social Institutions*. NY: Cambridge University Press.
Scott, James C. 1998. *Seeing Like a State*. New Haven: Yale University Press.
Sen, Amartya. 1986. "Rationality, Interest, and Identity." In *Development, Democracy, and the Art of Trespassing*, edited by Alejandro Foxley, et al. Notre Dame: University of Notre Dame Press.
———. 1993. "Capability and Well-Being." In *The Quality of Life*, edited by Martha Nussbaum and Amartya Sen, 30–53. Oxford: Oxford University Press.
———. 2002. *Rationality and Freedom*. Cambridge: The Belknap Press.
Shell, Marc. 1978. *The Economy of Literature*. Baltimore: Johns Hopkins University Press.
———. 1986. *Money, Language and Thought*. Berkeley: University of California Press.
Shiller, Robert J. 1995. "Conversation, Information, and Herd Behavior." *The American Economic Review* 85, no. 2: 181–85.
Silver, Morris. 1992. *Taking Ancient Mythology Economically*. Leiden: Brill.
Simmel, Georg. 1950. *The Sociology of Georg Simmel*. Edited by Kurt Wolff. New York: The Free Press.
———. 1955. *Conflict and the Web of Group-Affiliation*. New York: The Free Press.
———. 1971. *On Individuality and Social Forms*, edited by Donald Levine. Chicago: University of Chicago Press.
———. [1900] 1978. *The Philosophy of Money*. London: Routledge.
———. 1984. *On Woman, Sexuality, Love*. New Haven: Yale University Press.
———. [1908] 1995. *Soziologie. Untersuchungen über die Formen der Vergesellschaftung*. Frankfurt am Main: Suhrkamp.
———. 1997. *Simmel on Culture*. Edited by David Frisby and Mike Featherstone. London: SAGE.
Small, Albion. 1900. "The Scope of Sociology. IV. The Assumptions of Sociology." *American Journal of Sociology* 6, 1: 42–66.
———. 1905. *General Sociology: An Exposition of the Main Development in Sociological Theory from Spencer to Ratzenhofer*. Chicago: University of Chicago Press.

Smith, Adam. [1776] 1961. *An Inquiry into the Nature and Causes of the Wealth of Nations.* London: Methuen.

———. [1776] 1976. *An Inquiry into the Nature and Causes of the Wealth of Nations.* 2 Volumes. Oxford: Oxford University Press.

———. [1766] 1982. *Lectures on Jurisprudence.* Vol. V of the *Glasgow Edition of the Works and Correspondence of Adam Smith.* Indianapolis: The Online Library of Liberty.

———. [1762] 1985. *Lectures on Rhetoric and Belles Lettres.* Vol. IV of the *Glasgow Edition of the Works and Correspondence of Adam Smith.* Indianapolis: The Online Library of Liberty.

Sneath, David. 2004. "Property Regimes and Sociotechnical Systems: Rights over Land in Mongolia's 'Age of the Market.'" In *Property in Question,* edited by Katherine Verdery and Caroline Humphrey, 161–82. Oxford: Berg.

Snow, C.P. 1959. *The Two Cultures and the Scientific Revolution.* New York: Cambridge University Press.

Sobowale, Dele. 1996. "Budget '96: Much Ado About Nothing." *Sunday Vanguard,* 18 February: 19.

Solow, R. 1957. "Technical Change and the Aggregate Production Function." *Review of Economics and Statistics,* vol. 39: 312–20.

Solow, Robert M. 1997. *Learning From "Learning By Doing."* Stanford: Stanford University Press.

Speck, Frank G. 1926. "Land Ownership Among Hunting People in Primitive America and the World's Marginal Areas." *Twenty-second International Congress of Americanists (Rome)* 2: 323–32.

Spengler, Oswald. [1918] 1962. *The Decline of the West.* Abridged ed. New York: Alfred Knopf.

Spiegler, P. and W. Milberg. 2008. "The Taming of Institutions in Economics: The Rise and Methodology of the '*New* New Institutionalism.'" Mimeo. Department of Economics, University of Massachusetts-Boston.

Sprondel, Walter. 1973. "Sozialer Wandel, Ideen und Interessen: Systematisierungen zu Max Webers Protestantischer Ethik." In *Seminar: Religion und Gesellschaftliche Entwicklung,* edited by Constans Seyfarth and Walter Sprondel. Frankurt am Main: Suhrkamp.

Stack, C. 1974. *All Our Kin: Strategies for Survival in a Black Community.* New York: Harper.

Staveren, Irene van. 1999. *Caring for Economics.* Delft: Eburon Publishers.

Strathern, Marilyn. 1988. *The Gender of the Gift: Problems with Women and Problems with Society in Melanesia.* Berkeley: University of California Press.

Strecker, Ivo. 1988. *The Social Practice of Symbolization: An Anthropological Analysis.* London: Athlone.

Swedberg, Richard. 1990. *Economics and Sociology.* Princeton: Princeton University Press.

The African Guardian. 1993. 2 August: 28.

The Economist. 2003. 16 October.

The Guardian. 1996a. 21 August: 17.

The Guardian. 1996b. "Storm Over Budget Surplus." 17 September.

The Guardian. 1996c. "Mixed Reactions Trail Budget Performance." 18 September.

The Nigerian Economist. 1987. 6–19 January: 10.

The Nigerian Economist. 1988. "It's Spending Ease in '88." 6–19 January: 13–14.

The Saturday Newspaper. 1996. "The Budget of Faith." 17 February.

THISDAY. 1996. "The Budget of Faith '96." 17 February: 12–13.

Thomas, N. 1991. *Entangled Objects: Exchange, Material Culture, and Colonialism in the Pacific.* Cambridge, MA: Harvard University Press.
Timasheff, Nicholas. 1967. *Sociological Theory: Its Nature and Growth.* New York: Random House.
Tribe, Keith, ed. 1989. *Reading Weber.* London: Routledge.
———. 1999. "Adam Smith: Critical Theorist?" *Journal of Economic Literature* 37: 609–32.
Uzor, Mike. 1995. "Another Lost Year." *Policy,* 11 December 37.
Uzzi, B. 1997. "Social Structure and Competition in Interfirm Networks: The Paradox of Embeddedness." *Administrative Science Quarterly* 42: 35–67.
———. 1996. "The Sources and Consequences of Embeddedness for the Economic Performance of Organizations." *American Sociological Review* 61: 674–98.
Valeri, V. 1994. "Buying Women But Not Selling Them: Gift and Commodity Exchange in Halulu Alliance." *Man* (n.s.) 29: 1–26.
Veblen, Thorstein. [1899] 1953. *The Theory of the Leisure Class: An Economic Study of Institutions.* New York: Mentor.
Veblen, Thorstein. [1904] 1958. *The Theory of Business Enterprise.* New York: Mentor.
Velthuis, Olav. 2005. *Talking Prices: Symbolic Meanings of Prices on the Market for Contemporary Art.* Princeton: Princeton University Press.
Verdery, Katherine. 2003. *The Vanishing Hectare.* Ithaca: Cornell University Press.
Vianna, Francisco José de Oliveira. 1987. *História Social da Economia Capitalista no Brasil.* Belo Horizonte/Rio de Janeiro: Itatiaia/UFF.
Vico, Giambattista. [1744] 1984. *The New Science of Giambattista Vico.* Ithaca NY: Cornell University Press.
Vitebsky, Piers. 2001. "Withdrawing from the Land: Social and Spiritual Crisis in the Indigenous Russian Arctic." In *Postsocialism: Ideals, Ideologies and Practices in Eurasia,* edited by C.M. Hann, 180–95. London: Routledge.
Wallerstein, Immanuel. 2003. "Anthropology, Sociology, and Other Dubious Disciplines." *Current Anthropology* 44, no. 4: 453–60.
Waltzer, Michael. 1983. *Spheres of Justice: A Defense of Pluralism and Equality.* Oxford: Basil Blackwell.
Wardle, Huon. 2005. "A City of Meanings: Place and Displacement in Urban Jamaican Self-framings." In *Caribbean Narratives of Belonging: Fields of Relations, Sites of Identity,* edited by J. Besson and K. Fog Olwig, 79–93. Oxford: Macmillan,
Warsh, D. 2006. *Knowledge and the Wealth of Nations.* New York: W.W. Norton.
Weatherford, James. 1997. *The History of Money.* New York: Three Rivers.
Weber, Marianne. [1926] 1975. *Max Weber.* New York: John Wiley & Sons.
Weber, Max. 1916. "Die Wirtschaftsethik der Weltreligionen. Religionssoziologische Skizzen. Einleitung." *Archiv für Sozialwissenschaft und Sozialpolitik* 41: 1–30.
———. [1920] 1946. "The Social Psychology of the World Religions." In *From Max Weber,* edited by Hans Gerth and C. Wright Mills. New York: Oxford University Press.
———. 1949. *The Methodology of the Social Sciences.* New York: The Free Press.
———. 1958. *The Protestant Ethic and the Spirit of Capitalism.* New York: Charles Scribner's Sons.
———. [1921-22] 1972. *Wirtschaft und Gesellschaft. Grundriss der verstehenden Soziologie.* 5th ed. Tübingen: J.C.B. Mohr.
———. [1921-22] 1978. *Economy and Society: An Outline of Interpretive Sociology.* 2 Volumes. Berkeley: University of California Press.

———. [1920] 1988. "Einleitung." In *Gesammelte Aufsätze zur Religionssoziologie,* Volume 1. Tübingen: J.C.B. Mohr.
———. [1898] 1990. *Grundriss zu den Vorlesungen über Allgemeine ('theoretische') Nationalökonomie.* Tübingen: J.C.B. Mohr.
———. 1991. *Wirtschaftsgeschichte.* Berlin: Duncker und Humblot.
———. 1999. *Max Weber im Kontext. Literatur im Kontext auf CD-ROM 7.* Berlin: Karsten Worm InfoSoftWare.
———. 2003. *The Essential Weber,* edited by Sam Whimster. London: Routledge.
Webster. 1988. *New Lexicon Webster's Dictionary of English Language.* New York: Lexicon Publications.
West Africa. 1991. "Financial Discipline." 14–20 January: 12–13.
Whimster, Sam. 2002. "Notes and Queries." *Max Weber Studies* 3,1:74-98.
Whitehead, A.N. 1925. *Science and the Modern World.* London: Macmillan
Wilk, Richard R. 1996. *Economies and Cultures: Foundations of Economic Anthropology.* Boulder, CO: Westview Press.
Williamson, Oliver. 1975. *Markets and Hierarchies.* New York: The Free Press.
Wittgenstein, Ludwig. 1958. *Philosophical Investigations.* Englewood Cliffs, NJ: Prentice-Hall.
Wolf, Eric. 1964. *Anthropology.* New York: Prentice Hall.
Yan, Y. 1996. *The Flow of Gifts: Reciprocity and Social Networks in a Chinese Village.* Stanford: Stanford University Press.
Zeitlyn, David. 2004. "The Gift of the Gab—Anthropology and Conversation Analysis." *Anthropos* 99, no. 2: 451–68.
Zelizer, Viviana. 1985. *Pricing the Priceless Child: the Changing Social Value of Children.* New York: Basic Books.
———. 1994. *The Social Meaning of Money.* New York: Basic Books.
———. 1997. "How Do We Know Whether a Monetary Transaction Is a Gift, an Entitlement, or Compensation?" In *Economics, Values and Organization,* edited by Avner Ben-Ner and Louis Putterman, 329–36. Cambridge: University of Cambridge Press.
Zizek, Slavoj. 2000. "Da Capo Senza Fine." In *Contingency, Hegemony, Universality,* edited by Judith Butler, Ernesto Laclau, and Slavoj Zizek, 213–62. London: Verso.
Zucker, G.L. 1986. "Production of Trust: Institutional Sources of Economic Structure, 1840–1920." *Research in Organizational Behavior* 8: 53–111.

Index

abstract
    and concrete, 140
    models, 79
    money, 149
abstraction, 18, 22, 24 passim, 79
Adam Smith, 82–83, 86
    on money, 138
    on rhetoric, 152
    and self-love, 191
    and training, 92
alienable, 120, 124, 134
anthropologists, and capabilities, 92
anthropology
    and economics, difference of, 179
    and economics, troubled history of, 94
    and qualities, 141, 142
Appadurai, Arjun, 121, 124, 134, 189
Aristotle, 4, 13
associations and interests, 37–38
Austrian economics, 10

Babbage, Charles, 9, 88
    and capabilities, 92
base, 8, 64
Becker, Gary, 24, 25, 28, 70
becoming and become, dialectic of, in Spengler, 148
Bemba, 67
benchmark, 105, 107
Blaug, Mark, 46, 47, 59
borrowing between disciplines, 84
budget, rhetoric of, 113 passim
budgetary control, 104

calculative reason, 17, 18, 78. *See also* homo economicus, rational economic man
capabilities, and conversations, 91–92
capitalism, 1
cascading, 13, 64–65, 70. *See also* colonization
cash cropping, 77
chance, 102
checking accounts, 162
citations between disciplines, 84–85
class, and interests, 38–39
Colander, Mark, 47
collaboration, 95
colonization, 65, 76
    European, 75
    See also cascading
colonize, 25
commensuration, 76
commodities, and gifts, 118, 120–123
commodity, 11, 23
    and gift, 134–135
commodity phase, 121, 189, 190
commons, tragedy of, 70
community, 63
    types of, 146
community currencies, 153–154
con, in economics, 56
conjoint person, 66, 80n.3
content, 3, 5
    and form, 33
conversation, 9, 12
    across disciplines, 2
    type of, 88–94

conversations
    between disciplines, 82 passim
    in business, 130–133
    and capabilities, 91–92
    and commodity phase, 189
    political, 79
    and preferences, 91–92
cost-benefit analysis, 26
cross-fertilization, 83, 94
cultural
    capital, 1
    and economy, 184
    goods and social functions, 187–188
    goods as values, 187
    as values, histories, and news, 185, 186
culture, connotations of, 187

debasement, 65
Debtors Anonymous, 171–172
deduction, 7, 53, 63
Demsetz, Harold, 8, 9, 71 passim, 80nn.13–14
dialectic, 12
    in Spengler, 148
dialectical, 3, 5
dialectics, 64
    in economy, 74
    of form and substance, 19
disjoint person, 66, 80n.3
division of labor, 82–83, 86–87
    and Babbage, 88
    and disciplines, 92
drop pan, 139
Dumont, Louis, 23
Durkheim, Emile, 13, 20–22, 27

econometrics, 56–57, 59
Economic man, 21–22. *See also* homo economicus
economic values as instruments, 186, 187
economics
    and anthropology, 81
        troubled history of, 94
    as conversation, 180–181
    as study of values, 186
economists, and capabilities, 92
economy as culture, 186
efficiency, 71

Emerson, Ralph Waldo, 161–162
empiricism, 8, 51, 53
endogenous
    technology, 49
    variables, 65
entrepreneur as rhetor, 183
exchange value, 189
exogenous variables, 65
expression, 3
externalities, 65, 72–73, 76

fetishism of money, 136, 139
first fundamental welfare theorem, 43, 45, 46. *See also* Pareto, efficiency
form, 3, 5
    rhetorical, 63
form and content, as circular argument, 109, 116
formalist, 4–5, 6
formalist-substantivist debate, 15 passim, 85

garage sale, 122
general equilibrium, 47, 50, 51, 53
genres of conversation, 89–91
gift, 1, 11, 23
    and commodity, 134–135
    as free sample, 131
    as metaphor, 119
    in relation to commodity, 119, 120–123
gifts, as bribes, 128–129
government rhetoric, 115
Gregory, Chris, 23

Hardin, G., 70
Hayek, Friedrich von, 10, 14nn. 498–103
    and knowledge, 93
Herrmann, Gretchen, 122
Herskovits, Melville, 7
Hirschman, Albert, 195
holistic approach, 86
homo economicus, 5, 6, 8, 32, 41, 60, 68
    in ethnography, 76–77
    maximizing, 86
    See also rational economic man
hypothetico-deductive method, 7
hypothetico-deductivism, 46, 50, 51, 59

identity change, 75
ignorance, 99, 100, 106
imperialism of economics, 44, 59, 87
inalienable, 120
incommensurable goods, 190
individualist position, 25
induction, 7, 49, 50, 55, 59
institutions, and genres, 91
interest, 5-6
    and love, 170
interest-driven, 35-37
interests
    and associations, 37-38
    and class, 38-39
    dispersed, problem of, 95
    problem of different, 90-93
    and social relations, 42
internality, 65, 72-73
International Monetary Fund, 10, 46, 66, 108
international trade, 48
interpretation, 63
intuition, 51
invisible hand, 32, 44

Keynes, John Maynard, 14n.1, 139
Kletzer Effect, 8, 57-59
Knight, Frank, 7, 32
Knight-Herskovits exchange, 85
knowledge
    interpretation of dispersed, 90-93
    problem of, 95, 96n.9
Kopytoff, Igor, 121
Krugman, Paul, 48

labor value, 69
Leacock, Eleanor, 73 passim
legitimation, 66
Leontieff paradox, 48
lexis, 3, 8
lexis and logos in money, 156
Locke, John, 9, 68-89
    and money, 144
    on property, 144
logos, 3, 8, 140
long run, 104
long term, 100, 101

Macpherson, C.B., 68
magnitude and function, in Spengler, 148-150
Malcolm X, 137, 138
Malinowski, Bronislaw, 21-22
marginal utility, 36
market
    as conversation, 181-184
    talk, 191, 198
markets
    and bourgeois virtues, 198
    as culture, 177
    and externalities, 198
    and spillovers, 198
Martin Luther King, 174-175
Marx, Karl, 68-69, 151, 189
Mass-gift
    and commodity, 124, 125
    defined, 123
    and mass-manufacturing, 127
    types of, 126
material and ideal, 39-41
Mauss, Marcel, 22, 119-122, 197
McCloskey, Deidre, 3, 58-59, 178
McLuhan, Marshall, 3, 4
meaning, 3, 63
measuring rod, 78. *See also* commensuration
medium, 3
message, 3
methodological differences, 86-87
methodological individualism, 19, 45, 70
methodologies, 82
military rule, 98, 104, 105
Mill, John Stuart, 45
Mirowski, Philip, 3, 57, 83, 101
models, incomplete, 79
Modernist project, 28, 29
modernist tradition, 178
modernization, 78
monetarist policy, 103, 115
money, 136, 137-139 passim
    in conversations, 160-175
Montagnais-Naskapi, 73 passim
mutuality, 63

narrative, 65
    of Locke, 68-69

narratives, 8
    of legitimation, 78–79
    of possession, 67
national economy, idea of, 111, 115
neoliberal rhetoric, 112
New Economics, 43, 47, 50, 53
New Institutional Economics, 8, 9, 71, 95
New institutionalism, 8, 59–60

oikos, 13
    and connectedness, 193–194. *See also* sharing, community
optimal foraging theory, 23–24

Pareto optimality, 50. *See also* first welfare theorem
Pareto theorem. *See* first fundamental welfare theorem
Pareto, Wilfredo, 79
performance, 2
persuasion and valorization, 182
Polanyi, Karl, 16–18, 27
Polanyi, Michael, 101
pragmatism, 9, 14n.4, 44
preferences, 5, 6
    and conversations, 91–92
    and introspection, 93
property, 8
    and Locke, 144
public rhetoric, 111

rational choice, 7, 59
rational economic man, 17, 44. *See also* homo economicus
Ratzenhofer, Gustav, 33
reciprocity, 1, 17
redistribution, 17
res, 3
rhetoric
    and culture, 179–180
    as difference, 177
    meaning of, 3 passim
    and money, 160
    as persuasion, 2
rhetorical practices, 181
Robinson Crusoe, 72
robust, 49
romanticism, 18, 30n.3

Rose, Carol, 69
Rousseau, Jean-Jacques, 66

sales
    and samples, 129–133
    and social relationships, 128
sales people, 127, 128
sample gift, 126
samples
    free, 131
    as gifts, 123, 130–133
    and supermarket gifts, 134
scarcity, 45, 71, 76
separation, of disciplines, 88
shared interests, 64. *See also* interests
sharing, 73
short term, 100, 101
significance, 8
    abuse of, 58–59
Simmel, Georg, 6, 33–34
simplicity, 4, 5, 10
simplification, 19, 24 passim
Small, Albion, 33
Smith, Adam, 9, 17, 20, 32
social action, 36
social capital, 1
society
    and groups, 197
    and reciprocity, 197
Solow, Robert, 48
Spencer, Herbert, 20–22
Spengler, Oswald, 12
spillovers, 10
state talk, 191
Strathern, Marilyn, 23
structural adjustment, 10, 28, 111
structural adjustment policy, 98, 104, 105–110
style, 3
subjective perception, 38
submission to market, 98–99
subsidy, 107–110, 112
subsistence farming, 77
substance, 3
substantivist, 4–5, 6
sugar cane, 77
supermarket gift, 126
supermarket gifts, and samples, 134

switchmen, 39–41

tension, in debate between formalists and substantivists, 29. *See also* dialectics
total social fact, 160
trade, impersonal, 63
trade and scarcity, 76–77, 78
transaction cost, 72
Trobriand Islands, 21–22

uncertainty, 98, 106
use value, 189

valuation spheres, 191 passim
    and economists and anthropologists, 199
value in exchange, 140
value in use, 140
value realms, 64
values, incommensurate, 13
veiling, 66
verba, 3
virtualism, 28, 101, 102

Weber, Max, 6, 34–41